Journey Through the Wilderness

Garnet Wolseley's Canadian Red River Expedition of 1870

Paul McNicholls

Helion & Company

Helion & Company Limited
Unit 8 Amherst Business Centre
Budbrooke Road
Warwick
CV34 5WE
England
Tel. 01926 499 619
Email: info@helion.co.uk
Website: www.helion.co.uk
Twitter: @helionbooks

Published by Helion & Company 2019
Designed and typeset by Farr out Publications, Wokingham, Berkshire
Cover designed by Paul Hewitt, Battlefield Design (www.battlefield-design.co.uk)

ISBN 978-1-911628-30-9

British Library Cataloguing-in-Publication Data.
A catalogue record for this book is available from the British Library.

For Lyndy Anne

Contents

List of Images

List of Maps

Acknowledgments

The origins of this book go back to early 2016 when I was approached by Dr Christopher Brice of Helion and Company to produce a volume for a forthcoming series of books on Victorian military campaigns. I had met Chris in London a few years before when he was giving a talk at the National Army Museum. His preference was that my contribution to the series would be something from a Canadian perspective, and we settled on the Red River Expedition of 1870. This little known military episode in the early history of post-Confederation Canada, we agreed, would be a good topic of investigation given that it was the British Army's last campaign in North America and the first independent command of Garnet Wolseley, who would rise to become Commander-in-Chief of the British Army. Rather surprisingly given these twin factors, it had the added advantage of having received very little attention from military scholars of the Victorian period.

The same is not the case with the background story to the sending of the expedition in the spring of 1870, and a great amount of research and writing by Canadian scholars has been devoted to the events at the Red River Settlement over the course of the preceding winter.

I would like to start by recognizing some of the historians who blazed the trail for me. Arthur S. Morton, W.L. Morton, John S. Galbraith, E.E. Rich, George F.G. Stanley, Joseph Kinsey Howard, Desmond Morton, Gerald Friesen, and J.M. Bumstead were essential reading for me in understanding the goings on at Red River prior to the dispatch of the Wolseley expedition. For the Canadian political and military background, I am indebted to the works of C.P. Stacey, Donald Creighton, Richard Gwyn, J.L. Granatstein, Desmond Morton again, Stephen J, Harris and J. Mackay Hitsman. For the British political and military background, as well as biographies of Garnet Wolseley, I found the writings of Kenneth Bourne, Ged Martin, Ian F.W. Becket, Edward Spiers, Steven Corvi, Joseph Lehmann and Halik Kochanski insightful and helpful. This list is certainly not exhaustive and, if the reader wishes further detail, it is recommended that they consult the bibliography.

The Red River Expedition is the story of a military campaign with no battles; not even a skirmish. The real story is, as the book's title makes clear, the journey of the force through the wilderness to Fort Garry, the sight of modern day Winnipeg. Maps were, therefore, essential to assist the reader in understanding the obstacles and progress of the force. I am grateful to *Helion* for agreeing to the inclusion of so many and to George Anderson for expertly drawing them.

No book is written without the assistance and patience of a great many people, and this is certainly the case with the writing of this book. I would like to thank those at The National Archives at Kew, the Hampshire Archives, the Hove Public Library, The British Library, Library and Archives Canada, and the Toronto Public Library for the helpful assistance and support that was provided during my research. This list could have been a great deal longer if not for the fact that much information can now be found online and I would like to single out the University of Alberta in this regarding for placing so many primary documents relating to the history of the Canadian West online.

I would also like to add my gratitude to Professor Desmond Morton who corresponded with me by e-mail in the early days of my research and Professor Barry Gough who spoke with me on the telephone and by e-mail. Both provided assistance that I believe kept me on the right path at the beginning of my process into trying to come to grips with the events I was about to write about.

Dr. Christopher Brice, my editor at Helion, has done stellar work in making suggestions to the text and generally keeping me focused during the writing phase of the book. I would also like to thank him for approaching me to write the story of the Red River Expedition in the first place. He has taken a chance on a first time author and I hope the end product has shown his confidence was justified.

Many friends have supported me throughout the research and writing process. John and Sarah Verbeeten in West Sussex, and Julian Hill and Mike Higton in different parts of Surrey, have hosted me on more than one occasion during my research trips to England. Their hospitality and conviviality made these visits an even more enjoyable experience. In Canada, former Winnipeg resident Mike D'Amour responded helpfully to my requests for information on the geography of the region. Phil and Jayne Lin put their house on Vancouver Island at my disposal for several weeks while they were away so that I could have an undisturbed place to 'knuckle down' and write once the research phase was at an end. Phil has also shown great patience during many other visits in discussing various aspects of the expedition over a glass of single malt whisky. To all of these individuals I send my heartiest thanks.

It is of course my family that has borne the brunt of my obsession with the Red River Expedition over the past three years. My children, Andrew, Colin and Lauren, are now adults and have hopefully understood the constant distractions of their father. I'm not sure the same can be said of my granddaughter, Isla. It is to my wife Lyndy Anne, however, that the lion's share of my thanks must go. Not only has she proof read the manuscript and made helpful suggestions on numerous occasions, she has also patiently persevered with three years of her husband's constant ruminations and conversations regarding a minor military expedition from nearly 150 years ago. For her patience and forbearance during this process, I am most grateful and to her the book is dedicated with much love.

Paul McNicholls
Sooke, British Columbia, Canada, May 2019

Introduction

This is the story of the dispatch of a small military expedition to the Red River Settlement in the spring of 1870. Located along the Red and Assiniboine Rivers at the site of modern day Winnipeg in the Canadian province of Manitoba, the settlement was at the time part of the vast territories which for almost two hundred years had been administered by the Hudson's Bay Company. Strange as it seems to us today, in 1869 this land was not part of Canada. It was, however, well-known amongst the more than 12,000 residents at the Red River Settlement that the recently confederated Dominion of Canada would soon be taking over; the Hudson's Bay Company[1] was selling up and Ottawa was buying. This was a vast swathe of territory. The rights of the indigenous population, who had lived here for millennia prior to the arrival of Europeans, received scant consideration, and many of the First Nations peoples no doubt took a very different view as regards exactly who owned the vast piece of real estate that was about to be sold. It is not really surprising, therefore, that the Canadian Government gave little, if any, thought to consulting with the Red River residents to explain what was about to occur.

At this time just under half of the settlement's population was composed of the French-speaking Métis people; the mixed race descendants of French fur traders and First Nations women. With a quasi military organization stemming from their tradition of the buffalo hunt, the Métis were a force to be reckoned with. Of all those residing at Red River, Métis claims to legal land ownership were, however, also the most tenuous, and the uncertainty resulting from the lack of any assurances from the Canadian Government as to what would happen after the takeover, made them nervous. The arrival of Canadian road builders and surveyors in 1868 and 1869, together with the activities of a small group in the settlement that made up the Canadian Party, caused them to be even more wary of what lay ahead. The result was that they took matters into their own hands to force the Canadian Government to negotiate and give them the guarantees they had every right to expect. While many other residents at the settlement were also nervous of the changes that would be wrought by Canada's purchase of the HBC lands, the manner in which the Métis under their leader Louis Riel went about demonstrating their discontent caused consternation within the English-speaking communities. A serious misjudgement by Riel would ultimately result in a call to arms in English-speaking Canada as well.

The events of the winter of 1869/70 have successively been known as the Red River Rebellion, the Red River Uprising, the Red River Resistance, and the Red River Troubles. Whatever title one chooses to adopt, the consequences in Canada were politically far-reaching. They led directly to the creation of the new province of Manitoba, something the Canadian Government had not intended when negotiating for the purchase of the HBC territories. They also clearly demonstrated that there were significant divisions between English and French-speaking Canada, and these would re-occur again and again in the years ahead during times of national crisis. There was also the relationship between the Canadian Government and the Métis. Though a settlement was reached between Canada and the residents of Red River in the spring of 1870, a number of its terms were not carried through. The legacy of this is that Métis grievances continue in Canada to this day.

The unrest at the Red River Settlement would also lead to the dispatch from Canada of the Anglo-Canadian Red River Expeditionary Force, one of the lesser known military operations of the Victorian age. This campaign is the focus of this book. It was the last military campaign conducted by the British Army in North America and

1 Throughout the text, the Hudson's Bay Company will be described by its full name, or sometimes abbreviated to HBC or even 'the Company'.

the first independent command of Colonel Garnet Wolseley, a man who would rise to become Commander-in-Chief of the British Army. Wolseley would, in fact, utilize aspects of the transportation methods of the Red River Expedition in his much better known campaign on the Nile in 1884/85.

Given that the Red River Expedition provides the opportunity to learn more about Wolseley's methods of command at such an early stage in his career, it is somewhat surprising that there is such a paucity of modern scholarship on the topic. The story of the expeditionary force is one of detailed planning and organization and much of the credit for the success of the operation is down to Wolseley, though he was ably supported by his commanding officer Lieutenant-General James Alexander Lindsay. There would be very limited opportunities for re-supply during the trek to the Red River Settlement and so meticulous preparation was essential.

Disputes between the British military and the Canadian politicians and administrators were probably inevitable, particularly in light of the exceedingly tight timeframes the British imposed on themselves to get their troops to and from the Red River Settlement before the arrival of winter. One of the main reasons Canadian Prime Minister Sir John A. Macdonald pushed so hard for British participation was because he knew that, at this early stage in the country's development, Canada lacked the expertise to mount such an operation. Lindsay and Wolseley, however, were forthright and even at times disparaging towards Canadian efforts, again largely driven by the demands of their government as to the departure of their forces, and this did not help Canadian sensibilities. Having said this, many, though as we shall see certainly not all, of the British complaints during the planning stages had at least some merit. To add to all the difficulties, communication from the Canadian Government was not always as open as it should have been. The situation surrounding the chartering of the Great Lakes Steamers will be shown as a case in point. Matters were also not helped by the fact that once the time constraints of the British schedule really started to take hold, Wolseley began to see Canadian conspiracies everywhere. He demonstrated an uncanny ability to give offence to the Canadian Government's Department of Public Works man, Simon J. Dawson, and Dawson was certainly not shy about firing back when he felt he or his department had been maligned.

When one considers that the Red River Expedition's story is that of a military campaign without battles, it is surprising how many talking points there actually are. It was conducted against a backdrop of British military reorganization and retrenchment which saw the War Office in London withdrawing its garrisons from many parts of the empire, including Canada. The British Government of William Ewart Gladstone was reluctant to commit troops to the venture and did so only after repeated requests on the part of Sir John A. Macdonald in Ottawa. Gladstone's view of the expedition was also very different from Macdonald's. The Canadian Prime Minister and English-speaking Canada envisioned a punitive expedition and this was something Gladstone would not sanction. The terms of British participation were clearly laid out as being one of peaceful occupation of territory after a political settlement had been concluded. As we shall see, Wolseley, despite the clear orders under which he was operating, fell in much more closely with the views of English Canada as his force approached the Red River Settlement.

In Canada there was a significant linguistic divide between those who supported the expedition and those who did not. English Canada was enthusiastically behind the dispatch of a military force to the west; in fact they demanded one be undertaken. French Canada was opposed. The Canadian authorities were insistent that its contribution to the expeditionary force would be made up of one battalion from Ontario and one from Quebec. The inability to find recruits in French-speaking Canada, despite the rich militia tradition in the province, demonstrated just how badly divided Canada was.

Additionally, the unrest at Red River, with the consequent dispatch of the expeditionary force, was in no way the only problem facing Macdonald at this time. It was not even the only military issue facing him, as between 1866 and 1871 there were a number of raids across the border with the United States by Fenian American Civil War veterans bent on wresting control of Canada from the British Empire in the cause of Irish independence. The number of distractions facing the Canadian Prime Minister no doubt played a role in his failure to recognize the seriousness of the problem at the Red River Settlement as early as he should have.

Then there was the American dimension to the story. The United States also had aspirations to take control of the lands of the Hudson's Bay Company; the territory that today comprises the western provinces and territories of Canada. In point of fact, they also desired to take over Canada as it existed at the time as well. As the Red River Expeditionary Force proceeded on its journey west, there were points along the route where Wolseley and his men would pass near American controlled territory and one place where they actually needed to transit their ships through an American lock at the Sault Ste. Marie rapids. Washington was far from supportive of a military force moving into territory it was desirous of acquiring for itself and was determined to make matters as difficult as it could. As we shall see, however, this opposition would stop short of risking armed conflict with Great Britain.

The crux of the story, though, is the journey of the expeditionary force itself. Despite one recent Canadian history book describing the expeditionary force as marching " ... overland on the Red River trail from the head of Lake Superior ... "[2] the truth of the matter is that there was no Red River trail and the 'overland' route incorporated a great many rivers, lakes and portages, with numerous treacherous waterfalls and rapids thrown in for good measure. In 1870 there was quite simply no easy way to get from Canada to the Red River Settlement unless you went through the United States. The American Government would never have sanctioned the use of its territory by a foreign military force had permission been requested from Ottawa, but in any case the Canadian Government never considered this as an option. Nevertheless, certain individuals involved in the Red River story did use the American route to make their way to or from the settlement.

Perhaps the greatest controversy of the expedition's journey to Red River was the incomplete road from Thunder Bay on Lake Superior to Shebandowan Lake where the men would embark on their journey proper. Wolseley would after the event make some blunt accusations of what had been promised and what the failure to deliver on these 'promises' had meant to his ability to get his men underway in a timely manner. This controversy is carefully considered below.

Generally speaking, the story of the expeditionary force is one of great physical effort and endurance on the part of the men involved. The journey as a whole was carried out in almost continuous rain, with the men day after day laboriously moving their boats and supplies across rivers, lakes and portages. They were constantly soaked to the skin, subsisted on a monotonous diet, and were daily at risk from the dangers of the conditions in which they worked, all the while harassed by millions of ever-present insects. It really was a *Journey Through the Wilderness.*

Space is also given to the history of the Red River Settlement and the Red River Troubles, as they form the essential background to the dispatch of the military force in the spring of 1870. The story of these events can, however, be found in much greater detail in many excellent books.[3] Very little, on the other hand, has been written on the expedition itself. In most cases it garners a line or two, possibly a paragraph, in more general histories dealing either with the British Empire or the creation of the Canadian West. In the opinion of the author, it is high time to remedy this and also place the events surrounding its dispatch into their Canadian, Imperial and North American contexts.

---

2 Bryan Elson, *Canada's Bastions of Empire; Halifax, Victoria and Royal Navy 1749-1918*, (Halifax: Formac Publishing Company Limited, 2014) p59.

3 The Red River Troubles is a contentious subject in Canadian historiography and there are a wide range of views on the subject. See for example, J.M. Bumstead, *Trials and Tribulations: The Red River Settlement and the Emergence of Manitoba, 1811-1870*, (Winnipeg: Great Plains Publications, 2003), Gerald Friesen, *The Canadian Prairies: A History by Gerald Friesen*, (Toronto: University of Toronto Press, 1984), Joseph Kinsey Howard, *Strange Empire; A Narrative of the Northwest*, (St. Paul: Minnesota Historical Society Press, 1994, First published 1952), John S. Galbraith, *The Hudson's Bay Company as an Imperial Factor, 1821-1869*, (Berkeley: University of California Press, 1957), Arthur S. Morton, *A History of the Canadian West to 1870-71*, (London: Thomas Nelsons & Sons Ltd), W.L. Morton, *Manitoba: A History*, (Toronto, University of Toronto Press, 1957) , E.E. Rich, *The Hudson's Bay Company, Volume 3 1821-1870*, (Toronto: McClelland and Stewart, 1960) , and George F.G. Stanley, *The Birth of Western Canada; A History of the Riel Rebellions* (Toronto: University of Toronto Press, 1960, First Published 1936).

1

Furs, Settlers and 'A New Nation'

Almost from the beginning of European arrival on the vast continental landmass that we know today as Canada the fur trade was the staple of the economy, and by far and away the most important animal pelt was that of the beaver. Beaver hats were the height of fashion in Europe until the mid-nineteenth century and the appetite for beaver pelts was seemingly insatiable.

What began as a search for a navigable route to the orient, quickly led to a trade in furs with some indigenous tribes while conflict developed with others. The French established themselves in the St. Lawrence River valley, founding the city of Quebec in 1608. Initially, the First Nations peoples brought the furs from the interior to the French at Montreal. The Huron people jealously protected their role as the middlemen in the fur trade supply chain, but warfare with the Iroquois, who sought to wrest this control from them, caused French traders to venture into the interior to ensure the supply of pelts continued.

Known as the *coureurs de bois*, these hardy adventurers travelled deep into the continent's interior. Navigating up the Ottawa River, they traversed the vast network of rivers and lakes north and west of the St. Lawrence River valley and by the 1660's " ... were making a succession of adventurous voyages into the territories of the middle west and were building up a reliable notion of the geography of the region of the lakes and of the territory to the north and west."[1] By 1738 they had established forts in the area of the Forks, as the confluence of the Red and Assiniboine Rivers would become known.[2]

Despite the success of the fur trade, France's colony struggled and in 1663 the French Crown assumed direct control. While the trade in beaver pelts remained important, the aim was the creation of a self-sufficient settler colony along the lines of the English colonies further south along the Atlantic seaboard. The result was greater rules and regulations controlling the fur trade of New France, with dire financial consequences for those who failed to comply. Two *coureurs de bois* who fell afoul of French authority were Médard Chouart des Groselliers and his brother-in-law Pierre-Esprit Radisson. Finding their way to London, they convinced a group of influential Englishmen that the furs of the continental interior could be better accessed via Hudson's Bay. While the waters of the bay were free of ice for only a short time each year, the closer proximity to the fur bearing lands was an attractive proposition. The result was that in May of 1670 King Charles II gave a Royal Charter to the investors, including his cousin Prince Rupert, granting a monopoly to trade in furs in the region drained by all rivers and streams flowing into Hudson's Bay. This was the beginning of the Hudson's Bay Company, and while it is doubtful that Charles II had any comprehension of the enormous size of the territory he had turned over to the new commercial enterprise, the territory, soon to be known as Rupert's Land, gave the Company control of almost 1.5 million square miles; or over one third of what we know today as Canada. Much of the rest of modern day northern and western Canada became known as the North-Western Territory, and, given that no other European power had access to this equally vast tract of real estate, other than the Russians in what would become Alaska, the HBC would ultimately trade here too. This was formalized in 1859 when the British Government assigned the

1 E.E. Rich *The Fur Trade and the Northwest to 1857*, (Toronto: McClelland and Steward Limited, 1967), p19.
2 Charles N. Bell, *Old Forts of Winnipeg*, (Manitoba Historical Society, MHS Transactions Series 2, No. 3 Read 1927), pp6/7.

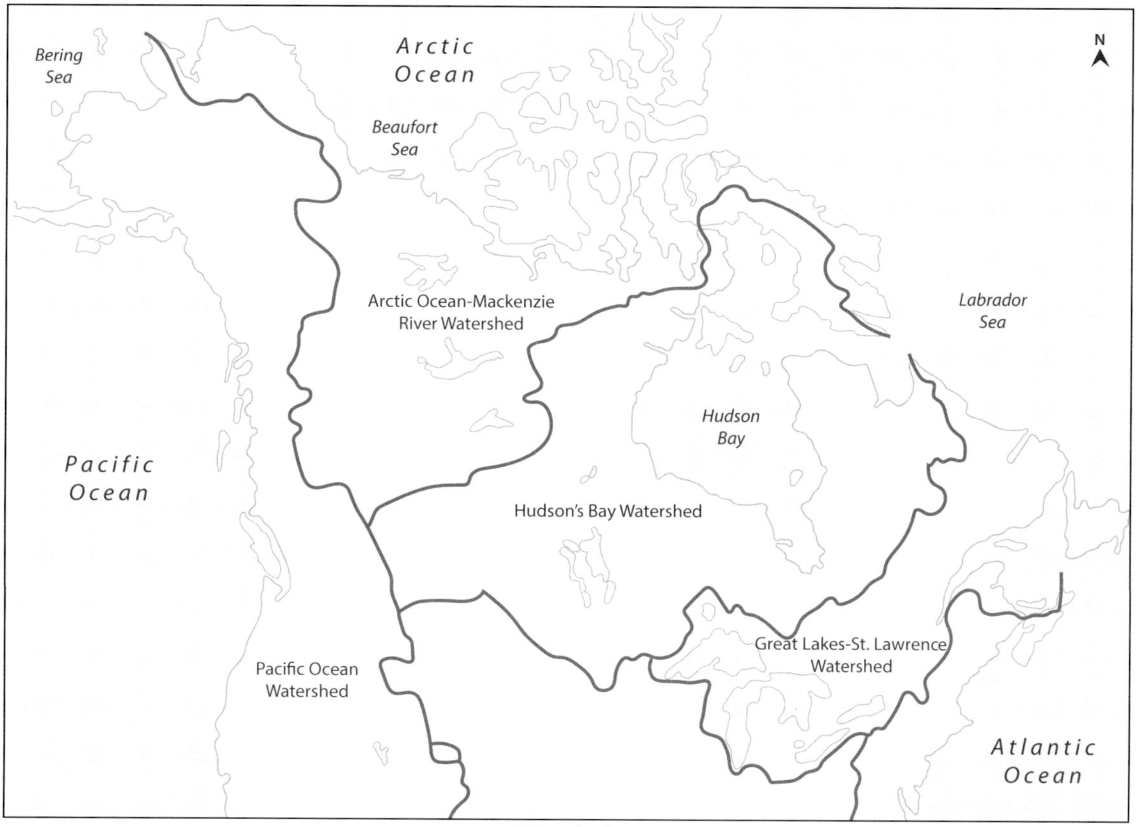

Watersheds.

administration of this area to the Company as well. Land grants of this enormity were truly breathtaking in their scale, and took little account of the people who were already living there.

The Company established a number of trading posts around the bay, the most important being York Factory at the mouth of the Hayes River, established in 1684. Business initially boomed to the detriment of the trade of New France, though various French expeditions overland and by sea against their new rival seriously disrupted the English trade until British sovereignty on the bay was confirmed by the Treaty of Utrecht in 1713. Defeat by the British at Quebec in 1759 and Montreal the following year, however, saw the end of New France. Aside from the islands of St. Pierre and Miquelon near Newfoundland, the French colonies on the Atlantic seaboard and the St. Lawrence region were now British territory.

While the fur trade was far from the primary reason behind the conflict with the French in North America, it now seemed secure and the demise of French power indicated that unfettered prosperity lay ahead for the Hudson's Bay Company. There was no need to venture into the interior of the continent in search of furs; HBC Factors and their employees could remain in their factories and forts and let First Nations trappers bring the pelts to them.[3] When the ice on the bay broke up, ships would arrive from England to collect the furs and supply the Company's employees with a new season's worth of trade goods.

In fact, the prosperity of the HBC was anything but unfettered. While the French could still periodically be a thorn in the side of the Company, as when a naval force attacked and captured York Factory in 1782, the main rivalry came in the form of a new company based on Montreal that had picked up the mantle of the old French

3 The Factor was the HBC's lead man at a fort or factory.

trade. Largely run by Scots and utilizing French-speaking workers, the North West Company as it became known would give the HBC a serious run for its money.

Unlike the HBC, which was an incorporated joint-stock company operating with a charter which specified a governor, deputy governor and a committee of directors, the North West Company was "a series of co-partnerships between small groups of men who were promoters, merchants or fur-trader explorers, or all three together or in turn."[4] They were not without competition of their own such as the New North West Company, also known as the XY Company, and John Jacob Astor's Pacific Fur Company. However, under the aggressive leadership of William McGillivray, they saw off their competitors and challenged the HBC itself for dominance of the fur trade of Rupert's Land and the North-Western Territory.

The success they achieved was based on a level of organization that, initially at least, the HBC was unable or unwilling to match. Given their remoteness from the rich fur bearing lands of the interior, the Montreal based company penetrated deep into the continent, going to the source of the furs, diverting them from the HBC factories on Hudson's Bay, and making a significant dent in the rival company's profits. A vast network of trading posts was established and, "by providing the officers in the field with a direct interest in the profits through their status as 'wintering partners', gave additional energy to its expansion."[5]

It required a highly developed organization and a monumental level of effort, but there were fortunes to be made and made they were. Its organization, however, was not without weaknesses. The trade required considerable capital investment each and every year on the part of the Montreal partners and, if its trade was interrupted or severed, these fortunes could quickly evaporate. Although its leading members apparently did not recognize it, the exceedingly long line of communication between Montreal and the rich fur lands of the Athabascan region of the continental interior, combined with the fact it was operating in an area where the sole right to trade had long ago been granted to its rival, made it particularly vulnerable to just such a severance of trade.

Each spring the Montreal based fur traders would set out on the long journey to their annual gathering place at Grand Portage on Lake Superior. Here they would meet with the wintering partners, those who had spent the winter at the trading posts in the interior. The Montreal partners would bring the trading goods for the next season's barter with the First Nations trappers and the wintering partners would bring the current season's furs. By 1803 the establishment of the border between British North America and the westward-expanding United States meant Grand Portage now fell within United States territory. Consequently, a new meeting place was established at Fort William on Thunder Bay, named for William McGillivray.

The mode of transport during this arduous journey was by heavily laden canoe. The canoes of the Montreal partners were larger as part of their journey took them onto two of the Great Lakes; Huron and Superior. The canoes of the wintering partners, known as *Canot du Nord*, were smaller so as to be more practical on the lakes and rivers of the interior. Both canoe types were powered by the navigational skill and brawn of French-speaking *voyageurs*. These were in a sense the descendants of the *coureurs de bois*. Even during the French period the entrepreneurial *coureurs de bois* were increasingly being squeezed out as control of the fur trade fell into fewer and fewer hands. Whereas the *coureurs de bois* had been involved in all aspects of the trade, the *voyageurs* were employees of the larger trading concerns. The *voyageurs* provided the unrelenting and back breaking toil along rivers, across lakes, and over the innumerable portages, to transport the trade goods to the interior of the continent and the furs to Montreal.

When the two groups met for their annual meeting, first at Grand Portage and later at Fort William, "for the month of July the depot was bursting with activity as over 1,000 men gathered to pass on trade goods and provisions to the winterers, and to pack the fur to take back to Montreal."[6] After catching up with friends, feasting and drinking, "when all the business had been completed, the wintering partners and their men set off again

4 Marjorie Wilkins Campbell, *The North West Company*, (Toronto: The Macmillan Company of Canada Limited, 1957), p1.
5 Galbraith, *Hudson's Bay Company*, pp4/5.
6 Keith Wilson, "Fur Wars", *Horizon Canada, Centre for the Study of Teaching Canada Inc.*, August 1985, p628.

Thomas Douglas, the 5th Earl of Selkirk.Credit: (National Archives Library / Library and Archives Canada / C-001346)

for their remote trading posts in their light *Canot du Nord* laden with provisions and trade goods, while the Montrealers returned home with the precious furs."[7]

The HBC viewed their rivals as upstarts and derisorily referred to them as 'the pedlars from Montreal.' The Nor'Westers, largely dominated by Scots merchants, referred to the HBC as 'the English.' There was a degree of irony in this as, although the HBC's headquarters was in London, large numbers of its employees in Rupert's Land were Scots and Orcadian. The diversion of the furs from its factories on the bay forced a response, and the HBC spread its tentacles to create its own fur posts in Rupert's Land and the North-Western Territory. Frequently these were located close to, and sometimes even adjacent to, the forts of their upstart competitors. The rivalry between the two enterprises was fierce, but the philanthropic activities of a Scottish lord after 1811 added a new dimension that would lead to a decade of open violence between the two enterprises.

"An aristocrat with a social conscience", the altruistic Thomas Douglas, the 5th Earl of Selkirk, was born near Kirkcudbright in Scotland in 1771.[8] Although he was the seventh son, the deaths of his six elder brothers resulted in him inheriting the earldom upon the death of his father in 1799. Over the course of his travels, he had been particularly moved by the plights of Scottish highland crofters, displaced to make way for large scale sheep farming, and Irish peasants in the aftermath of the uprising of 1798. For a loyal peer of the realm such as Selkirk, emigration to the empire seemed the logical solution. He looked to British North America and, after establishing settlements with different levels of success on Prince Edward Island and in Upper Canada, set his sights on the Red River Valley in Rupert's Land.

> Why Selkirk chose the forks of the Red and Assiniboine rivers for the focus of his new emigration plan is something of a mystery, but perhaps the popularity of the site in the previous century and company officer's praise for the fertility of its land influenced him. Equally important, no doubt, was the exhaustion of the fur resources of this district, the proximity of the buffalo plains (which stretched west of the River between the valleys of the Assiniboine and the Missouri), and easy access to the company transportation route from York Factory.[9]

7 Wilson, "Fur Wars", p628.
8 Keith Wilson, "Settlement at the Forks," *Horizon Canada, Centre for the Study of Teaching Canada Inc.*, October 1985, p747.
9 Friesen, *Canadian Prairies*, p71.

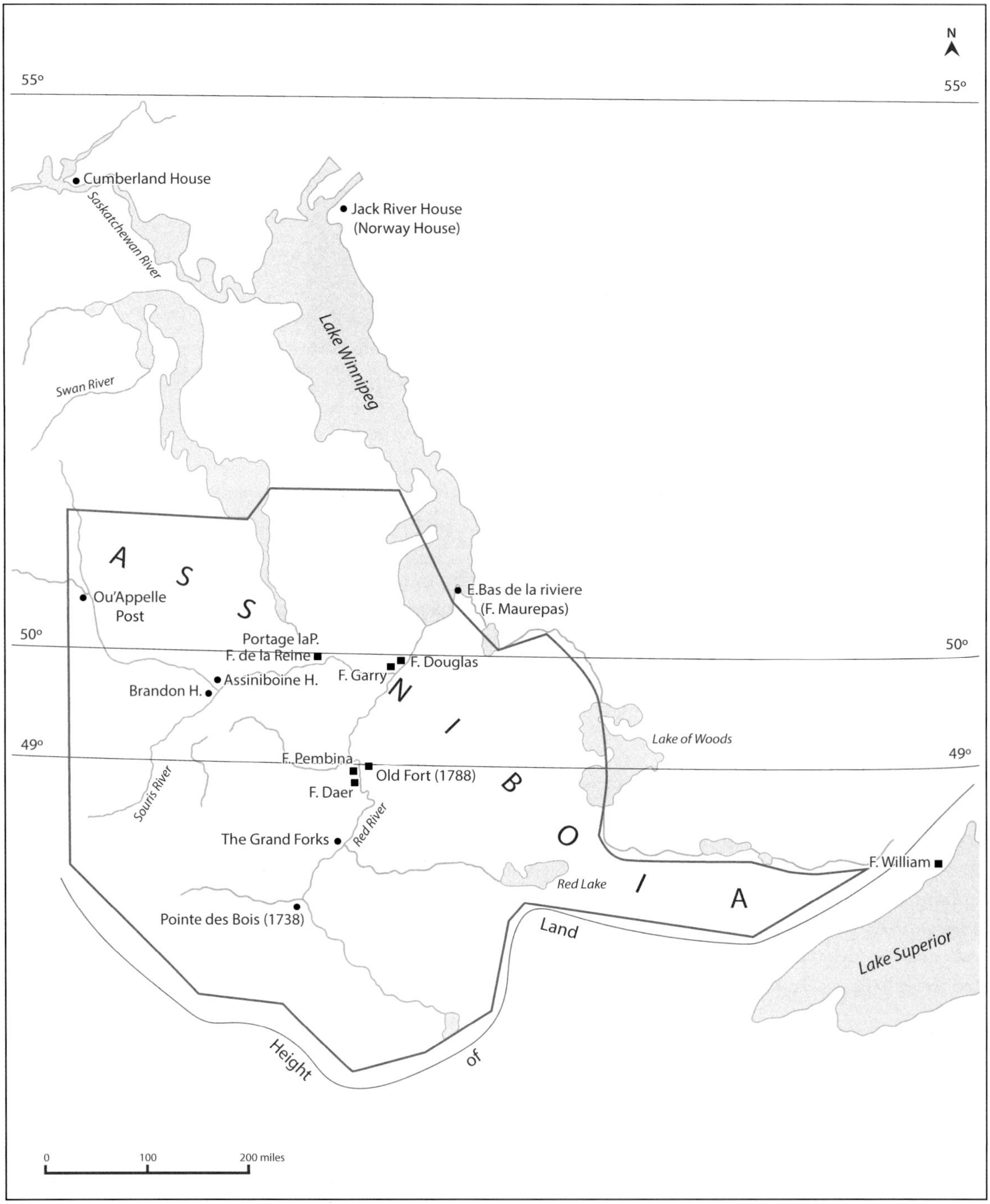

Selkirk Land Grant.

Initial approaches to the British Government did not meet with success. In its view the land fell within the jurisdiction of the HBC and traditionally the Company had been opposed to settlement within its territory. However, by 1808 a downturn in the Company's trade due to the loss of markets in Europe brought about by the Napoleonic Wars, caused the HBC's governing committee to rethink its position. It might after all not be such a bad idea to have a settler colony on its territory. "The colony would furnish provisions for the posts and boat brigades; it would supply country-bred men for the service and offer sanctuary to retired servants and their dependants; ... finally it would confirm the Company's title to the soil, flouted by the Montreal traders, through actual occupation."[10] The Company's financially restrained position also meant a drop in its share price and Selkirk, together with his allies, made large purchases. They did not have a controlling interest, but they had gained 'a strong voice'.[11]

In May 1811 Selkirk was granted a concession of 116,000 square miles centred on the junction of the Red and Assiniboine Rivers that would become known as Assininboia. Even within the ranks of the HBC many remained skeptical of the wisdom of establishing a settler community within fur trading lands. The response from the leaders of the North West Company in Montreal, however, went much further. The region was an important crossroad on their canoe route from Montreal through Fort William to the interior of the continent. In 1809, they had constructed Fort Gibraltar at the confluence of the Red and Assiniboine Rivers. The mouth of the vast Saskatchewan River system, located at the north end of Lake Winnipeg, furnished a route as far west as the Rocky Mountains and provided access to the headwaters of the Columbia River which flowed into the Pacific Ocean. From Cumberland House on the Saskatchewan River, it was also the gateway, via Frog Portage, to the Mackenzie River basin and the rich fur lands of the Athabasca region. The fact that Selkirk was also a major HBC shareholder led to a strong suspicion by William McGillivray, together with the rest of the North West Company leaders, that the actions of the earl had more to do with crippling their trade than it did with philanthropy. While the matter is open to debate, the weight of evidence, particularly in light of what would subsequently take place, supports the notion that altruism was at the heart of Selkirk's motivation. Nevertheless, "the man with the plow was to be placed across the vital route by which all North West transportation moved" and the North West Company wasted no time in setting about destroying the nascent colony before its business could be ruined.[12] William McGillivray's brother, Simon, wrote, "He [Selkirk] must be driven to abandon it, for his success would strike at the very existence of our trade."[13]

It was, however, not solely the North West Company that wished to see an end to Selkirk's dream. The company's transportation link was both long and arduous, and high caloric nourishment to sustain the extreme physicality of the men's exertions was crucial to the success of the trade. The North West Company's success in its competition with the HBC was based on its organization and this included providing the necessary foodstuffs for the men working the canoes. "Corn, flour, and pork grease from Detroit and Michilimackinac fed the brigades across [Lake] Superior" and over the height of land beyond Fort William to Lake Winnipeg.[14] "The plains south of the Assiniboine and Saskatchewan [Rivers] teemed with buffalo, and these furnished the pemmican for the northbound canoemen."[15] Buffalo pemmican, made from thinly cut slices of meat, dried hard and pounded almost to a powder, then mixed with melted fat and sometimes berries, was the staple food for the central portion

10 Morton *Manitoba*, pp44/45.

11 Gray, John Morgan, "DOUGLAS, THOMAS, Baron DAER and SHORTCLEUCH, 5th Earl of SELKIRK," in Dictionary of Canadian Biography, vol. 5, University of Toronto/Université Laval, 2003–accessed May 29, 2017.

12 Douglas MacKay, *The Honourable Company; A History of the Hudson's Bay Company*, (Toronto: McClelland and Stewart, 1949), pp134/35.

13 Mays, Herbert J., "MACDONELL, MILES," in Dictionary of Canadian Biography, Vol 6, University of Toronto/Université Laval, 2003-accessed June 9, 2017.

14 Morton, *Manitoba*, p39.

15 Morton, *Manitoba*, p39.

of the canoe route. Its nutritional value was the fuel that sustained the *voyageurs* during their journey to the trading posts in the interior of the continent.

To provide sufficient amounts of pemmican the buffalo began to be hunted on a more or less commercial scale, rather than simply to supply the needs of the First Nations peoples of the plains as had traditionally been the case. Initially this hunt had been conducted by the aboriginal peoples themselves; the Assiniboine and Cree. Over time, it was competed for and then taken over by a new group of people descended from European men involved in the fur trade and First Nations women.

Marriages *à la façon du pays* (according to the custom of the country) between European men and First Nations women were inevitable as soon as male employees from both fur trading enterprises began taking up residence in the interior of the continent. At first, the HBC had tried to stop such relationships, but this opposition was lifted after 1739, and was thereafter actively encouraged as a way of building trade connections with the indigenous people supplying the beaver pelts. While these marriages could become lifelong, the First Nations tradition was that they could be dissolved when either party became dissatisfied with the arrangement.[16] Consequently, a great many of the offspring of these relationships simply became members of the mother's First Nations tribe. In a much smaller number of cases, children accompanied their fathers who chose to return to the European world after their service in the wilderness was at an end. Over time, however, a third group developed into a new distinct people of mixed race ethnicity with their own customs and traditions. In Rupert's Land there were two distinct branches of this new mixed race group, one French-speaking and the other English-speaking. Today the two groups have largely coalesced into a single people known as the Métis. In the formative years, though, the two were separate and at the time of the Red River Expedition, the term Métis referred to the French-speaking group only.[17]

For the most part, the English speakers were those descended from the marriages of Scottish, Orcadian, and English HBC employees to First Nations women. At this time they were referred to as 'Countryborn.' In the case of the Métis, " ... their offspring established a distinctive culture based on a combination of European and native customs ... .They erected their log cabins on the waterfront, cultivated peas and potatoes ... , created a distinctive costume that combined native moccasins and leggings with European ruffled shirts and waistcoats, and established control over the middle rungs of the fur trade economy."[18] Most importantly for the events about to unfold, "by 1810 they had established roles as buffalo hunter and provisioners to the North West Company."[19]

While it did not happen overnight, as a result of their crucial role in maintaining the food supply, the Métis people of the Red River region were by the end of the eighteenth century beginning to see themselves as a "self-conscious and culturally distinct people;" 'a New Nation.'[20] They viewed the severing of the communication route caused by the creation of Assiniboia, and its consequent impact on the pemmican trade, as just as big a threat to their livelihood as the North West Company did to its. This made the two natural allies and the riding and shooting skills of the Métis, honed by years of experience on the buffalo hunt, made them formidable opponents.

Under the leadership of Miles Macdonell, the newly appointed Governor of Assiniboia, the first group of Selkirk settlers reached the Forks in the summer of 1812. In fact, these were employees of the colony rather than true settlers and it was their job to prepare the groundwork for the real colonists who would follow. With all of the intrigues by the North West Company they were a disgruntled group by the time they arrived, though their difficulties were just a foretaste of what was to come.

16 Sylvia Kirk, "Women in Between, Indian Women in Fur Trade Society in Western Canada", *Historical Papers/Communications historiques*, 12 (1), 1977 pp30–46.

17 In this book the term Métis will refer to the French-speaking group only and not, as is common today, both the English and French-speaking people of mixed race ethnicity.

18 Friesen, *Canadian Prairies*, p 68.

19 Jennifer S.H. Brown, "The Métis: Genesis & Rebirth," in Francis, R. Douglas and Palmer, Howard (Editors), *The Prairie West, Historical Readings (2nd Edition)*, (Pica Pica Press, Text Book Division of the University of Alberta Press, 1992), p109.

20 Bob Beal, & Rod Macleod, *Prairie Fire; The 1885 North-West Rebellion*, (Edmonton: Hurtig Publishers, 1984), p13.

The initial party arrived too late in the season to plant crops and there was insufficient time to construct shelter before winter set in. The majority of the new arrivals moved to the HBC post at Pembina, south of the Forks but still within the borders of Assiniboia. Macdonell and a small group remained and began the construction of Fort Douglas, named in honour of Lord Selkirk. While they were less than pleased by their arrival, the first contacts with the North West Company men and the Métis went fairly well, and relations were in fact better than they were with the HBC representative at Pembina. Macdonell seems to have had an uncanny ability to rub people the wrong way, though the arrival of the first group of actual settlers in late October 1812 exacerbated the mounting pressures he found himself under regarding food supplies and adequate shelter for his charges. The Selkirk settlers moved back to the Forks in the spring of 1813 and were joined by another group of arrivals who had made the journey from York Factory, but when the crops failed they were again forced to move to Pembina for a second winter.

While it is highly likely that sooner or later there would have been a confrontation between Selkirk's settlers and the North West Company and their Métis allies, over the winter of 1813/14 Macdonell made a cardinal blunder making a clash inevitable. His ongoing concern over the supply of food caused him to issue a proclamation forbidding "the taking of any 'flesh, grain or vegetables' out of Assiniboia" for a period of one year unless special licence was received from Macdonell himself.[21] Whether intended or not, " ... from the point of view of the Nor'Westers and the Métis, the 'pemmican proclamation,' as it came to be known, was an open declaration of war. It interfered with the livelihood of the Métis, who supplied the pemmican, and it threatened the trade of the Nor'Westers, who relied upon the staple to feed their trading parties."[22]

Over the summer of 1814 the crisis heightened as Macdonell's representatives confiscated all the pemmican they could lay their hands on. An immediate resort to violence by the Nor'Westers and Métis was narrowly averted by the conclusion of an agreement between the two sides whereby the pemmican would be restored in return for a guarantee that food would be supplied for the settlers the following winter. Nevertheless, tensions returned to a boiling point the following October when the North West Company repudiated the agreement. In fact, the Montreal merchants went much further than simply reneging on their promise to supply food. "They pressed the young metis men of the district to harass the colony, ... to commence open hostilities against the enemy in the Red River, ... and they conducted a campaign of terror in 1815 including the destruction crops, the theft of animals and implements, and the burning of some houses."[23]

Having returned from York Factory with yet another group of settlers, Macdonell had reached the end of his tether and wrote to Selkirk offering to step down as governor should a replacement be sent out. A number of the settlers had also had enough of North West Company intrigue and Métis harassment and accepted an offer from the Nor'Westers of free passage to Upper Canada. Fearing an imminent attack, in June of 1815 Macdonell gave himself up and was transported back to Montreal by North West Company officials. Shortly thereafter, the remaining colonists retreated to Jack River House near the northern end of Lake Winnipeg. It seemed that Selkirk's dream had come to an untimely end.

Upon hearing that his settlement was in jeopardy, Selkirk embarked for North America. When he arrived in New York in October he was greeted with the news that, to all intents and purposes, its existence was already at an end. He journeyed to Montreal to confront the Nor'Westers and prepared to journey to Assiniboa armed with the powers of Justice of the Peace. However, in March of 1816 he heard that all might not be lost after all. It seemed the fortunes of the colony had been reversed through the actions of two men, Colin Robertson and Robert Semple.

Colin Robertson was leading an HBC expedition into the Athabasca fur country when he met the dispossessed Selkirk colonists who had opted to accept safe passage to Upper Canada heading in the opposite direction. After hearing of the depredations they had suffered, he chose instead to lead them back to the settlement. Robertson

21 Wilson," Settlement", pp747/748.

22 Mays, Herbert J., "MACDONELL, MILES," in Dictionary of Canadian Biography, Vol 6, University of Toronto/Université Laval, 2003-accessed June 9, 2017.

23 Friesen, *Canadian Prairies*, p75.

was a man of action and believed that force had to be met with force. In October 1815 he seized Fort Gibraltar from the Nor'Westers and only returned it when he received assurances that the actions of the company and their Métis allies would cease. He rebuilt Fort Douglas and spent the winter there. Not a man to wait on events, in March of the following year, when he again saw signs of aggressive action against the settlement, he seized Fort Gibraltar from the North West Company for a second time.

Robert Semple was Macdonell's replacement as governor of Assiniboia, and he arrived at the Forks a month after Robertson with a new party of settlers. On the surface the arrival of these two men gave the appearance that the tables had been turned on the North West Company and the Métis, and the Selkirk colonists had regained the initiative. This, however, was not the true state of affairs as there were some very real differences between the two men as to how the settlement should be run. Robertson favoured an aggressive response to the Nor'Westers and their Métis allies and argued for the disruption of the supply lines with their trading posts in the interior. The less dynamic Semple believed that securing adequate food supplies for the colony should be the first priority. The two clashed and on June 11th, 1816 Robertson left the colony. The timing of this loss of a leader more attuned to the circumstances with which the settlement was faced could not have been worse.

On June 19th a force of Métis some 60 to 70 strong under Cuthbert Grant reached the settlement. Semple made no attempt to defend the fort and went out with 25 settlers and HBC men to meet with Grant's party. At some point Semple must have recognized the danger because he sent back to the fort for a cannon. The two groups met at an area known as Seven Oaks. A verbal altercation escalated to violence and 20 of Semple's party were killed, including the governor himself, for the loss of one of Grant's men. Fort Douglas surrendered the following day and the settlers were again dispersed.[24]

Meanwhile, early in 1816 before the events at Seven Oaks had taken place, the North West Company's spring brigade left Montreal with the belief that it was time for decisive action. "In 1816 a larger party than usual left, and advance elements had gone ahead with clear instructions to finish off the settlement, preferably with a force of Indians, but by storming the fort if necessary."[25] At roughly the same time, Selkirk, having been unsuccessful in his efforts to have the British authorities in Canada take action to protect his colony, decided to take matters into his own hands. Employing a force of soldiers from the recently disbanded Swiss-German de Meuron and de Watteville regiments, which had fought on the British side in the War of 1812, along with a few Glengarry Fencibles, he set out in the wake of the North West Company's spring brigade with 12 boat loads of supplies and arms for the colony. He had originally intended to bypass Fort William, but on July 25th at Sault Ste. Marie he learned of the Seven Oaks massacre and the consequent destruction of his colony. He was roused with anger and proceeded directly to the North West Company's summer meeting place where the annual gathering was underway. His soldiers took control of the fort and nine of the Nor'Wester partners were arrested, including William McGillivray himself. While the partners were sent back to Montreal, Selkirk spent the winter at the fort and impounded the North West Company furs that fell into his possession. In the depths of winter a party of his soldiers was dispatched on ahead and, after an arduous trek in very difficult conditions, they took the North West Company fort at Lac la Pluie, then Fort Daer at Pembina, and finally Fort Douglas at the Forks in January 1817. Selkirk followed in the spring arriving at the Red River Settlement on June 21st.

The events at Red River had created a considerable stir garnering the attention of Sir John Sherbrooke, the new British governor in Montreal, the Earl of Bathurst, the Colonial Secretary in London, and even the Prince Regent. The cause of this attention undoubtedly had a lot to do with a peer of the realm operating his own private army, and Selkirk had twice ignored warrants for his arrest that reached him at Fort William. In all likelihood, though, it was largely driven by the fact that Selkirk had forced the government in London to act on a matter

24 Hartwell Bowsfield, "SEMPLE, ROBERT," in Dictionary of Canadian Biography, vol. 5, University of Toronto/Université Laval, 2003–, accessed March 13, 2018, and George Woodcock, "ROBERTSON, COLIN," in Dictionary of Canadian Biography, vol. 7, University of Toronto/Université Laval, 2003–, accessed March 13, 2018.

25 Gray, Selkirk.

where it preferred to abstain.[26] British policy had always been to remain aloof from the vast domains of the HBC, and successive governments were determined to leave it to the Company to provide defence and order.[27]

Selkirk was wounded by the repudiation of his actions by the British Government that followed his return from Red River. He was angered that London viewed the affair as a trade war with fault found on both sides. "It took no notice of Selkirk or the settlement as special factors."[28] He returned to Canada and, during the various hearings and inquiries that followed, his health went into decline. He returned to England and then to the south of France in search of a healthier climate. He died there in April 1820.

The fur wars, however, did not just destroy the health of Lord Selkirk, they seriously damaged the financial well-being of both companies, though the HBC had been better able to weather the storm. The vulnerability of the North West Company partners had been laid bare by the disruption in their trade. As early as 1818 William McGillivray was floating the prospect of a merger, to which Selkirk was completely opposed, and while he was alive the prospects were not good. The commission of inquiry held in Montreal into the goings on in Rupert's Land had included a recommendation on the merits of amalgamation.[29] The Colonial Office reached the same conclusion having had enough of the disruption and violence resulting from the rivalry. In 1821, with Selkirk's opposition no longer a factor, the two companies were combined and the name of the North West Company passed into history.[30]

Within a short time the merger would look more like a takeover by the HBC and the headquarters of the new company would be located in London, not Montreal. Indeed, recognizing that their monopoly worked best when isolated from more settled areas and aiming to avoid any new competition from traders in Canada, the great North West Company canoe route largely fell into disuse and for the most part Rupert's Land and the North-Western Territory became cut off from British North America to the east. The border between British North America and the United States established after the Revolutionary War, and then extended by the London Convention from Lake of the Woods to the Rocky Mountains in 1818, meant that any land route from Canada to the lands of the HBC in the west would not be an easy one. This was a simple matter of the geography of the region. The boat brigades of the North-West Company had done exceedingly well in the face of these obstacles, but they were obstacles nonetheless and any larger force looking to move west from Canada could only do so with great difficulty. The HBC had their preferred route from York Factory on Hudson's Bay. This was also a difficult journey, but was now the route of choice for the dominant HBC.

The easier path from Canada to the west was south of the Great Lakes, but this was now United States territory. In 1821 this was a land sparsely populated by Native American peoples, but over the succeeding decades matters would change as American settlers moved into the country. The HBC might have successfully isolated itself from Canada, and in so doing sought to preserve its monopoly over the fur trade, but by the mid-Nineteenth Century a settler frontier would arrive on its southern flank bringing with it far-reaching ramifications for the Company and the people who lived within its territory.

26 Bumstead, *Trials*, pp31/32
27 Galbraith, *Hudson's Bay Company*, p3.
28 Gray, Selkirk.
29 Galbraith, *Hudson's Bay Company*, p5.
30 The North West Company name has, however, been resurrected. In 1987 a group of investors purchased the HBC's Northern Stores Division. They now operate as the North West Company and trace their lineage back to the original organization.

2

Confederation, the Militia and the Fenian Threat

By the middle of the Nineteenth Century British North America was made up of seven colonies, five on the eastern side of the continent and, between 1858 and 1866, two in the west. The vast lands of the HBC lay in between. The five eastern colonies were Newfoundland, Nova Scotia, New Brunswick, Prince Edward Island and Canada. In the west there were Vancouver Island and British Columbia, though these would join together in 1866. Communication in the east was largely waterborne with some rudimentary roads, but railway construction from the late 1830s onwards would revolutionize the way people and goods were moved. Communication from Canada to the HBC lands was virtually non-existent.

The St. Lawrence River Valley of New France had become the British Province of Quebec in 1763 and then, to mollify the United Empire Loyalists moving up from the United States in the aftermath of the American War of Independence, had been divided into Lower and Upper Canada in 1791. The Durham Report following the rebellions of 1837 resulted in the two Canadas being joined together once again in 1841. Despite the majority of the European population residing in French-speaking Canada East, or more accurately because the majority resided here, there was a single legislature with an equal number of seats for both Canada East and Canada West.

This had been acceptable to the residents of Canada West at the time, but by the 1850s the language balance in Canada had irrevocably altered. There had been an influx of English-speaking arrivals most of whom gravitated to Canada West. English and Scots came in roughly equal numbers, but, owing to the famine in Ireland, many more came from here. This resulted in the people of Canada West calling for more seats on its side of the legislature; Representation by Population, or as it was popularly known at the time, 'Rep by Pop'.

There were a number of drivers that would lead in 1867 to the Confederation of the Province of Canada, Nova Scotia and New Brunswick into the new Dominion of Canada. Political deadlock in Canada East and West, the threat of invasion from the United States during and after the American Civil War, and encouragement from Great Britain, where anti-imperialist sentiment had been gaining momentum for several decades, were all factors. The British North America Act, which brought the new country into existence, also made provision for Prince Edward Island, Newfoundland, British Columbia, and, most importantly for this story, the HBC territories of Rupert's Land and the North-Western Territory, to join 'on equitable terms' at a later date.[1]

Without Confederation, acquisition by Canada of the territories controlled by the HBC would have been a non-starter, though by 1869 the HBC was certainly willing to sell if a buyer could be found. Canada East would never have sanctioned the addition of a huge swathe of new territory to the Province of Canada, with its inevitable colonization by English-speaking settlers. This would have tipped the balance far too heavily against the French-speaking side of the province. Confederation, however, divided the lands of the Province of Canada

1 There are a litany of books dealing with Canadian Confederation. Two good examples are: Donald Creighton, *The Road to Confederation; The Emergence of Canada, 1863-1867*, (Toronto: Macmillan of Canada, 1964) and W.L. Morton, *The Critical Years; The Union of British North America 1857-1873*, (Toronto: McClelland and Stewart, 1964).

Sir John A. Macdonald, the first prime minister of the Dominion of Canada. (Notman Studio/Library and Archives Canada/C-010144)

into the two new provinces of Ontario and Quebec within the new Dominion of Canada.[2] The compromises reached during the Confederation negotiations left language and education as a responsibility of the provincial governments rather than the federal government. This meant that French language and culture could be protected within Quebec and, assuming the dominion government in Ottawa was willing to act in acquiring the HBC lands, French Canada would not oppose such a move.

It is somewhat ironic, therefore, that John Alexander Macdonald, the dominant man in Canadian politics during this era, the most important Father of Confederation, and the visionary who saw the critical importance for the new country's survival in taking control of Rupert's Land and the North-Western Territory, had prior to Confederation been a supporter of the *status quo* in the Province of Canada. Described in 1871 by one observer, who will become a very important part of the Red River Expedition story, as " ... the only man of really statesmanlike ability in the Canadian Ministry," the Scottish born Macdonald was an astute politician and a master dealmaker.[3] Highly intelligent, though not a particularly gifted orator, where it suited his purpose he would confuse or delay matters, earning him the sobriquet of 'Old Tomorrow'. He used conviviality, humour, and cajolery to persuade, but when this proved unsuccessful was not averse to exerting raw political power. If all else

2 The origins of the term "Dominion" is interesting, especially in light of the fact that this was the first time it was used in this context. Later the other major settler colonies (Australia, New Zealand, and South Africa) would also be referred to as Dominions. In the 1930's there was the great debate as to whether "Dominion Status" should be granted to India. The Canadian delegates pondered long and hard over what to call the new Canadian creation. They had originally thought of the Kingdom of Canada, but it was decided that this might offend the United States. They settled on Dominion.

3 Garnet Wolseley (An Officer of the Expeditionary Force), "Narrative of the Red River Expedition," *Blackwood's Edinburgh Magazine*, Vol. CVIII July – Dec 1870 and Vol CIX Jan – Jun 1871, London 1870 and 1871 (Published in 3 parts Dec, 1870 and Jan. and Feb. 1871, Part 1 p715.

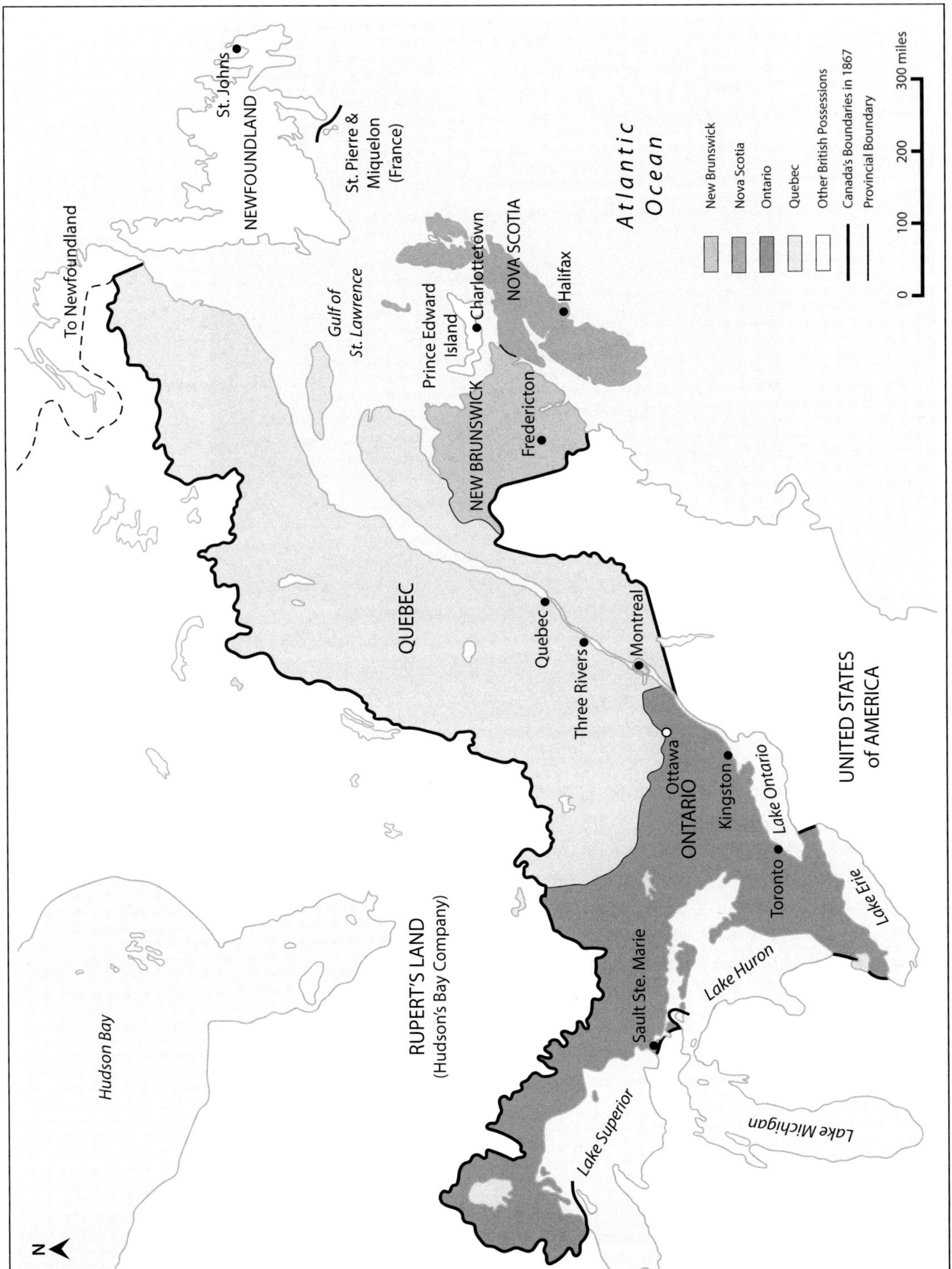

Canada in 1867.

failed there was always the distribution of patronage appointments, and Macdonald ensured that he maintained control of these.[4]

His life away from the political arena was wrought with many challenges and tragedies. His first wife, plagued by chronic ill health, died in 1857. The first of his two sons died at just 13 months of age. A second marriage in 1867 produced a daughter with severe mental and physical disabilities. Perhaps unsurprisingly, Macdonald also had a problem with alcohol. He is perhaps best characterized as being an intermittent binge drinker. His bouts of drunkenness were problematic, but they were periodic and for the most part he was able to function in the face of his personal and political challenges, though he would revert to the bottle at the height of the Red River troubles in April 1870.[5]

Macdonald had opposed the idea of colonial union when it had first been mooted by the Reformers of Canada West in 1859. The Conservatives were not the majority party in Canada West and his ability to maintain a hold on political office was largely due to his alliance with George-Etienne Cartier and the Bleu bloc, which held political sway in Canada East. Opposition to 'Rep by Pop' made both he and the Conservatives unpopular with much of the electorate in Canada West, but he recognized that increasing the number of seats in the west was much more beneficial to his political opponents.[6] He also knew that a federation separating the legislatures of Canada East and West would make it much more difficult for both he and his party to maintain its hold on political power. However, when it became clear that the Canadian legislature had reached a political impasse resulting from the need to obtain a double majority on legislation pertaining to the province as a whole, he recognized that something had to be done. When Reform's George Brown offered in June of 1864 to join any coalition government that would seek a way out of the impasse, Macdonald readily agreed to join with Cartier and Brown in the Great Coalition, believing that " ... if change was inevitable he preferred confederation to the other options available."[7]

Canadians did not embrace the idea of political union with the other British North American colonies from any strong desire for independence. In fact, quite the reverse was the case. If anything it was the British who were urging their colonists to think more clearly about their political future.[8] Nevertheless, once he had made up his mind, Macdonald became the champion of colonial federation, and it was he who " ... not so much created a nation as manipulated and seduced and connived and bullied it into existence against the wishes of most of its own citizens."[9] It was no surprise that Sir John, as he became after Confederation, was the new country's first prime minister.

While the feared American invasion had not materialized either during the Civil War or in its aftermath, as the United States focused on reconstruction and westward expansion after the North's victory, the threat had played its part in encouraging both British and British North American leaders to focus on a colonial union. Nevertheless, in the post-Civil War years a real invasion threat did manifest itself in the form of the Fenian Brotherhood, an Irish Republican organization based in the United States. Attacks would also take place in Great Britain in 1867, but in the North American colonies it took the form of a series of raids originating from south of the border.[10] The

4 See Richard Gwyn, *John A., The Man Who Made Us: The Life and Times of John A. Macdonald Volume One 1815-1867*, (Vintage Canada, 2008), pp2/3, Bruce Hutchison, *Mr. Prime Minister, 1867-1964*, (Don Mills: Longmans Canada Ltd, 1964), pp8-10, & Johnson and Waite, Macdonald.

5 Ged Martin, "Sir John A. Macdonald and the Bottle," *Journal of Canadian Studies/Revue d'études Canadiennes*, Volume 40, Number 3, Fall 2006.

6 J.K. Johnson and P.B. Waite "MacDonald, Sir John Alexander", in *Dictionary of Canadian Biography*, Vol 12, University of Toronto/Université Laval, 2003-accessed June 19, 2017.

7 Philip Buckner, "Macdonald, Sir John Alexander (1815-1891)", *Oxford Dictionary of National Biography*, Oxford University Press, 2004-16, online edn, p4.

8 H.V. Nelles, *A Little History of Canada, Third Edition*," (Don Mills: Oxford University Press, 2017), pp126/27.

9 Gwyn, *John A*, p459

10 Denis Richards and J.W. Hunt, *An Illustrated History of Modern Britain 1783-1964*, (London: Longman Group Limited, 1973), p183.

attacks were carried out largely by Irish veterans of the American Civil War, beginning in 1866 with a reccurrence in 1870/71, though the threat was ever-present throughout the period. One of these incursions, resulting in the Battle of Eccles Hill south of Montreal on the border with Vermont, was fought on May 25, 1870. This coincided with the opening moves of the Red River Expeditionary Force's journey to Fort Garry. It is an important point to make that the dispatch of the force to the Red River Settlement was not the only military matter on the new Canadian Government's plate at this time. Indeed, a major concern of the British military authorities once the expedition to the HBC lands was underway, as we shall see, was the protection from Fenian incursions of its extended line of communication and supply.

The Fenian raids brought about a significant change in the mind-set of Canadians regarding their military and the defence of their borders. Given that two-thirds of the Red River Expeditionary Force would be made up of Canadian volunteers, it is worthwhile taking a brief look at how the Fenian threat unfolded as well as the state of the Canadian militia in 1870.

Throughout 1865 and into 1866 the Fenians made no secret of their intentions towards Britain's North American colonies. It was believed that taking control of British colonial possessions, or even simply threatening them, would force the British Government to free Ireland. London responded with an increase of the garrison strength in North America and by the summer of 1866 it stood at 11,741 men in Canada, with a further 4,969 in Nova Scotia.[11]

The first raid at Campobello in New Brunswick in April 1866 proved farcical for the Fenians, but their attack across the Niagara River, resulting in the Battles of Ridgeway and Fort Erie at the beginning of June, were a greater threat and demonstrated the lack of training and preparedness of Canada's militia force.

Historically the defence of Britain's North American colonies had involved the stationing of a garrison of Imperial troops which, in the event of an emergency, would be backed by local forces. This had been the case in New France prior to 1763 as well. Every able-bodied male was liable to service, though militia gatherings tended to be social occasions; for the most part " ... annual musters ... to keep alive in the public mind the consciousness that personal service was demanded and obligatory."[12] Little in the way of tactical training took place, but in spite of this a militia myth developed in the period after the War of 1812 that the defeat of the American invasions had resulted primarily from the actions of locally raised men rather than the professionalism and discipline of the British regulars. The militia did at times provide solid service between 1812 and 1814, but it was without question the presence of British regulars that saw off the attempted American invasions; not forgetting the valuable assistance from allied First Nations warriors.[13]

Following the granting of responsible government in the Province of Canada in 1849, and concurrent with Britain's move away from protectionist economic policies in favour of free trade, there were repeated cries in London for Canadians to take on a much greater responsibility for their own defence.[14] British North Americans, on the other hand, tended to hold the view that their defence was the responsibility of the Crown. The 1846 Militia Act did for the first time embrace the concept of volunteer local troops, as opposed to universal compulsory service, though accomplished little else. At the start of the Crimean War in 1854, however, "the colonies burst forth in military fervour" to man the posts of the British formations called away to fight the war against Imperial Russia.[15] Even on the far distant Pacific coast, James Douglas, the Governor of Vancouver Island,

11 Desmond Morton, *A Military History of Canada*," (Edmonton: Hurtig Publishers, 1985), p89.

12 C.F. Hamilton, "Defence 1812-1912," in Adam Short and Arthur Doughty (editors), *Canada and Its Provinces, A History of the Canadian People and Their Institutions*, (Toronto: T. & A. Constable at the Edinburgh University Press for the Publishers Association of Canada, 1914), p380

13 J.L.Granatstein, *Canada's Army; Waging War and Keeping Peace*,"(Toronto: University of Toronto Press, 2002), Chapter 1, "The Militia Myth Canada Arm's to Confederation".

14 Responsible Government was the establishment of parliamentary self-government in the Province of Canada. It was granted in the other British North American colonies at around the same time. Previously, while there had been elections to the provincial legislature, the government was made up of individuals who sat at the discretion of the Governor-General. After 1849 the government was drawn from the majority party or a coalition of parties in the legislature. The government was, therefore, "responsible" to the majority in legislature for its time in office.

15 See Morton, *Military*, p46 and Granatstein, *Canada's Army*, p18.

stated his willingness to organize attacks on Russian trading posts if so ordered.[16] In the Province of Canada a new militia act was passed in 1855 which, in addition to the maintenance of the traditional Sedentary Militia, provided for an Active Militia of a little over 4,000 men with training paid for by the government.[17] In 1858 a regiment for service overseas with the British Army, the 100th (Prince of Wales's Royal Canadian) Regiment of Foot, was raised in Canada.[18] However, by the end of the decade enthusiasm for the militia had again waned, and by 1862 militia volunteers in the whole of British North America amounted to 19,000 men, roughly 3% of the males of military age.[19]

The threat posed by the onset of the American Civil War saw a new militia act tabled in the Canadian legislature. It proposed an Active Militia of 50,000 men with a similarly sized reserve; a significant increase over all previous militia bills. John A. Macdonald argued the case for the government, but the bill was strongly opposed and ultimately defeated resulting in the resignation of Cartier's Ministry. Having rushed Imperial troops to Canada in the wake of the Trent Affair, news of the bill's defeat was received with anger in London, a response that many Canadians were at pains to understand. After all it was not their quarrel that was placing them at risk of attack.[20] There might have been some logic to this perspective, given for example Britain's construction of Confederate commerce raiders such as the CSS Alabama. However, a number of actions by colonists in British North America, perhaps most notably the St. Albans Raid in October 1864 when a Canadian court released captured Confederate raiders on a technicality, also angered the United States Government.[21] Consequently, the British position that its North American colonies take a more participatory approach to their defence, was perhaps not as unreasonable as many colonists viewed it.

The new government of John Sandfield Macdonald[22] successfully passed two acts in 1863; one dealing with the non-sedentary militia and one dealing with volunteers. While they may not have gone as far as the British Government would have liked, the Province of Canada was now willing to spend $500,000, whereas eight years before just $10,000 had been deemed sufficient.[23] The volunteer strength was to be increased to 35,000 men, a considerable accomplishment in its own right, but the great achievement was the establishment of schools for the training of officers.[24] "The services of several regiments of the regular army were utilized, and classes of officers and candidates for commissions were formed at Toronto and Quebec, and later at Montreal, Kingston, Hamilton, and London."[25] No officer was to be promoted, except provisionally, until he had successfully passed the course and by April 30th, 1866 over 700 first class certificates and 1400 second class certificates had been awarded.[26] Supplemental training was provided in 1865 by a three-week camp at Laprairie under a certain Colonel Garnet Wolseley.[27] "The Schools were a great success and brought a small measure of professionalism to the militia – for the six years of their existence."[28]

---

16 Morton, *Military,* p79.

17 C.P. Stacey, *Canada and the British Army 1846-1871 (Revised Edition)*, (Toronto: University of Toronto Press, 1963), p93.

18 Stacey, *British Army*, pp105/106.

19 Hamilton, "Defence", p400.

20 The Trent Incident occurred in October of 1861, when an American naval frigate intercepted the British mail packet RMS Trent and removed two Southern diplomats. The war was not going well for the Union at this point and it seemed a distinct possibility that the cause of the Confederacy might prevail. Not wishing to risk an expansion of the war, after several months President Lincoln released the diplomats.

21 Morton, *Military*, p83.

The St. Albans Raid was one of a series of pinprick raids carried out by Confederate forces along the Canadian border which culminated in an attack on the town of St. Albans, Vermont in October 1864. The retreat of the raiders back into Canada, and their subsequent release by a Canadian court, which deemed they could not be extradited because they were soldiers operating under military orders, was not looked upon favourably by the government of the United States.

22 No relation to John Alexander Macdonald.

23 Stacey, *British Army*, p150.

24 Hamilton, "Defence", p403.

25 Hamilton, "Defence", p404.

26 Hamilton, "Defence", p405

27 Hamilton, "Defence", p405

28 Granatstein, *Canada's Army*, p21.

The Fenian threat and the raids that followed changed the mind-set of British North Americans militarily as well as politically. "For St. Patrick's Day 1866, more than fourteen thousand Canadians volunteered for duty."[29] Once the early raids began, "both the people and the political authorities [which] had hitherto showed only a mild interest in military matters; now ... were shocked into making an effort to rectify the weakness and errors which the Fenian Raids had bared."[30] The attacks provided Canadians with an external threat and one which was arguably more manageable than a full-blown invasion by the American Army. This made Canada's militia more important. "A small citizen force could have done little to block Grant and Sherman, but it was the appropriate defensive response against bands of Fenians rarely more than a thousand strong ... ."[31] Regardless, the effect of the raids resulted in Canadians taking the military situation and military training more seriously and this would be demonstrated in their much improved performance when the attacks were renewed in 1870/71.[32]

There was one more militia act prior to the onset of the crisis at Red River and this was the first of the newly created dominion in 1868. Given the raised profile the Fenian raids had given to defence, no lesser personage than George-Etienne Cartier specifically requested the militia portfolio. He had been prime minister when the 1862 bill had failed and his government had resigned on the issue. He took this step so " ... his great influence in Quebec might be utilized to make the government's military policy acceptable to the people of that province, ... [and] because the militia portfolio was regarded in 1867, as one of the most important departments."[33] The 1868 act extended the Province of Canada's militia system to the new Dominion of Canada as a whole. The strength of the Active Militia was set at 40,000 volunteers, divided into nine military districts of which Ontario, with 21,816 Active Militia members and 293,536 in the Reserve Militia, had four and Quebec, with 12,637 in the Active Militia and 202,579 in the Reserve, had three. Two of Quebec's districts were predominantly French-speaking. Nova Scotia and New Brunswick had one district each.[34]

To properly understand the Canadian militia at the time of the outbreak of the Red River troubles, one also must recognize that it was a political as well as a military force. From its early days "volunteer officers ... developed great skill in jockeying for preferment, an early indication that the militia was a political force much more than a military one."[35] Politics and militia went hand in hand. Militia officers tended to be men of high social standing, either sitting members of the Canadian legislature and later parliament or men with serious political influence. "In the first seven parliaments after Confederation" as many as a quarter of all MP's "held some kind of militia commission."[36] Parliamentary debates dealing with the militia's annual estimates became known as 'Colonel's Day', and non-military MPs tended not to be in attendance in the house.[37] "Appointments, promotions, contracts, discipline, even the replacement of worn out uniforms were guided by partisan considerations ... ."[38] As we shall see, there would be political considerations to be reckoned with when it came to the raising of the Canadian component of the Red River Expeditionary Force.

29 Morton, *Military*, p89.

30 George F.G Stanley, *Canada's Soldiers, 1604-1954; The Military History of an Unmilitary People*, (Toronto: The Macmillan Company of Canada, 1954), p231.

31 Ged Martin, *Britain and Origins of Canadian Confederation, 1837-67*, (London: Macmillan Press Ltd, 1975), p40.

32 See: Hereward Senior, *The Last Invasion of Canada; The Fenian Raids of 1866-1870*, (Toronto: Dundurn Press, 1991).

33 Stanley, *Soldiers*, p234.

34 Stanley, *Soldiers* p235 & Morton, *Military*, p90.

35 Granatstein, *Canada's Army*, p18.

36 Desmond Morton, "The Militia Lobby in Parliament: The Military Politicians and the Canadian Militia, 1868-1897," in Adrian Preston and Peter Dennis (Editors) *Swords and Covenants*, (London: Croom Helm Ltd, 1976), p76.

37 Morton, "Militia Lobby", p75.

38 Morton, "Militia Lobby", p75.

3

The Withdrawal of the British Garrisons

The ink was hardly dry on the British North America Act in 1867 when the Canadian Government found itself confronted with a new and uncomfortable reality regarding the defence of its borders. "The Britain of the 1860's was largely anti-imperial in spirit and in practice, more interested in contracting its responsibilities than in extending its imperial frontiers and developing its relationship to distant colonies."[1] The industrial revolution had made Britain economically preponderant in the world and the abandonment of mercantilist principles in the mid-1840s, leading to the adoption of the Manchester School of liberal economics with its emphasis on free trade, resulted in trade with the rest of the world outside of the empire roughly doubling between 1857 and 1875.[2] In 1844 just prior to the abandonment of the Corn Laws, one of the key events along the path to free trade, Britain exported as much to the United States as it did to all of its colonies combined (£8 million), and colonial administration was a burden on the British taxpayer to the tune of £4 million a year. In contrast, an embassy in Washington and a few consulates around the country cost just £15,000.[3]

There were those in the British Government and elsewhere in the establishment who went so far as to take the view that the existing colonies were liabilities, " ... expensive to administer, costly to defend, and they exposed Britain to needless foreign entanglements."[4] Lord Palmerston might forthrightly state " ... there may be much to be said for the theory put forward by some, that our colonies are an encumbrance and an expense, and we should be better without them, but that is not the opinion of England, and it is not mine."[5] However, he was an old man when he penned these words and would not long be a factor on the political scene. His views did not reflect those of the up and coming men such as William Gladstone, who in December 1868, three years after Palmerston's death, formed a new Liberal administration elected on a platform of fiscal responsibility. The new prime minister made no secret of his dislike of the state of affairs regarding Britain's colonial garrisons and, as early as 1861, had said " ... that it was necessary for colonies to learn self-defence if they were to develop into great free communities ... ."[6] Now as prime minister, Gladstone was intent on conducting a thorough reappraisal and reform of Britain's army and the country's military commitments.

Successive British governments had fretted over their relations with the United States during the decades following the War of 1812, though the numerous border disputes and war scares that sometimes followed had

---

1 C.P. Stacey, *Canada and the Age of Conflict; Volume 1: 1867-1921*, (Toronto: University of Toronto Press, 1984), p40.

2 Bernard Porter, *The Lion's Share; A Short History of British Imperialism 1850-1970*, (London: Longman Group Limited, 1975), p65.

3 Morton, *Military*, p78.

4 Nelles, *Little*, p117.

5 Donald Creighton, *John A. Macdonald; The Young Politician*, (Toronto: The Macmillan Company of Canada, 1952), p361.

6 Stacey, *British Army*, p204. There were others in Gladstone's Government who agreed with the prime minister as regards colonial commitments. In 1872 Lord Sherbrooke told the new Governor-General of Canada, Lord Dufferin, "now you ought to make it your business to get rid of the Dominion." See Stacey, British Army, P 125. John Bright at the Board of Trade believed that the separation of Canada and Britain would be good for both countries, and even Lord Granville, the Colonial Secretary, looked with favour upon Canada's eventual independence. See Stacey, British Army, op. cit. p205.

Prime Minister William Ewart Gladstone. (*Illustrated London News*, ILNO-1874-0207-0009-F)

always been resolved by negotiation, or in one case arbitration.[7] However, concern over war with the United States reached an acute stage with the rise of American military power during the Civil War. Britain feared that should the Union's army march north, there was little it could do to prevent its North American territories from being overrun. This was confirmed by a 'frighteningly realistic' report authored by Lieutenant-Colonel William Francis Drummond Jervois of the Royal Engineers, a noted expert on the design and construction of forts. After a visit to British North America in 1863, it was " ... frankly admitted that the western part of the province of Canada was indefensible."[8] Jervois " ... recommended that Halifax, Montreal and Quebec be fortified and that British regulars be concentrated at the last two cities. He did not believe that the Great Lakes could be held and concluded that defence west of Montreal was impossible."[9] The political maelstrom this unleashed in Canada resulted in Jervois' return to British North America and the production of a second slightly more optimistic report. This outlined how victory in a war with the United States could be achieved through a combination of the construction of temporary fortifications in the direction of Hamilton and naval control of Lake Ontario. This would allow a strategic withdrawal east and, with the arrival of winter, it was thought that a stalemate on land would result. While all of this was going on, the Royal Navy would blockade the American coast with the result that Wasington's trade would be strangled and a British victory attained. His conclusion regarding large parts of Canada being indefensible, however, remained largely unchanged.

It was not just the risk of war with the United States, however, that was causing the British Government to re-think its commitment to imperial defence. From London's perspective imperial garrisons were not specifically a Canadian issue, they were rather a British issue that involved Canada. Britain was a global power and, as such,

7 The dispute surrounding the San Juan Islands, on the Pacific coast lying between the mainland and southern Vancouver Island, and known as the Pig War, was settled by the arbitration. The dispute began in 1859 and lasted for 12 years until it was resolved by the German emperor in favour of the United States. See E.C. Coleman, *The Pig War; The Most Perfect War in History*, (Stroud: The History Press, 2009).

8 Creighton, *Confederation*, p86.

9 Winks, Robin W. Winks, "JERVOIS, Sir WILLIAM FRANCIS DRUMMOND," in Dictionary of Canadian Biography, vol. 12, University of Toronto/Université Laval, 2003–accessed May 13, 2016.

Secretary of State for War Edward Cardwell. (*Illustrated London News*, ILNO-1865-0318-0008-F)

had to take a much broader view of its worldwide responsibilities and commitments. It was the Royal Navy that allowed Britain to flex its military muscle on the world stage. Though much improved since the Crimean War, the army was still dwarfed by its major European rivals, and for much of the Nineteenth Century up to this point had largely been broken up and based in overseas colonial garrisons. As far back as 1827 the Duke of Wellington had noted that of 110 battalions of foot in the army, only 40 were stationed in Great Britain and Ireland, 20 were in India and 50 were on garrison duty throughout the empire.[10] By the mid 1830's 80% of the cost of empire to the British taxpayer was as a result of the expense of the overseas garrisons.[11] In addition to fiscal matters, whenever a crisis arose across the globe, including threats of war with France in 1840 and again in 1850/51, or the actual outbreak of war in the Crimea in 1854 and India in 1857, there was the perennial struggle to find sufficient troops to meet requirements. In 1861 there were garrisons in no less than 34 overseas possessions or dependencies and because Britain's was a maritime empire, there was also a constant flow of troops at sea in transit from one garrison to another.[12]

In Canada the formation of the Royal Canadian Rifles in 1840 helped in small part to alleviate this continual movement of men. Raised from long service veterans from other regiments and stationed permanently in Canada, it was said that the RCR had more medals than any other regiment in service, though its primary purpose was to man the frontier posts and prevent other members of the British garrison from deserting to the United States.[13] They were, however, never the equivalent of a regular line battalion of infantry due to the age of the men and the fact that there was no provision for reserves.[14] The RCR received higher rates of pay, as well as grants of land upon retirement which, it was hoped, would entice the men to remain in Canada at the end of their service. Over 500 did, with more than half going on to serve in the militia.[15]

10 Stacey, *British Army*, pp53/54.
11 Stacey, *British Army*, p39.
12 Hamilton, "Defence", p393.
13 Hamilton, "Defence", p394.
14 J. Mackay Hitsman, *Safeguarding Canada, 1763-1871*, (University of Toronto Press, 1968), p155.
15 Roberts, Rick, "Records of the Royal Canadian Rifles," Global Genealogy & History Store, http://globalgenealogy.com/globalgazette/canada-military/british-in-cda/roal-cdn-rifles-1840.htm

By the time Gladstone's Government came to power, Britain's focus was fixedly on Europe and the rise of Prussia. While Canadian politicians struggled with the issues that would lead to Confederation, Prussia had embarked on a series of wars that had re-structured central Europe. The Second Schleswig-Holstein War in 1864 had been followed by the Austro-Prussian War in 1866. The Franco-Prussian War would follow in 1870/71. If the British had been inclined to intervene or try to exercise their influence on the continent, they had very limited means militarily of doing so. The British Army was largely stationed overseas in its colonies and a major overhaul was long overdue.

The man appointed Secretary of State for War, with the task of pushing through this reform and bringing the army's costs under control, was Edward Cardwell. Throughout his political career the new War Secretary had developed an unfavourable view of the how the War Office operated. He sought "'to obtain the greatest amount of efficiency at the smallest cost,' and this could only be successfully accomplished by means of 'a complete reformation of a system now universally pronounced to be unsatisfactory.'"[16]

Cardwell would only begin the fundamental reform of the British Army and it would be left to future Secretaries of State for War to carry on with this work. For the purposes of the Red River story, suffice to say that his work spelled the end of the colonial garrisons in Canada, as well as other self-governing settler colonies. Henceforth, military establishments would be reserved for imperial stations such as the naval bases Gibraltar, Malta and Halifax, as well as India and Ireland, and Cardwell wasted no time in putting his plans into action. In 1869, he proposed to reduce the total forces in the colonies from 50,000 to 26,000[17] and, despite protests from Canadian politicians, his decision to reduce the number of British troops in Canada from over 16,000 in 1868/69 to just over 6000 in 1869/70 met with no significant criticism at Westminster, demonstrating once again " ... the dissatisfaction of Parliament with the old colonial arrangements."[18]

A renewed crisis with the United States stemming from the rejection by the American Senate of Britain's offer of settlement for losses sustained to Union shipping during the Civil War, did not deter Cardwell from his plan for the withdrawal of the garrisons either. Assistance would be given for the raising and training of local forces, arms would be supplied at cost price, and there would be a loan guarantee for fortifications if the Canadian government wished to take advantage of it; but, as Lord Granville, the Colonial Secretary,' communicated to the Governor-General Sir John Young in February 1870, aside from 2,000 troops stationed at Halifax, only one battalion of infantry and one battery of garrison artillery would remain in Canada for the present year and these would be concentrated at Quebec. The Canadian Government had made it known that it was unwilling to assume the cost of the Royal Canadian Rifles and so the decision was made to disband them.[19] All other British troops stationed in Canada would be withdrawn at the end of 1870.[20]

Canadians in general were less than pleased with these decisions, though Ottawa had done little to ingratiate themselves with the British military as Cardwell announced his department's decisions. One example involved the small British force that remained at Toronto. The Secretary of State for War, recognizing its isolation, had wanted it withdrawn. At the behest of Sir Charles Windham, the commander of British forces in Canada, they were kept in place, but only after Cardwell had extracted a personal commitment from Windham that he would take responsibility for ensuring that Canadian forces would be available to support them in the event of an emergency. However, when a Fenian crisis arose and Windham requested the calling out of 3,000 volunteers to bolster his isolated garrisons, Minister of Militia Cartier refused citing that parliament had not voted on funds for such an enterprise.[21]

As has already been noted, the aim of the Cardwell reforms was to bring about an improvement in the British Army's capability in the wider world and were not aimed specifically at Canada. However, this does not mean

16 Giles St. Aubyn, Giles, *The Royal George; The Life of H.R.H. Prince George Duke of Cambridge, 1819-1904*, (London: Constable, 1963), p136.

17 Stacey, *British Army*, p208.

18 Stacey, *British Army*, pp209-212.

19 Stacey, *British Army*, p214.

20 Stacey, *British Army*, pp226/227.

21 Stacey, *British Army*, pp219/220.

London did not have specific reasons for taking these steps in North America. As Professor Desmond Morton has noted, the removal of the garrisons "... served notice that no sane British government would again contemplate war with the United States and, whatever an occasional eccentric soldier might imagine, no sane Canadian politician would expect it."[22] Unfortunately for Canada, the decision on the withdrawal of the garrisons coincided with a belated realization in Ottawa that trouble was brewing in the lands of the HBC; territory that in 1869 Canada was preparing to purchase. Very shortly the Canadian Government would find they had need of British military support. The question would be whether the British would be willing to cooperate.

22 Morton, "Militia Lobby", p76.

4

The End of the Fur Trade Monopoly

With the merging of the two fur trading enterprises in 1821, the old North West Company route from Fort William largely fell into disuse and communication with the trading posts of the interior was maintained through York Factory on Hudson's Bay. Assiniboia remained under the control of the Selkirk family until 1834 when it reverted to the HBC. Its size was reduced when in 1818 the United States and Britain established the international boundary from the Northwest Angle at Lake of the Woods to the Rocky Mountains as running along the 49th parallel. All territories south of this line were now within the United States. In 1838 Assiniboia was re-defined as being those lands lying within 50 miles of the junction of the Red and Assiniboine Rivers. It came to be ruled by a governor and appointed council with the first governors being servants of the Selkirk family. After the lands reverted to the HBC, the governor was appointed by the Company, though both he and the council remained very much overshadowed by Sir George Simpson, 'the little emperor'; the HBC's omnipotent man in the north-west between 1825 and his death in 1860.

After 1821 the Red River colony grew, though it did not exactly prosper. Floods occurred in 1826, 1852 and 1861 and there were periodic plagues of grasshoppers, as well as droughts.[1] The North West Company's Fort Gibraltar was renamed Fort Garry, after Nicholas Garry a deputy governor of the HBC who had been their representative in the Northwest during the amalgamation. It became the Company's administrative hub in the region, as well as the meeting place for the Council of Assiniboia. After it was destroyed in a flood, a new fort was built nearby in 1835. It became known as Upper Fort Garry to differentiate it from a second fort that had been built twenty miles downstream on higher ground in 1830. This second fort was known as Lower Fort Garry and sometimes the Stone Fort.[2]

The population at the settlement was diverse. Selkirk's Swiss-German soldiers had for the most part moved on; however the descendants of his settlers, by this time referred to as the Kildonan Scots, remained. Then there were the retired HBC employees. While the Company had never been fully convinced of the merits of combining the fur trade and colonization, an assortment of Company officers and servants had settled at the Forks after their work in the fur trade was at an end. They were largely Scots and Orcadian with some English and, together with their First Nations wives and children, they quickly settled into a sedentary agricultural life. These were the people that came to be known as 'Countryborn'. In 1836 thirteen families made up largely of Lincolnshire farmers arrived to add to the settlement's mix. There was also a smattering of French-Canadian immigrants and it was " ... from this group [that] most of the leaders of the French-speaking community of Red River were to trace their origin."[3]

Then there were the Métis. Pembina was more convenient for the buffalo hunt, nevertheless, by 1823 most had been persuaded to settle at Fort Garry. The tradition and draw of the hunt, however, meant that they were less attentive to the settled way of life on the farm and, together with their view of themselves as the shield of the

1 MacKay, *Honourable*, p258.
2 Bell "Old Forts" pp11/12.
3 Morton, *Manitoba*, p63.

settlement against marauding Sioux war parties, " ... served to perpetuate ... their strong sense of identity, their belief that they were a 'new nation.'"[4]

Regardless of the language of the Red River settler, lots were laid out in the tradition of French Canada, each farm " ... bound to the river's edge; not a single farmstead ... built away from the water side, not a lot ... laid out without its river frontage."[5] Over time the settlement spread out along the Red and Assiniboine Rivers to Pembina in the south and Portage-la-Prairie in the west, with each settler group living within its own parishes. French-speakers resided along the Red River south of Upper Fort Garry to the United States border at Pembina and west along the Assiniboine River. English-speaking parishes were found north of Fort Garry along the Red River towards Lake Winnipeg and west along the Assiniboine from Poplar Point to Portage-la-Prairie. Legal ownership of the land was complex. The titles of the Kildonan Scots and those of the 'Countryborn' had either been recorded in the HBC records or were long-term grants. The Métis, on the other hand, were simple squatters and this would complicate matters when Canada looked to take over.

By 1870 the population of the settlement had risen to 12,000. 48.1% were French-speakers of mixed race ethnicity, 34.1% were English-speakers of mixed race ethnicity, 13.1% were white and 4.7% were First Nations. Where there had been 600 mixed race families in residence in 1835, there were more than 2500 families thirty-five years later.[6]

In 1821, as part of the terms of the merger, the new company was granted a twenty-one year licence to trade exclusively in the lands west of Rupert's Land. When in 1837 the HBC applied to the British Government for a renewal of this licence, though it was granted for a further twenty-one years, " ... a special clause was inserted granting the Crown authority to annex any part of the Company's chartered territories for the purpose of establishing a Crown colony."[7]

By the 1840's the arrival of the American settler frontier south of the 49th parallel was fundamentally changing the Hudson's Bay Company's world. There was the very real risk of the American settlers continuing their advance into HBC territory. This was accompanied by a general sense of lawlessness at the Red River itself as locals from all of the settlement's communities sought to exploit the changed circumstances by breaking the HBC's monopoly and trading directly with the United States. The Territory of Minnesota, created in 1849, had a population of just 6077 in 1850. By 1870 the State of Minnesota, established in 1858, had a population of over 172,000.[8] The isolation of the HBC lands, the fundamental piece of the equation that had made their monopoly on trade a viable business model, was quickly withering away.

The advent of the railway, and a riverboat service on the Red River as far as Pembina in 1858, meant " ... the Red River colony was being drawn into the American economy by a transportation system linking it with the United States. The imminence of American absorption was symbolized by the extension of the United States postal service to Pembina in 1857."[9] St. Paul lay just 470 miles away and, while this was roughly the same distance as Fort William or York Factory, these were " ... marked by portages and dangerous waters and through rugged country."[10] The trip from Lake Superior to Red River could take up to three weeks and a rival Canadian postal service failed as a result. On June 14th, 1860 there were only six letters in the outgoing Canadian mail whereas almost eight hundred pieces of mail and newspapers were sent via the American service.[11] The Company lands

4 Morton, *Manitoba*, p63.
5 Morton, *Manitoba*, p85.
6 R. Louis Gentilcore, (Editor), *Historical Atlas of Canada; Volume 2 The Land Transformed 1800-1891*, (University of Toronto Press, 1993), Plate 18.
7 Stanley, *Western Canada*, p21.
8 Galbraith, *Hudson's Bay Company*, p336.
9 Galbraith, *Hudson's Bay Company*, p336.
10 Morton, *Critical Years*, pp24/25.
11 Gerald E Boyce, "Canadian Interest in the Northwest, 1856-1860," (Unpublished Thesis mspace.lib.umanitoba.ca 1960), p167.

were being drawn inexorably into the American orbit and the viability and survival of the HBC was becoming a major question mark.

In 1846 there was a war scare between Great Britain and the United States as a result of the Oregon Boundary Dispute.[12] Sir George Simpson wrote to London expressing concern for the safety of the Company's territories should war break out, though it seems he was more interested in convincing the British Government to send a military force for the maintenance of law and order at the Red River Settlement itself rather than protection of the HBC's lands from the threat of American invasion. He would write:

> The presence of military establishments in the Interior can be productive of little benefit to us at any other point than Red River Settlement, & there one is absolutely necessary to the existence of the Fur Trade, not in reference to any difficulty with the United States only, but as a means of protection against the inhabitants of the Settlement, as with the feeling at present on the minds of the half-breeds, it will be quite impossible to protect the trade or inforce our laws without the presence of military at that point … .[13]

In spite of reservations from one as venerable as the Duke of Wellington himself, on June 26th, 1846 a detachment of the 6th Regiment of Foot, comprising approximately 300 officers and men, along with a few gunners and engineers, under the command of Major John Crofton, sailed from Cork, Ireland bound for Hudson's Bay. They arrived at York Factory on August 8th and, after an arduous journey up the Hayes River, were safely in residence at Upper and Lower Fort Garry by October 6th. In fact, the Oregon Boundary Dispute was settled before they arrived, but the force would remain at the settlement for two years and, according to Red River resident Alexander Ross, they were a popular addition to the community. This might have had something to do with the money they brought into the local economy, but they were certainly a stabilizing influence at the unruly settlement as well.[14]

Interestingly, the British considered utilizing the Métis as irregular troops should hostilities break out with the United States. The views expressed at this time are a revealing window into how the British looked upon the people who would challenge Canada a quarter of a century later. In 1845 British Lieutenants Warre and Vavasour were sent west from Canada to report on the defensibility of the north-western territories, particularly Oregon. As they took the same route the Red River Expedition would take in 1870, it is interesting to note they reported that, while it was possible to send troops overland from Fort William, heavier ordnance would have to come by way of York Factory. As any British expedition sent from Canada would of necessity been composed primarily of infantry, rather interestingly they stated " … that a small body of cavalry and artillerymen would be the best types for the occasion; they could form a 'core' of regiments raised among the half-breeds."[15]

Lord Cathcart, the recently appointed commander of British troops in North America, also felt that forming a native corps " … of a warlike and hardy race" could in the event of war serve to rally the tribes on the American side of the frontier, " … it being well known that they cherish a deadly hatred towards the Americans."[16]

Major Crofton as well spoke very highly of the Métis.

---

12 The Oregon Boundary Dispute came about as a result of rival British and American claims to the territories west of the Rocky Mountains. The initial American position had been for control of all lands as far north as 54°40'. The British had proposed that the border should follow the Columbia River. In 1846 it was agreed that the border should continue along the 49th Parallel to the Pacific Ocean with all of Vancouver Island going to the British. It was vague as to where the border would fall between the mainland and Vancouver Island which later resulted in the Pig War between 1859 and 1871.

13 Morton, *Canadian West*, p808.

14 Alexander Ross, *The Red River Settlement; It's Rise, Progress, and Present State*," (London: Smith, Elder and Co., 1856), pp364/365 & Morton, *Manitoba*, p76.

15 Morton, *Canadian West*, p808.

16 See: Cooke, O. A. and Hillmer, Norman, "CATHCART, CHARLES MURRAY, 2nd Earl CATHCART," in Dictionary of Canadian Biography, vol. 8, University of Toronto/Université Laval, 2003–, accessed March 26, 2018. Also, William R. Morrison, "The Sixth Regiment of Foot at Lower Fort Garry," in *Canadian Historic Sites: Occasional Papers in Archaeology and History* – No. 4, Ottawa, 1970, pp168/169.

> They are a tall, strong, and active race of men. They are the best horsemen and marksmen in the country. If it should ever be considered expedient by Her Majesty to raise a body of irregular cavalry in this country, there exist in the half-breed the most eligible material I have ever seen in any country and I have seen the Risalus of India and the Arabs.[17]

Simpson too, despite his reservations about the security at the Red River Settlement, in response to questions from Cathcart, responded with enthusiasm regarding the military abilities of the Métis, stating that:

> ... the inhabitants of Red River ... would be effective either as Cavalry or Infantry. They are excellent horsemen, quite remarkable for activity on foot; and from the constant use of the snow shoe in the winter, could during that season, when the employment of horses would be impracticable, on account of the depth of the snow, perform journeys on foot which the Whites would be unequal to.[18]

He went so far as to put forth the idea that, in the event of war, four Royal Naval warships should be stationed at the mouth of the Columbia River on the Pacific coast together with a large body of marines and 2,000 Métis and Indians.[19] Quite what the Métis themselves would have made of these discussions had they known of them was never put to the test.

The British Red River garrison was withdrawn in 1848; it had never been intended that it would be permanent. The troops were replaced by a group of military pensioners. Though much was promised as far as the quality of these men, they were ineffectual in maintaining the HBC's authority and equally bad as farmers. The result was a return to the state of lawlessness and uncertainty that had prevailed in 1846.

Matters came to a head in 1849 following the indictment of Guillaume Sayer and three others, charged with illegally trading furs. The trial was a raucous and intimidating affair with armed Métis present. The pensioners demonstrated their ineffectiveness by staying away. The jury returned a decision of guilty but recommended mercy and no penalty was imposed. "This 'pardoning' led to the assumption by the armed crowd that the accused had been acquitted and they swarmed away shouting 'trade was free.'"[20] While strictly speaking this was not the case, the HBC never again attempted to enforce its monopoly and a bustling trade developed with St. Paul. The old order in the Northwest was as good as dead and Governor Simpson made no secret of his view that the heyday of the fur trade monopoly was over. In 1856, he told John Shepherd, the newly elected governor in London " ... it would be wise to sell the company's rights before the British government became aware that they were worthless."[21]

The new state of affairs after the Sayer trial saw fur sales with Minnesota increase " ... from $5,000 in 1845 to $40,000 in 1855 and an average of over $150,000 annually in the following several years."[22] The Métis once again carved out an economic niche for themselves, as their forebears had done, and took control of the carrying trade between the Forks and St. Paul. Goods were carried in two wheeled Red River carts and after 1850 they became so numerous they were organized into brigades. Where there had been only six carts in 1844 there were 102 in 1851 and by 1869 there were 2,500, stirring up clouds of dust on the prairie trails, the ungreased wooden axles shrieking.[23] According to Canadian traveller and poet Charles Mair, who would also play a role in the events at Red River during the troubles, "to hear a thousand of these wheels all groaning and creaking at one time is a sound never to be forgotten – it is simply hellish."[24] By 1858 even the HBC had accepted the merits of the easier transportation route south of the border and was beginning to bring some of its supplies through St. Paul as well.

17 Stanley, *Western Canada*, p127.
18 Morrison, "Sixth Regiment", p168.
19 Barry Gough, *Britannia's Navy; On the West Coast of North America 1812-1914*, (Heritage House Publishing Company Ltd, 2016), p88.
20 Morton, *Manitoba*, p77.
21 Galbraith, *Hudson's Bay Company*, p338.
22 Friesen, *Canadian Prairies*, p102.
23 Wilson, "Settlement", p751.
24 Wilson, "Settlement", p751

British soldiers would yet again make the long trek to Red River in 1857. Governor Simpson seized on a report of American cavalry on the plains near Pembina and convinced Lord Palmerston of the need for a garrison.[25] This time it was a company of the Royal Canadian Rifles and, in spite of the Warre and Vavasour report of 1845 regarding the viability of the overland route from Fort William, as with the 1846 expedition, the men travelled via York Factory.[26] This time however they came from Canada, leaving Montreal on June 23rd, 1857. They reached York Factory at the end of August and by October were at Fort Garry.[27] By 1861 the War Office in London was no longer willing to foot the bill for the maintenance of the garrison and the HBC declined to pay for its replacement. Its withdrawal signified the end of effective Company rule at the Red River Settlement.[28]

A further request for a military garrison at Fort Garry, this time from the resident Roman Catholic bishop and the local settlers worried about Sioux warriors moving up from Minnesota, was made in March of 1863. The British Government, however, had scant interest in adding to its list of garrisons in remote outposts of empire and no action was taken. The Colonial Secretary took the view that the HBC was responsible for the defence of Rupert's Land and, if the local population was that concerned, they should form their own volunteer militia.[29]

In 1857, with the HBC's licence two years from expiry, a Select Committee of the House of Commons met in London to determine the future of the Company's concession. It reviewed all aspects of operations, but key to the Red River story, "they tried ... to discover whether the plains of the Northwest could be used for any other purpose than the fur trade, and whether the Company's licence should be renewed, or some commercial and political changes recommended."[30] The Select Committee sat for over forty days and heard from twenty witnesses. The report that followed recommended that the licence should be renewed, but that areas suited for settlement, such as the valleys of the Red and Saskatchewan Rivers, should be ceded to Canada when the Canadian Government was in a position to accept them.[31]

Even before the sitting of the Select Committee, however, both the British and Canadian Governments had determined there was a need for more information regarding the soil and climate of the region. This resulted in the dispatch of two separate expeditions to the Northwest, one British and one Canadian. The British under Captain John Palliser sailed from England in May 1857 and the Canadians set out two months later. Initially the Canadian party was headed by George Gladman, a retired HBC officer, with Simon James Dawson, an engineer born in Scotland in 1818 and a man who will become important in the Red River Expedition story, and Henry Yule Hind a Cambridge trained professor of chemistry and geology. Both expeditions made their way across Lake Superior and then canoed and portaged their way to the interior. The Canadians were wracked with dissension from almost the outset. Gladman fell out with the other two and withdrew. Hind and Dawson ultimately conducted two separate expeditions and then clashed with each other during the report stage.[32]

Both British and Canadian reports agreed that, contrary to the views the HBC had espoused for as long as anyone could recall, and were still being given voice by Sir George Simpson during the hearings of the Select Committee, there were vast tracts of potential farmland to be found in the Northwest. "Hind ... waxed lyrically over the truly 'fertile valleys of the west,' calculating that between the Red River and the south branch of the Saskatchewan, there were eleven million acres of fertile and arable land."[33] Dawson was even more optimistic and

25 Morton, *Critical Years*, p28.

26 Stanley, George F.G.: "A Soldier at Fort Garry," in *The Beaver, Governor and Company of Adventurers trading into Hudson's Bay*, Winnipeg, Autumn 1957, p10.

27 Stanley "Fort Garry", p11.

28 See Morton, *Manitoba*, p103 and Friesen, *Canadian Prairies* p114.

29 Hitsman, *Safeguarding*, p182.

30 Morton, *Manitoba*, p95.

31 At the time of the licence renewal in 1838, the British Government had established its right to set up crown colonies on HBC lands. One was established on Vancouver Island in January 1849 and a second on the mainland (British Columbia) in the aftermath of the Select Committee in 1858.

32 Elizabeth Arthur, *Simon J. Dawson, C.E.*, (Thunder Bay Historical Museum Society, 1987), pp5-11.

33 Bumstead, *Trials*, p131.

proposed the construction of a road from Thunder Bay to Upper Fort Garry, which the Canadian Government declined to undertake due to cost.[34] Palliser's report, published shortly afterwards, agreed that there were millions of acres of prime agricultural real estate, but cautioned that there was a large area of dry belt, an area of desert like conditions, that became known as Palliser's Triangle. In this regard, Palliser was correct.

Though the Canadians were perhaps overly confident and Palliser too pessimistic, both were positive as regards the potential for agricultural exploitation.[35] Combined with the recommendations of the Select Committee, there was now ample information to support the cause of Canadian expansionists. "Science had ... confirmed what the continental expansionists had long known instinctively: the Northwest could not only be settled, but as the Canadian government would insist in 1864, was 'capable of sustaining a vast population.'"[36] It now remained to be seen what the Canadian Government would do. There was also the question of what action the American expansionists would take.

34 Arthur, *Dawson*, & Arthur, Elizabeth, "DAWSON, SIMON JAMES," in Dictionary of Canadian Biography, vol. 13, University of Toronto/Université Laval, 2003–, accessed April 4, 2018.

35 Morton, Manitoba, op. cit. p100.

36 Bumstead, *Trials*, p132.

5

The Control of the Northwest

The fur trade monopoly had evaporated in the wake of the Sayer trial and the HBC lands appeared to be moving inexorably into the economic orbit of Minnesota. The most likely, and in many ways the most logical, long term future for Rupert's Land and the North-Western Territory seemed to be that they would move into its political orbit as well. American annexationists such as James Wickes Taylor, who would become an informant for the American State Department at Fort Garry during the Red River troubles, Joseph Wheelock, editor of the *Daily Press* in St. Paul, Minnesota, Financier Jay Cooke, and William Marshall, who would visit Red River at Cooke's behest in April 1870, certainly believed that the Northwest would fall under the control of the United States especially if it could be made dependent on communications through Minnesota; and this was already well underway.

The problem for American annexationists before the outbreak of the Civil War, however, was the balance that successive United States administrations were determined to maintain between slave and non-slave owning territories.[1] Any increase in the latter could upset the delicately poised equilibrium. Additionally, in 1857 an economic panic dried up the supply of credit leaving little money for the policies of the expansionists.[2] Americans were otherwise occupied during the Civil War itself, but concurrently with this cataclysmic conflict, in Minnesota between 1862 and 1864 there was a vicious local war underway between the settlers and the Sioux.

With the victory of the Union armies in 1865, and the slave versus non-slave balance no longer a matter of concern, interest from the American frontier states in acquiring the HBC territories reasserted itself. Though never getting out of committee stage, in 1866 a bill was introduced in the House of Representatives in Washington to purchase the lands of the HBC for $10 million and admit Nova Scotia, New Brunswick, Canada East and Canada West into the American Union as new states. This was followed in March of 1868 by the passing in the Minnesota State Legislature of a resolution calling for the annexation of the HBC lands to the United States, though it found no support in Washington. Annexationists took heart when Ulysses S. Grant became president in March 1869. Both he and his Secretary of State, Hamilton Fish, " ... were expansionist-minded not only in regard to the North West Territories, but to Canada ... " as well.[3] At an early cabinet meeting Grant went so far as to make clear that " ... the acquisition of Canada was among his principal policy goals."[4] However, Grant and Fish were 'responsible men' and aspiring to acquire these lands did not mean they were willing to do so at the risk of fomenting an 'international incident'.[5] Prime Minister Macdonald would certainly worry over the attitudes and actions of American politicians in both Washington and the western border states, but he had correctly assessed just how far they were willing to go when he wrote in January 1870 " ... that the United States Government are

1 Friesen, *Canadian Prairies*, p110 & Morton, *Critical Years*,. p25.
2 Friesen, *Canadian Prairies*, p110.
3 Hartwell Bowsfield, "The United States and the Red River Settlement," *Manitoba Historical Society Transactions*, Series 3, Number 23 1966-67 Season, p9.
4 Richard Gwyn, *Nation Maker; Sir John A. Macdonald: His Life, Our times, Volume Two: 1867-1891*, (Vintage Canada, 2012), p96.
5 Bowsfield, "United States", p6.

The prairie border between the HBC Territory/Canada and the United States in 1870.
(*Illustrated London News*, ILNO-1870-0129-0016-F)

resolved to do all they can, *short of war,* [author's emphasis] to get possession of the western territory … ."[6] Grant was not about to risk triggering a crisis with the British over their North American territories and the simple truth of the matter was, without support from Washington, the aspirations of the Minnesota annexationists rested on very shaky foundations.[7]

Another potential outcome for the HBC's lands was that Britain would turn the fertile belt into a crown colony. As we have seen, provision for the establishment of crown colonies in Rupert's Land and the North-Western Territory had been made in the late 1830s, and there was precedent in the creation of the colonies of Vancouver Island in 1849 and British Columbia in 1858. Such action, viewed with hindsight, would also likely have removed the cause for the troubles that would break out at the Red River Settlement in 1869. As stated on more than one occasion, however, the principles of free trade and anti-imperialism were in the ascendant in London at this time and British governments, whatever their political stripe, were not interested in taking on the costs or responsibilities of additional territories unless it was deemed unavoidable. "From 1859 to 1868 the Colonial Office declined to undertake responsibility for ending the Company's regime and setting up a Crown colony. The successive colonial secretaries wished Canada to assume the burden of government between [Lake] Superior and the Rockies and contented themselves with acting as mediators between the Company and the

6 Sir Joseph Pope, "Correspondence of Sir John Macdonald; Selections from the Correspondence of the Right Honourable Sir John Alexander Macdonald, G.C.B.," (New York and Toronto: Doubleday, Page and Company, 1921), Macdonald to C.J. Brydges January 28, 1870, p124.

7 Morton, *Critical Years*, pp228/229. Macdonald also had concerns about encouragement from Great Britain not only when it came to American aspirations in the HBC lands, but in Canada as well. The United States had been angered by British support for the Confederacy during the Civil War and President Grant, along with other senior American officials, would have been happy to settle their outstanding grievances with Great Britain by the ceding of its North American territories to United States. As has already been noted, a number of British politicians would have been happy to see Great Britain divest itself of its North American responsibilities, including its connection with Canada. Secretary of State Hamilton Fish had gone so far as to sound out the British Minister in Washington, Sir Edward Thornton, regarding London's reaction to an American takeover. His response was that Britain would stand aside if Canada wished to join the Union. Needless to say, Sir John was not pleased when he heard of this, but when word got back to Thornton, his clarification to Fish was hardly a resounding endorsement for Canadian independence. See Gwyn, *Nation Maker*, pp96/97.

ambitious colony."[8] The Parliamentary Select Committee had made plain its view that the future of the HBC lands lay with Canada.

The first Canadian indications of interest in the HBC's lands began in the late 1840's. Two newspapers, the *Globe* and the *North American*, with George Brown and William McDougall as their respective editors, initially became critics of the HBC's rule and then "protagonists of Canadian acquisition of Rupert's Land … ."[9] Momentum gathered pace in 1856 and 1857 from the twin drivers of Toronto business interests looking to develop a larger economic hinterland for their city and the shortage of good farmland in Canada West. Brown was the constant in both of these camps given his connections with the Toronto business community and also the political support his Reform movement received from the agricultural community. However, the same economic panic in the United States that shelved the ambitions of the Minnesota annexationists also had an impact in Canada. The result was that the Canadian Government did not feel able to take on any additional territory at this time.

Aside from the poor state of the finances, there was also the already mentioned impact acquisition of the HBC lands would have had on the political balance in the province's legislature. The annexationist movement was championed by English-speaking Protestants. Canada West's population was already outstripping that of the French-speaking Canada East. A takeover of the agricultural lands of the HBC would only have exacerbated the problem and French Canada would simply not have stood for it. For this reason, prior to Confederation John A. Macdonald and his close ally George-Etienne Cartier had shown little interest in the annexation of the Northwest. Even as late as 1865 Macdonald had stated " … that he was 'quite willing personally to leave that whole country a wilderness for the next fifty years.'"[10] Once Confederation had been achieved, however, he recognized that if the new dominion was to survive and prosper in the face of the growing size and strength of the United States, it would have to expand into the HBC territories and ultimately bring British Columbia into the union as well. "Whereas before he had been worried at the prospect of an overgrown colony assuming the burden of western dominion alone, he was eager now that the expansion of Canada across the content should be completed."[11]

As we have seen, provision had been made in the British North America Act for the entry of Rupert's Land and the North-Western Territory into the dominion.[12] In 1865 it had seemed that it would be a simple matter of paying compensation to the HBC for the territory to become a part of Canada. The British Government had agreed to finance Canada's acquisition, but negotiations were surprisingly protracted and difficult, though this was partly due to a change of government at Westminster whilst discussions were underway. Cartier and William McDougall travelled to London to work matters out and the deal was finally brokered in March of 1869 after the Colonial Secretary, " … Lord Granville brought the representatives of the two parties to the Colonial Office, saw each in different rooms, going from one room to the other, and finally succeeded in getting terms agreed to."[13] The HBC territories would be transferred to Canada for a sum of £300,000 with the Company retaining 5% of the land in the fertile belt as well as property around its trading posts amounting to 50,000 acres.[14] Upon ratification in Canada's Parliament, the transfer date was fixed as October 1st, 1869 with it later being amended to December 1st. The new territory would be administered by a Lieutenant-Governor and Council, with McDougall himself appointed as the first incumbent.[15]

8 Morton, *Manitoba*, pp108/109.
9 Galbraith, *Hudson's Bay Company*, p334.
10 Johnson and Waite, Macdonald.
11 Donald Creighton, *John A. Macdonald; The Old Chieftain*, (Toronto: The Macmillan Company of Canada, 1955), p24 & Gwyn, *Nation Maker*, pp89/90.
12 Stanley, *Western Canada*, pp37/38.
13 Lord Edmond Fitzmaurice, *The Life of Granville George Leveson Gower, Second Earl Granville K.G., 1815-1891, Volume 2*, (London: Longmans, Green and Co., 1905), from Sir Robert Meade's notes, p25.
14 Stanley, *Western Canada*, p41.
15 Stanley, *Western Canada*, p42

The one major flaw in this whole process was that no one had consulted with the residents of the Company's lands, including those at the Red River Settlement. Though warnings had been given going as far back as Henry Yule Hind, " ... at no time from 1857 to 1869 ... did the Canadian ministers ever consider the matter as one requiring consultation with or assurances addressed to the people of the Northwest."[16] No discussion took place with the HBC employees in Rupert's Land and the North-Western Territory either and, given that their futures were at risk, they were understandably hostile. William Mactavish, Governor of Rupert's Land and Assiniboia, according to Macdonald's latest biographer, believed that it was in the best interests of the people of Red River that they join the United States at once.[17] He was gravely ill with tuberculosis, but when he stopped in Ottawa on his way back from London, he found that no one wished to hear the advice he had to proffer. He wrote to Alexandre-Antonin Taché, the Roman Catholic Bishop in Rupert's Land, that " ... although I have been for forty years in the country, and Governor for fifteen years, I have not been able to cause any of my recommendations to be accepted by the Government. Those gentlemen are of the opinion that they know a great deal more about this country than we do."[18]

In fairness to Macdonald, he had a great deal on his plate at the time and this included the threat posed by the Fenians, as well as a movement on the part of Nova Scotia to secede from the union in the immediate aftermath of Confederation. Consultation does not appear to have crossed the minds of the British either, despite it being British territory that was being transferred, though London viewed its involvement as that of a broker bringing together Canada and the HBC. In fact, " ... one of the greatest transfers of territory and sovereignty in history was conducted as a mere transaction in real estate."[19] Trouble was on the horizon but nobody was paying sufficient attention.

16 Morton, *Manitoba*, p117.
17 Gwyn, *Nation Maker*, p92.
18 Stanley, *Western Canada*, p64.
19 Morton, *Manitoba*, p117.

6

Trouble at the Red River Settlement

The hand writing had clearly been on the wall for some time that major changes were in the offing for the Red River Settlement.[1] The impacts of the Civil War and Confederation had wrought significant shifts in both the Canadian and American political and economic landscapes, while "Red River and the Northwest ... remained static and isolated under the nerveless rule of the Council of Assiniboia and the Hudson's Bay Company ... ."[2]

The improved communication links through the United States had resulted in a small increase in the number of settlers and merchants residing in the region. The former were mostly Canadian while the latter a mix of American and Canadian. The settlers tended to make their way up the Assiniboine River to Portage-la-Prairie, while the merchants constructed warehouses along the Red River close to the Forks. "The rude little village, the product of free and international trade in the locality ... was ... named Winnipeg to distinguish it from Fort Garry."[3] The settlers at Portage-la-Prairie broadly speaking were supportive of annexation to Canada; the Canadian merchants vehemently so.

The region got its first newspaper, *The Nor'Wester*, in 1859. It was really aimed at English-speaking Canada rather than the settlement itself and in many ways parroted the views of Toronto's *Globe*, arguing aggressively for an end to HBC control and annexation to Canada. Its intemperate attacks alienated many within the Red River community where many locals took the view that, despite the many imperfections of the Company, it " ... was the only barrier to the total collapse of law and order in the region."[4] The tone of *The Nor'Wester's* articles would mislead many in Ontario as to the true feelings of the residents at the Red River settlement. This would prove to be a mistake, as at no time had the majority there expressed themselves as being favourably disposed to a Canadian takeover.[5]

The newspaper eventually fell into the hands of Dr. John Christian Schultz, the boisterous leader of the Canadian Party at the settlement, a man Macdonald referred to as 'cantankerous'.[6] Though viewed favourably when he first arrived at the beginning of the 1860s, Schultz was soon distrusted and disliked by most of the older English and French-speaking residents at the Forks. "Many regarded his business practices as not merely shrewd, but unscrupulous."[7] It was, however, his politics and views on annexation that caused the most trouble. He championed a takeover by new Protestant, English-speaking settlers and in 1869 wrote to the brother of the newly appointed Lieutenant-Governor designate that the vote should be withheld from the settlement's inhabitants until "we get an immigration of Canadians with Canadian principles."[8] His Canadian Party was never

1 Morton, *Manitoba*, p105.
2 Morton, *Manitoba*, p110.
3 Morton, *Manitoba*, p103.
4 Doug Owram, *Promise of Eden; The Canadian Expansionist Movement and the Idea of the West 1856-1900*, (Toronto: University of Toronto Press, 1992), p82.
5 Stanley, *Western Canada*, p49.
6 Pope, *Macdonald*, from Macdonald to Sir John Rose November 23, 1869, p106.
7 Clark, Lovell, "Schultz, Sir John Christian," in Dictionary of Canadian Biography, vol. 12, University of Toronto/Université Laval, 2003–, accessed September 21, 2016.
8 Lovell, Schultz.

very numerous, but its antics brought about a renewal of general lawlessness that rendered the efforts of the colony's special constables ineffectual. "They so challenged all the fundamentals of the old order in Red River as to give the impression that they were trying to bring about anarchy. That indeed was to be the result, though it was not the intent, of their agitation."[9]

Into this volatile mix in 1868 was added the arrival of a party of Canadian road builders. In the years between 1862 and 1868 there had been a lack of rain at the Red River Settlement and this was followed by a grasshopper plague in 1865. In 1868 the combination of drought and another grasshopper infestation resulted in widespread crop failure. To add to the misery that year, both the buffalo hunt and the fishery were poor as well. A hungry winter on a scale not seen since the colony's formation was a very real possibility and relief programs were established in both Canada and the United States. Canadian relief came in the form of surveyors and labourers tasked with the construction of a road from the Northwest Angle of Lake of the Woods to Upper Fort Garry. This was part of the road that had been proposed by Simon J. Dawson in 1859.[10] Work began in November 1868 under John Allan Snow, who had arrived with 16 tons of provisions in October.[11] Snow found local labour difficult to find. Nevertheless, progress was made in 1868 and 1869 despite disputes over pay with some of his Canadian workers. One of these was a man named Thomas Scott, who we shall meet again.

The arrival of the Canadian road builders created suspicion and uneasiness amongst many of the settlement's residents prompting warnings from William Mactavish to the Minister of Public Works and soon to be Lieutenant-Governor designate of the Northwest, William McDougall. Nevertheless, in 1869 a Canadian survey party arrived, led by Lieutenant-Colonel John Stoughton Dennis, to survey lots for prospective settlers.[12] The situation reached a breaking point when the surveyors began staking out claims that neither conformed to the river lot system of the settlement nor appeared to respect existing ownership rights. The result was a confrontation with a group of Métis, and despite Dennis's repudiation of the actions of his surveyors, the damage had been done.

Matters were made worse by the close connection that had immediately been established between Dennis and his men and Schultz and the Canadian Party. Inflammatory letters, written by survey party member Charles Mair, published in *The Globe* as well as other Canadian newspapers, had not gone unnoticed either. The Métis, the group with the most tenuous legal title to the land, knew that the HBC and the Council of Assiniboia were in no position to provide the assurances they required. They determined they would have to act for themselves and make their own terms with Canada.

Louis David Riel was just twenty-five years old in 1869. Identified by Bishop Taché, the Roman Catholic Bishop of Rupert's Land, for his scholarly potential, he was in 1858 sent to Canada to train for the priesthood. The young Riel " ... showed himself to be intelligent and studious, with a capacity for charming others, but he could also be moody, proud, and irritable."[13] In 1864 the death of his father, a leader of the Métis opposition during the Sayer trial, appears to have seriously impacted the young man. Always introverted and " ... subject to moods of depression ... ,"[14] he withdrew from his studies and took a job as a clerk in a Montreal law office. He hoped the money he earned would assist his family back at Red River, but unhappy and bored with his legal studies and having been involved in a failed romance, he made his way back to the settlement. He arrived in July of 1868 as the reality of Canadian expansionist aspirations was beginning to set in amongst the Métis.

Louis Riel became one of the central figures in the events at Red River following the announcement that a deal had been reached for the transfer of the HBC lands to Canada. In October, as tensions rose, a Métis National Committee was formed with Riel appointed secretary. With the armed discipline of the buffalo hunt behind

9 Morton, *Manitoba,* p111.

10 See Chapter 4.

11 Bowsfield, Hartwell, "SNOW, JOHN ALLAN," in Dictionary of Canadian Biography, vol. 11, University of Toronto/Université Laval, 2003–, accessed July 23, 2018.

12 Read, Colin Frederick, "DENNIS, JOHN STOUGHTON," in Dictionary of Canadian Biography, vol. 11, University of Toronto/Université Laval, 2003–, accessed July 23, 2018.

13 Thomas, Lewis H., "RIEL, LOUIS (1844-85)," in Dictionary of Canadian Biography, vol. 11, University of Toronto/Université Laval, 2003–, accessed April 9, 2018.

14 Thomas, Riel.

them, almost overnight the Métis had become the arbiters of authority at Red River and Louis Riel, as their new leading light, showed himself more than willing to utilize what was essentially an irregular military force in what he saw as the just cause of his people. While his preference was for a consensus within the Red River community as a whole, he quickly demonstrated his willingness to use the military arm of the Métis to back up his demands with intimidation and force whenever he believed his vision was being challenged. This is not to say that the Métis did not have legitimate grievances; they most certainly did. However, the English-speaking communities did not face the same land ownership issues as the Métis and so did not view the arrival of the Canadians with the same trepidation.

One of the major objections by the Métis to the Canadian takeover was the appointment of the brash and annexationist William McDougall as Lieutenant-Governor. Even *The Globe* questioned McDougall's appointment, writing "If Wm. McDougall is sent up to Fort Garry with a ready-made counsel composed of men completely ignorant of the country and the people, the strongest feelings of discontent will be aroused."[15] Riel was determined to deny him entry into what was still HBC territory and issued a written proclamation to this effect. The Lieutenant-Governor designate had travelled from Canada through the United States. After crossing the border at Pembina, on November 2nd, 1869 he found himself confronted by an armed party of Métis resulting in his ignominious retreat back into the United States. Simultaneously Riel secured his power base at Red River itself when a force of four hundred of his supporters took control of Upper Fort Garry. There was no opposition from the HBC. The morale of the Company's employees was in a low state in any case due to the terms of the sale of the HBC's lands, but in reality resistance against such an overwhelming show of local force would have been pointless and foolhardy. Possession of the fort with its stores and its strong defensibility was something of a masterstroke on Riel's part and gave the Métis " ... effective control of Red River until late the following spring, the earliest time that Canadian troops could reach the territory."[16]

The response within the community as a whole to this escalation was mixed. While there were opponents of Riel from within the Métis community, the majority supported him, and whenever threatening action was taken by other groups, most notably the Canadian Party, even the less committed Métis tended to rally around their charismatic leader. Neither Riel nor his supporters had rejected the rule of the Crown and, despite his forceful actions in blocking McDougall and taking control of the upper fort, there had been no serious outbreak of violence. The 'Countryborn' and Kildonan Scots communities, however, though somewhat nervous of Canadian intentions themselves, were unwilling to throw their weight behind what many saw as an act of rebellion. The English-speaking settlers at Portage-la-Prairie appear to have been supportive of Canadian annexation, which is not surprising as they were largely recent arrivals from Canada. This support, however, did not translate into a willingness to oppose the Métis military wing. The same could not be said of Schultz and the Canadian Party and there were frequent calls from this group to foment opposition to Riel and the Métis. Despite their hardline stance, however, their actions were consistently slow and ineffective, and tended only to inflame the situation.

Bishop Robert Machray, the Anglican Bishop of Rupert's Land, was sympathetic to the concerns of the Métis and had in 1868 written to the Duke of Buckingham, the Colonial Secretary at the time, " ... requesting that the government clarify the titles of squatters and that a small detachment of soldiers be sent to maintain the peace." No action was taken. As the situation at Fort Garry began to deteriorate, Bishop Machray voiced his criticism of the actions of the Canadian Party, the Canadian surveyors, and the failings of the Canadian Government in properly preparing the community for the takeover. He was, however, also staunchly opposed to the taking up of arms by Riel's men, but acted as a stabilizing influence in the settlement trying to keep the hotheads in the English-speaking parishes in check.[17] The English-speaking community, consisting largely of farmers, would in all

15 Stanley, *Western Canada*, p65.

16 See Morton, *Manitoba*, p123 and Beal and Macleod, *Prairie Fire*, p20.

17 Hackett, Christopher, "MACHRAY, ROBERT," in Dictionary of Canadian Biography, vol. 13, University of Toronto/ Université Laval, 2003–, accessed May 24, 2018.

Louis Riel and his council during the troubles at Red River. The American William Bernard O'Donoghue is sitting to the Métis leader's immediate left. (Toronto Public Library TS-1-B-402C-Riel-003

likelihood have been quickly overwhelmed had an attempt been made to oppose the Métis by force of arms. This hesitancy to fight, however, should not be confused with agreement on their part as to what was occurring at the Red River Settlement. All of this, of course, meant that the consensus Riel sought was going to be very difficult to find.

Four days after the seizure of Upper Fort Garry, Riel invited the English-speaking communities to elect twelve representatives (ten from the English-speaking parishes and two from Winnipeg) to meet with an equal number of Métis delegates. This was the First Convention which had its inaugural meeting on November 16th. The key points of substantive discussion revolved, firstly, around whether or not the actions of the Métis in blocking McDougall's entry into the settlement constituted an act of rebellion, secondly, with Riel's intentions towards American intervention, and, thirdly, Riel's proposal around the formation of a provisional government.

The discussions were stormy, but initially at least tended to deal with trivial matters. Then, a proclamation from Governor Mactavish was introduced, drafted at McDougall's request, characterizing the recent events as 'unlawful' and urging the delegates to disperse. Based on this, James Ross, the Kildonan Scot who had been leading the discussion for the English-speaking delegates, referred to the Métis as being in a state of rebellion. Riel responded emphatically. "If we are rebels, we are rebels against the Company that sold us, and is ready to hand us over, and against Canada that wants to buy us."[18] He emphatically denied that they were in rebellion against the authority of the Crown, which he believed had not given final authority to the transfer and Riel used his oratorical skills to urge the English-speaking delegates to present a united front with the Métis towards Canada.

On November 23rd Riel set upon the idea of forming a provisional government to initiate negotiations with the Canadian Government. A number of his supporters were at first unenthusiastic, being concerned that this might be seen as rebellion against the Crown, but they were eventually won over. There was, however, no getting

18 George F.G. Stanley, *Louis Riel*, (Toronto: The Ryerson Press, 1963), p69

onboard on the part of the English-speaking delegates who, believing that there was something "vaguely illegal about the plan," were unwilling to support it[19]

Riel rejected the assertion that he was willing to call for American intervention in support of the Métis cause. Fear of such a move was a major consideration in the thinking of Canada's leaders and there were most certainly Americans within Riel's inner circle, particularly in the early days of the troubles. Men such as Enos Stutsman, Oscar Malmros, and Fenian sympathizer William Bernard O'Donoghue, strongly favoured American annexation. There has been speculation that it was Stutsman who put the idea of the provisional government in Riel's head.[20] However, although O'Donoghue would remain by Riel's side until the end of the troubles, it is likely that the Métis leader kept the Americans at Red River close at first only because he did not yet feel strong enough to openly discard them. He was willing to accept their sympathy and support, but they disappeared from the centre of events as soon as he felt he no longer needed them. At no point does it appear that Riel ever seriously considered calling on American support, " ... except as an implied threat or as a last resort."[21]

On December 1st Riel presented the convention with a List of Rights. It contained 14 points dealing with such matters as "representation in the Canadian parliament, guarantees of bilingualism in the legislature, a bilingual chief justice, and arrangements for free homesteads and Indian treaties."[22] The English-speaking representatives felt able to support the List of Rights after word arrived at the settlement that McDougall had symbolically crossed the border on the night of November 30th and read out a proclamation to the effect that the Company's rule was at an end and their lands were now part of Canada. As we shall see, McDougall had over-stepped the mark, but the English speakers at Red River Settlement now accepted, incorrectly as it turned out, that the government of Assiniboia and the HBC's territories had lapsed and their convention delegates thought that McDougall should be brought to the settlement so that negotiations could commence immediately. Riel's viewpoint was different. He strongly argued that McDougall must not be allowed into the territory until Canada's parliament had ratified the List of Rights. "He dismissed the English with contempt, and at that the First Convention was dissolved."[23]

After William McDougall had been stopped at the border on November 2nd, Sir John A. Macdonald had contacted the British Government stating his wish that the takeover be delayed as Canada had a right to expect a peaceable assumption of power. The Colonial Office greeted the news with 'astonished disapproval'.[24] Lord Granville, the Colonial Secretary, quickly came to the realization, however, that " ... we could not force the territory on Canada, if they put up their backs," and informed Prime Minister Gladstone accordingly.[25] McDougall, impatiently biding his time south of the border at Pembina, had been told to do nothing until he heard definite news that the transfer had taken place. Having had no further word, and under the influence of the Canadian Party who advised that a proclamation by him would result in an English-speaking uprising against the Métis, he made the dubious assumption that the transfer had taken place on schedule.[26] His concern was that if the HBC government had in fact ceased to exist as of December 1st, lacking a declaration that Canada was now in charge, the Métis would be free to act as they saw fit. What if Riel chose to invite the Americans to intervene? In a moment of farce, he crossed the border in the dead of a cold winter's night and read out his proclamation to the empty prairie.[27]

McDougall cut a rather lonely and forlorn figure as he waited in isolation at Pembina for news that Canada had taken control of the HBC lands. Consequently, one is able on a certain level to find some degree of sympathy for the actions he deemed to be necessary on that cold and snowy prairie. Nevertheless, he had seriously over-

19 Stanley, *Riel*, p71.
20 Stanley, *Riel*, p70.
21 Morton, *Manitoba*, p125 & Stanley, *Riel*, p65
22 Thomas, Riel.
23 Morton, *Manitoba*, p129.
24 Creighton, *Old chieftain*, p49.
25 Creighton, *Old chieftain*, p49
26 Friesen, *Canadian Prairies*, p121.
27 Rea, J.E. "Red River Stand-off," *Horizon Canada, Centre for the Study of Teaching Canada Inc.*, April 1986, p1349.

stepped his authority. The Lieutenant-Governor designate had, after all, been instructed to bide his time until news that Canada had definitely taken control reached him and this he had not done. McDougall's declaration to the open prairie, together with his scuttle back across the border to the warmth of his lodgings in Pembina, could by themselves be viewed as rather comical. However, he had also taken the highly inflammatory step of appointing Lieutenant-Colonel John Stoughton Dennis, the man who had been in charge of the survey party that had inflamed the Métis earlier in the year, as 'Lieutenant and Conservator of the Peace' with authority to raise a body of armed men to enforce Canadian authority, disarm the Metis and reoccupy Fort Garry. It was Dennis's arrival at the settlement on December 1st with a copy of McDougall's proclamation that informed the residents of what had happened the night before. One can only imagine what went through McDougall's mind when on December 6th he received a communication from Canada, dated November 19th, telling him on no account to try and assert authority on HBC territory until definite instructions to do so were received.[28]

The prime minister was incandescent with anger when he found out about the proclamation. "McDougall had displayed Canada's impotence to Americans and Metis alike," and various reports from Minnesota were keeping Washington apprised that Canada's assumption of power in the Northwest was not proceeding smoothly.[29] On December 8th, the Senate in Washington passed a resolution asking the president for clarification regarding the presence of McDougall on American territory, together with information regarding the opposition of the Red River residents to his assumption of office.[30] As for the instruction he had given to Dennis, together with rumours that Dennis was in communication not just with local First Nations tribes but also with Sioux warriors displaced by the wars south of the border, McDougall received on December 24th a very pointed communication from Joseph Howe, the Secretary of State for the Provinces. He was informed that he had used the queen's name and organized an armed force in HBC territory without authority. Howe spoke of 'grave occurrences' which had caused 'great anxiety,' and told McDougall that even under the sanction of law, such action would not be taken lightly " ... considering the fearful consequences which might ensue, were the Indians, many of them but recently in contact with the white inhabitants of the neighbouring states, to be drawn into the conflict." Finally, McDougall was informed that his actions were "under the circumstances entirely illegal [and] the Governor General and Council cannot disguise from you the weight of the responsibility you have incurred."[31] By the time this stinging missive was written, McDougall was already on his way back to Canada. He would never assume the position of Lieutenant-Governor.

Dennis had little success in raising his force. The most obvious source of manpower was the Canadian Party, but most of the English-speaking settlers in the community refused to rally to his call to arms. Word of what he was up to also made its way to the Métis who were angered by his activities, particularly the rumours of his agitation amongst the local First Nations peoples and especially the Sioux. Tensions were again on the rise. Those Métis who had so far withheld their support, now rallied to Riel and he once again demonstrated his willingness to draw on the military arm for a swift and decisive act.[32]

The seizure of the upper fort at the beginning of November had secured HBC stores for his supporters, however, the several tons of supplies brought into the settlement by John Snow back in October 1868 were located at John Schultz's store in Winnipeg village. In the midst of winter in an isolated outpost such as the Red River Settlement, after the poor crops of recent years, supplies of food on this scale were of great import to those wishing to maintain or take control. Dennis ordered Schultz to withdraw his men from such an exposed position so close to the Métis stronghold at the fort, but the Canadian Party leader was unwilling to relinquish his hold

28 Stanley, *Western Canada*, p77.
29 Desmond Morton, *A Short History of Canada (Fifth Edition)*, (Toronto: McClelland & Stewart, 2001), p102.
30 Stanley, *Western Canada*, p60.
31 The National Archives, CO 42/684, Department of Secretary of State for Colonies.
32 Morton, *Manitoba*, p129.

over such a valuable asset. On December 7th the Métis surrounded the store, capturing and imprisoning Schultz and around fifty of his supporters.[33] The next day Riel proclaimed a provisional government.

Perhaps somewhat belatedly, Prime Minister Macdonald realized that he had a serious problem on his hands at the Red River Settlement. Canada's insistence on the delay of the transfer meant that the Northwest remained, for the time being at least, British territory. Nevertheless, ever the dealmaker, Sir John was determined to send his own Special Commissioners to Fort Garry to effect a resolution of the problem. He would later write, "He [Bishop Taché] is strongly opposed to the idea of an Imperial Commission, believing, as indeed we all do, that to send an overwashed Englishman, utterly ignorant of the country and full of crotchets, as all Englishmen are, would be a mistake. He would be certain to make propositions and consent to arrangements which Canada could not possibly accept."[34] Despite the insulting tone of Macdonald's comment, admittedly written in a private letter to Sir John Rose his personal confidant in London, what is clear is that Macdonald was determined to seize control of the forthcoming negotiations. What is equally clear is that Gladstone's government had no interest in assuming such a direct role in the affairs of Red River by sending out an Imperial Commission. The British were looking to divest themselves of responsibility not to increase it. The way was clear for Macdonald to take the lead.

Sir John recognized that the Métis had reason to be dissatisfied, telling Cartier in late November, "all that those poor people know is that Canada has bought the country . . . & that they are handed over like a flock of sheep to us; and they are told that they lose their lands ... . Under these circumstances it is not to be wondered at that they should be dissatisfied, and should show their discontent."[35] However, the prime minister could also present a harder visage. In February 1870 he wrote privately to Sir John Rose that "we must never subject the government there to the humiliation offered to MacTavish. These impulsive half-breeds have got spoiled by this emeute, and must be kept down by a strong hand until they are swamped by the influx of settlers." [36]

The most important of the three commissioners sent by Macdonald to Red River was Donald Smith, the future Lord Strathcona, and aside from Governor Mactavish, the HBC's most senior officer in North America. Smith " ... was empowered not only to seek to calm suspicion, but also to take such steps, in concert with Mr. McDougall and Governor Mactavish, as may seem most proper in effecting the peaceable transfer of the country and the government from the Hudson Bay authorities to the Government of the Dominion."[37] This included the liberal use of bribery as he saw fit. Smith arrived at Fort Garry on December 27th, the same day that Riel, the real power in any case, became head of the new provisional government.

The two first met on January 6th, 1870 and Smith quickly concluded that he would have to make his case directly with the people of Red River rather than with Riel and his council. There was nowhere indoors that could accommodate such a large number with the result that on January 19th he addressed an outdoor gathering of nearly one thousand people in temperatures of minus 20 degrees Fahrenheit from a balcony at Upper Fort Garry.[38] The meeting went so long that it had to be reconvened the following day. [39] Smith's aim was to assure the residents of liberal treatment from the Canadian Government once the takeover had occurred. The result was that

33 One of those taken at the Schultz store was Peter MacArthur, a Scot who had arrived at Fort Garry to work on the road in 1869. Writing 65 years later just before his death, he was critical of the HBC for not sharing the funds of the purchase with its employees, as this caused 'bitter discontent' and turned them against the takeover. He was most critical, however, of the Canadian Government's representative at Red River (Lindsay Russell) for not distributing the provisions at Schultz's store in light of the crop and buffalo hunt failures. He wrote: "It is my considered opinion that if the Surveyor-General had distributed the provisions when asked, there would have been no rebellion." Peter MacArthur, "The Red River Rebellion," *Manitoba Pageant*, Spring 1973, Volume 18, Number 3, http://www.mhs.mb.ca/docs/pageant/18/redriverrebellion.shtml

34 Pope, *Macdonald*, Macdonald to Sir John Rose Feb 23, 1870, p128.

35 Gwyn, *Nation Maker*, p110 & Johnson and Waite.

36 Pope, *Macdonald*, Macdonald to Sir John Rose Feb 23, 1870, p128.

37 Morton, *Manitoba*, p132.

38 Donna McDonald, *Lord Strathcona; A Biography of Donald Alexander Smith*, (Toronto: Dundurn Press, 1996), p154.

39 The previous day it had been -35F. and seven people froze to death. This exceeded the total number of deaths associated with the whole episode of the troubles at Red River, the expedition and even the aftermath.

Riel suggested the formation of another convention, with the English and French-speaking communities electing twenty delegates each to hammer out the basis of a settlement.

Smith has left us an interesting description of the Métis leader:

> Riel may have his faults, but he is decidedly a man out of the common. In the first place, his appearance is striking; he is swarthy, with a fine head, a large brow, and a piercing eye. His manner is very restless, and his assumption of dignity and coolness is constantly interrupted by explosions of temper, which as quickly subside again. He seems fairly well-educated and on the whole is regarded here as a remarkable, but an ill-balanced man.[40]

Regarding the comment on lack of balance, there are numerous allegations of irrational or headstrong behaviour on Riel's part during the winter of 1869/70. It was reported on one occasion that he burst into the room of the gravely ill Governor Mactavish to heap abuse on him and threaten him with execution.[41]

The elections to the Second Convention in the French-speaking parishes were particularly acrimonious as Riel attempted to ensure those chosen were his supporters.[42] When the convention finally met, despite the equally heated discussions between the English and French-speaking representatives, and amongst some of the Métis delegates as well, a new List of Rights was hammered out.[43] There was also agreement for a representative Provisional Government, with a council of twenty-four members elected equally from the French and English-speaking parishes together with an executive of four headed by a president. After much debate Riel was elected president.

Three delegates were selected to carry the Provisional Government's demands to Ottawa; one each representing the French, English and, somewhat surprisingly, American communities at Red River. Finally, on February 11th, with the work of the convention concluded, an agreement was reached for the release of the remaining prisoners captured at Schultz's store and still being held at Fort Garry. It seemed that all had been satisfactorily resolved.

In fact, a number of the Fort Garry prisoners had already escaped, including Schultz himself, Charles Mair, and Thomas Scott, an Ulster Protestant who had been in Canada for seven years before arriving at Red River as part of the road construction crew. By all accounts, Scott was a rowdy and bigoted man who, along with three others, had been fined for assaulting John Snow, the foreman on the road project in 1868, over a pay dispute. Most of the escapers had retreated to the English-speaking community at Portage-la-Prairie, though Schultz himself had taken refuge with the Kildonan Scots.

Just prior to the agreement hammered out by the Second Convention, a plot was hatched to force the release of the remaining Fort Garry captives. A party from Portage-la-Prairie set out on February 10th, but were delayed for four days by a blizzard. During this time one of their scouts was captured carrying messages encouraging some of Riel's Métis opponents to attack the homes of his supporters and so draw men away from the fort. As with the earlier attempt by Lieutenant-Colonel Dennis to raise a force of men, this again had the effect of rallying Métis opinion around Riel.

The Portage-la-Prairie party was led by Major Charles Boulton, a Canadian born former British Army officer who had come to the settlement as part of Dennis's survey party in 1869. According to Boulton, he tried to talk the hotheads in the group, such as Mair and Scott, out of the affair and only went along with them to try and keep them under control. On February 14th they met with Schultz's group, though the Canadian Party leader brought word that he had been unsuccessful in persuading the Kildonan Scots to throw in their lot with the enterprise. By this time news had reached the would-be jail breakers that the prisoners were already being released. This should have brought an end to this poorly thought out and executed affair. However, as the party began to make their

40 McDonald, *Strathcona*, p158.
41 Mactavish died on July 23, 1870.
42 McDonald, *Strathcona*, p158.
43 McDonald, *Strathcona*, p159.

way back to their homes, they foolishly passed very near to Upper Fort Garry. An armed Métis party emerged from the fort, surrounded the 'rescuers' and took them prisoner. Schultz was not among the captives, but Boulton and Scott were. Boulton along with three others were sentenced to death, though pleas from Donald Smith and the leaders of the English-speaking community ultimately caused Riel to show clemency.

Just why Riel chose to imprison Boulton's party is unclear and it is not an absolute certainty that it was he who actually gave the order. If it was the Métis leader's doing, it was likely due to the fact that the Canadian Party would simply not go away. Whenever it seemed that Riel had gained control of the situation and the political vision he had for the Métis was in the ascendant, there were the Canadians yet again threatening to thwart and overturn his achievements. But even now all was not lost. The three delegates were preparing to leave for Canada with the Second Convention's List of Rights. Even with all of the disorder and disruption that had gone on, outside of government circles, there had been little interest in Canada towards the events at Red River. Macdonald was in a positive frame of mind and, albeit in derogatory language, he was talking of Riel going to Ottawa and making him a senator.[44] Riel would not be making the trip to the Canadian capital, at least not at this time, but a deal was still there to be done. The situation was, however, about to be turned on its head.

Thomas Scott, the belligerent and pugnacious Orangeman, was back in jail at Upper Fort Garry. He repeatedly hurled insults at his Métis guards and generally made himself difficult. His stubbornness, recklessness and physical size made him a difficult and intimidating man to handle. On top of this he showed a level of contempt for his captors that clearly demonstrated his feeling that they were somehow inferior. It is, however, also possible to sympathize with the man. He was in prison for opposing a political regime with which he, along with a great many others in the community, did not agree, and as he had demonstrated on several occasions, he was prepared to stand up for what he believed were his rights. He may also have been suffering from dysentery and, in the uncomfortable and cold conditions prevalent at the fort, this would not have left him in a settled frame of mind. His constant taunting finally brought matters to a head. In the highly charged environment of the fort, his apparent view that the pardoning of Boulton and the others had been a sign of weakness by Riel, was a miscalculation. The Métis guards told Riel that something must be done about Scott or they would take matters into their own hands. On March 3rd he was tried by a Métis tribunal and, despite dissenting views, was found guilty by a majority. Pleas from Smith this time fell on deaf ears; Riel told him "we must make Canada respect us."[45] Scott was executed the following day.

The killing of Scott changed everything. What had been viewed in Canada as an inconsequential series of events on a distant frontier now became front page news especially for English-speaking Canadians. "Scott's death provided Schultz and Mair with the symbol they needed to arouse the people of Ontario."[46] Both had made good their escapes to Canada in the aftermath of the botched rescue mission. Mair was already a member of the fledgling Canada First movement in Ontario, a small elitist group of young Canadians dedicated to a vision of Canada's destiny being to possess the west and populate it with English-speaking Protestants. He introduced Schultz to the movement's leaders, including George Denison, a former militia officer turned military author. Denison, Schultz and the other members of Canada First worked with considerable success in Ontario to stoke the fires of revenge for the killing of Scott. Denison was a sworn enemy of Minister of Militia George-Etienne Cartier, after his failure to attain the post of Assistant Adjutant-General of Cavalry, and was angered by what he

44 Macdonald would write: "Everything looks well for a delegation coming to Ottawa including the redoubtable Riel. If we once get him here, as you know pretty well by this time, he is a gone coon. There is no place in the ministry for him to sit next to Howe, but perhaps we may make him a senator for the territory." Letter to Sir John Rose Feb 23, 1870, Pope, *Macdonald*, p128.

45 Morton, *Short History*, p103.

46 Beal and Macleod, *Prairie Fire*, p24.

The killing of Thomas Scott at Fort Garry. ("Shooting of Thomas Scott" by Guilmette, *Canadian Illustrated News*)

saw as a lack of action on the part of the Canadian Government over the events at Red River. Following the death of Scott, he would find that " ... a spacious field for his talent of bellicose propaganda" had opened up for him.[47]

The three Red River delegates set out for Canada towards the end of March. They carried with them a List of Rights, though it was not the one agreed to by the delegates of the Second Convention. Riel and the other members of the Provisional Government's executive had amended the list without consultation with the legislative council. The changes included the demand that the Northwest be admitted as a province rather than a territory, something Smith during the negotiations had been adamant would be unacceptable to the Canadian Government, and that amnesty be granted for all members of the Provisional Government. At the last moment provision for a senate and denominational schools, as in Quebec, were added, probably at the instigation of Bishop Taché.[48]

There was a delay when two of the three delegates were arrested on their way to Ottawa and held for two weeks, but Macdonald secured their release and from then on, while negotiations led by the French-speaking representative Father Noël-Joseph Ritchot were far from easy, steady progress was made. Provincial status was accepted, though the new creation, to be named Manitoba, was miniscule compared to what had been envisioned by Riel and the Provisional Government. The rest of the former HBC lands were to become a territory ruled from Ottawa with its local headquarters at Upper Fort Garry.

It was left to Cartier to wind up the negotiations when on April 28th Sir John had 'taken to the bottle.'[49] Then two days after the first reading of the bill, Macdonald suffered an attack of gallstones that incapacitated him for over a month. It was, therefore, Cartier who took the lead in parliament as well, which given the height of feeling in English Canada over the killing of Scott, was not such a bad thing. "Macdonald's convenient indisposition cooled off many overheated passions; the Liberals and the Orangemen knew they had nothing to gain from attacking Cartier on the matter ... [and] the Bill passed with an overwhelming majority."[50] Royal Assent was

47 See Carl Berger, *The Sense of Power; Studies in the Ideas of Canadian Imperialism, 1867-1914*, (Toronto: University of Toronto Press, 1970), p57, David Gagan, *The Denison Family of Toronto 1792-1925*, (University of Toronto Press, 1973), p29, & Lt.-Col. George T. Denison, *Soldiering in Canada; Recollections and Experiences*, (Toronto: George N. Morang and Co., 1900), p173.

48 Morton, *Manitoba*, p140.

49 Alastair Sweeny, *George-Etienne Cartier*, (Toronto: McClelland and Stewart Limited, 1976), p210 & Creighton, *Old chieftain*, p67.

50 Sweeny, *Cartier*, p210.

Sir George-Étienne Cartier. (Library and Archives Canada; Copyright: Expired)

received on May 12th, 1870, with the Manitoba Act to come into effect on July 15th.[51] There would be a new Lieutenant-Governor as well, after what Sir John described as McDougall's 'most wonderful failure' during his mission to the Northwest.[52] Adams G. Archibald, from Nova Scotia, was " ... talented, fair-minded and anxious to heal the wounds of the resistance."[53]

When Ritchot returned to Red River with the details of the agreement, Riel expressed his satisfaction and on June 24th the Red River Assembly convened and voted in favour of the Manitoba Act. There was, though, one important matter that remained unresolved and that was the question of amnesty. It will be recalled that this had been added by the Red River Executive to the List of Rights on the eve of the delegates' departure for Canada. While earlier in the Red River troubles the Governor-General, Sir John Young, had offered a general amnesty to all who laid down their arms, this had not been made public until March. In any event, the killing of Scott had changed everything. English Canada was on the rampage calling for revenge and the Canadian Prime Minister was in serious political difficulty. Agitation begun by Canada First quickly spread as the Orange Lodges around Ontario threw their support behind some form of action being taken. Under these circumstances it was impossible for Macdonald to issue an amnesty and not lose the support of Protestant Ontario.

Ritchot and Taché urged Cartier to act. He quietly promised much, but delivered nothing. In reality there was little he could do. In an attempt to get out of their difficulty, the Canadians hung their hat on the technicality that, as the transfer of Rupert's Land had not taken place on December 1, 1869, legally Red River was outside of Canada's jurisdiction and so amnesty could only come from the Queen. Governor-General Sir John Young optimistically reported that something would be coming, but it was not.[54] Little notice had been taken in Westminster of the events in the Northwest, but when faced with Canada's request on the amnesty question, London took the view

---

51 The Manitoba Act gave the new province a bicameral legislature, as in Quebec, (The upper chamber was abolished as a cost cutting measure in 1876. Quebec's upper chamber would remain until 1968), four seats in the Canadian House of Commons and two in the Senate, guaranteed language protection and denominational schools, confirmed existing property rights, and set aside 1.4 million acres for the Métis and their children. The Manitoba Act in Statutes of Canada, printed by Brown Chamberlain, Ottawa, 1870.
Controversy has plagued these latter sections of the act ever since. Scrip was available for land if proof of birth in Manitoba prior to 1871 could be shown. However, "Métis landholders were harassed, while new laws and amendments to the Manitoba Act undermined their power to fend off speculators and new settlers. Of the approximately ten thousand people of mixed descent in Manitoba in 1870, two-thirds or more are estimated to have departed in the next several years." Brown "Métis", p111.

52 Pope, *Macdonald,* Macdonald to the Hon. John Rose, January 21, 1870, p121.

53 Rea, "Red River", p1351.

54 Sweeny, *Cartier*, pp210/211.

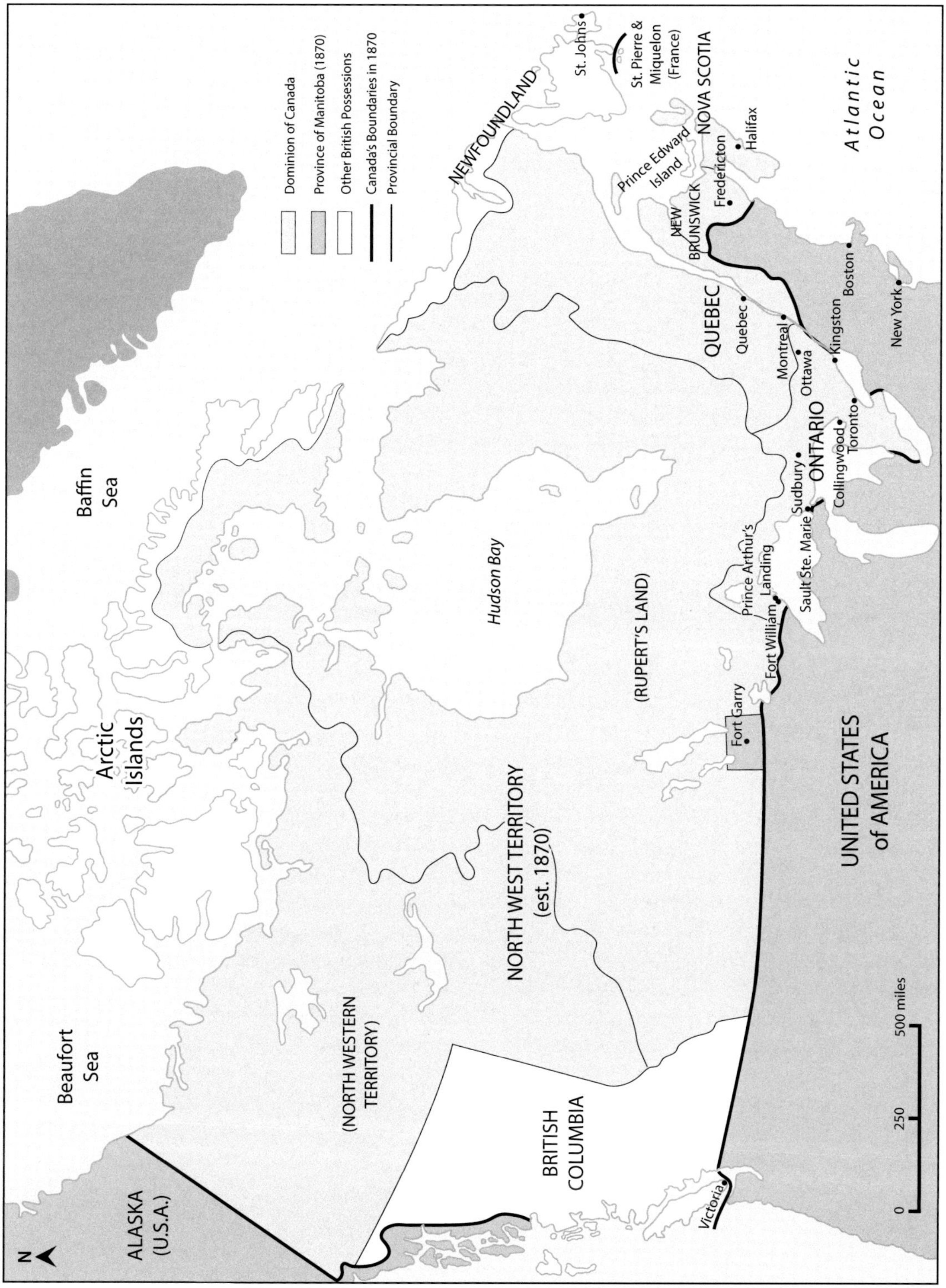

Canada in 1870.

that action on its part would be inappropriate when the Canadians were so divided themselves. Canada would have to resolve the situation on its own. In the short term it never did.[55]

Ottawa's concession to the inflamed passions of Ontario was the dispatch of a military force to take control of the new province. Not only would this help pacify the anger in Ontario, but, if the British could also be persuaded to contribute troops, it would demonstrate to the Americans a greater level of strength in the region than if Canada were to act alone. But Britain was withdrawing its garrisons and it remained to be seen if Gladstone and Cardwell would be willing to play along with Canadian aspirations.

55 Stanley, *Western Canada*, pp144-168.

7

An Expedition is Conceived

As matters began to unfold at the end of December, Macdonald was still thinking in terms of a negotiated settlement with Riel. He had some sympathy with Métis claims and when Colonel Garnet Wolseley, the British Army's Deputy Quartermaster-General in North America offered to accompany Donald Smith on his mission, Sir John declined. He wrote privately:

> It would never have done for Colonel Wolseley to have gone with him. Smith goes to carry the olive branch, and were it known at Red River that he was accompanied by an officer high in rank in military service, he would be looked upon as having the olive branch in one hand and a revolver in the other. We must not make any indication of sending a military force until peaceable means have been exhausted.[1]

Prior to the killing of Scott there had been little excitement in Canada regarding the events in Rupert's Land and the British had also taken virtually no notice. Nevertheless, quite soon after the events at Red River had finally caught Macdonald's attention, he began to think that a military expedition might be necessary and was clearly willing to use force if the Métis refused to come to terms. In the same letter as quoted previously, he wrote truculently:

> Should these miserable half-breeds not disband, they must be put down, and then, so far as I can influence matters, I shall be very glad to give Colonel Wolseley the chance of glory and risk of the scalping knife.[2]

Five weeks later, his tone remained unchanged. "I think the best plan will be to send a mixed expeditionary force of a small body of Regulars with some light artillery so as to shell the Forts in case they are held."[3]

The prime minister was not alone in his early contemplation of the dispatch of a military expedition together with a ready acceptance of the use of force. In February a Canadian Privy Council memorandum laid out that, with the Red River delegates scheduled to arrive in Canada in the spring, it was of the 'first importance' to send a military force to Fort William at the head of Lake Superior for dispatch to Fort Garry as soon as weather permitted. It was noted that the ice at Sault Ste. Marie had normally cleared by April 25th and so the expedition could be at Fort William on Thunder Bay by May 1st. The memorandum emphasized that the force must be led by a British officer 'of reputation' and contain Imperial troops. It was felt that a column of around one thousand men would suffice, with two or three hundred being regulars. The Privy Councillors even suggested that the bulk of the British contingent could be drawn from either the Rifle Brigade or the Kings Royal Rifle Corps, battalions of both regiments then being garrisoned in Canada.

Three reasons were listed in support of the importance of British involvement. First, it would send a message to the Americans that Britain continued to maintain an interest in its North American domains. Second, British

1 Pope, *Macdonald*, Macdonald to George Stephen, December 13, 1869, pp112/113.
2 Pope, *Macdonald*, Macdonald to George Stephen, December 13, 1869, pp112/113.
3 The National Archives, CO 42/695 Jan 26, 1870.

'prestige' would more likely result in a successful outcome to the operation rather than using 'untried volunteers only.' This was an acceptance on the part of the Canadian authorities that the new country's militia was not yet up to the task of undertaking an operation such as this alone. Finally, hostility towards Canada had arisen at the settlement that was not felt for Great Britain. The Métis were less likely to take up arms against British troops, but even if there was resistance, it would not have the same degree of animosity or result in bitterness and humiliation.[4]

Two more reasons were contained in the document; the legal points that Canada had no jurisdiction outside of its present borders and so no power to order its militia on an operation outside of the Dominion's borders.[5] Due to Macdonald's insistence on the delay of the transfer of Rupert's Land and the North-Western Territory to Canada, these lands remained HBC territory.

The memorandum went on to detail that contracts had already been entered into for the construction of boats to transport the men and material along the waters of the route, and they would be ready by April 1st. "Before that time every preparation as to men, transport, munitions of war and supplies should be perfected, so that the Force may be assembled at Fort William by the 1st of May."[6] Speed was clearly important to the Privy Councillors due to concerns regarding the response the Americans might take to the events at Red River. In the early spring the roads in Minnesota would be impassable. It was, therefore, crucial that the troops be well on their way " ... before the Insurgents can receive material help in the way of men and arms from the United States." The 'insurrection' needed to be 'put down' " ... before any considerable assistance from the United States can be obtained."[7]

Talk of British troops putting down an insurrection in Rupert's Land was not likely to sit well with a man like William Gladstone. There were two clear questions to be answered. First, would British troops be allowed to participate in a military expedition? After all, the decision had already been made that the garrisons were leaving, and on top of that, the Northwest was a part of Britain's domains towards which successive governments had shown very little interest. Second, assuming London did agree, would British participation take place along the lines that the Canadians envisaged?

On February 12th, 1870 the Governor-General, Sir John Young, wrote to Lord Granville, the Colonial Secretary, laying out the case to 'at once' make preparations for the dispatch of an expeditionary force with British participation.[8] By February 24th he was writing to London again in search of a response.[9] At first Lord Granville was opposed, noting on Christmas Day 1869, "the more I think of it the more I doubt the expediency of sending Imperial troops to Red River."[10] By March he had relented and on the 5th of the month it was agreed that Britain would allow a small contingent of its troops to go to Red River early in the spring " ... to act in conjunction with a force of Canadian Militia with the view of restoring order in that Settlement."[11]

The news was communicated to Governor-General Young by telegraph the following day, but there were conditions. The transfer of the HBC lands to the Dominion must be concurrent with the dispatch of the troops and 'adequate' terms must be granted by the Canadian Government to the 'half-breeds'.[12] It seems that Macdonald may have been the recipient of some advance notice or accurate gossip regarding the British decision. On February

4 It could be argued that this alleged reluctance on the part of the Métis to take up arms against British troops was simply the unsupported view of Canadian politicians who had no experience of what was actually going on in the minds of those at the Red River Settlement. However, the statements of Riel and other members of the Métis community regarding aspirations of loyalty to the Crown are well documented. See for example Stanley, *Riel*, pp69-71

5 TNA, CO 42/684, Committee of Canadian Privy Council.

6 TNA, CO 42/684, Committee of Canadian Privy Council.

The author found no documentation indicating that Wolseley was in any way involved in these discussions. Given, however, that he had been in contact with Macdonald regarding his participation in Donald Smith's mission to Fort Garry in December 1869, it is always possible that he was consulted.

7 TNA, CO 42/684, Committee of Canadian Privy Council.

8 TNA, CO 42/684, Committee of Canadian Privy Council.

9 TNA, CO 42/684, Committee of Canadian Privy Council.

10 Stanley, *Western Canada*, p129.

11 The National Archives, CO 42/684, Colonial Office Minute.

12 TNA, CO 42/684.

In the original Colonial Office document the word 'adequate' replaces 'reasonable' which is crossed out. 'Inhabitants' is also crossed out and replaced with 'half-breeds,' though, rather than interpreting this as a racial slur, it is more likely it was written

23rd, 1870 he wrote to Sir John Rose in London, "I received your cable yesterday to the effect that Her Majesty's Government will cooperate in the expedition. I am very glad of this. Even if the force does not go, the agreement of England to cooperate with us will be immensely satisfactory to us, and show that England has no intention of abandoning her colonies … ."[13]

Even after the decision had finally been taken, however, the soul searching in London continued. The same day that the telegraph was received in Ottawa, Gladstone wrote to Granville laying out a number of concerns surrounding the operation, including 1) whether an error had been made "in handing the Red River people over to Canada without their consent"; 2) his confusion regarding the actual mission of the military force, as he had believed it " … was intended only to subdue outliers not to overawe the community;"; and 3) wondering if it was too late to reach a negotiated settlement before the force embarked on its journey in May.[14] Granville replied that he had doubts as to whether the 'Red Riverites' should have been consulted, but he firmly believed they should have been managed better. "We are to blame in not having seen this, but the Dominion and the Company, who knew so much more than we did, seemed so certain of their business … ."[15] Canada, he continued, was 'tolerably sanguine' of the Red River delegates going to Ottawa, however, "the Canadians are fully alive to the extreme danger of bloodshed. I see no alternative to our standing by the Canadians, and if so the prompt assertion of authority is probably the safest."[16]

On the other hand, Lieutenant-General Sir John Michel, the commander of Britain's forces in North America between June 1865 and October 1867, was staunchly opposed to British participation. During his tenure he had also been against either the establishment of a crown colony in the Northwest or the joining of the HBC territories with Canada. This had nothing to do with any anti-imperialistic sentiment on his part; his opposition was simply due to the poor state of communications between Canada and Rupert's Land.[17] Taking a similar view to that voiced by the Duke of Wellington during the Oregon Crisis in 1846, he privately wrote that Fort Garry would become a trap should American forces intervene, and he viewed this eventuality as a very real possibility. "You can only escape by Hudson Bay, of which the waters are only open six weeks in the year and then only with a perfectly friendly free state in your rear."[18] Officially he questioned whether it was " … too much to say that England is risking a disgrace for an apparently small cause?"[19]

Nevertheless, the political decision had been taken. As yet, though, no commanding officer had been appointed and neither British nor Canadian troops had been assigned to the enterprise. In fact, at this crucial juncture there was no senior British officer in Canada west of Halifax. In February Sir Charles Windham, the Lieutenant-General Commanding in North America, had died. Given the intent to retain Halifax as an imperial naval base after the garrisons had been withdrawn from the rest of Canada, the headquarters of British forces in North America had consequently been transferred here, with Sir Hastings Doyle, the popular and efficient British commander in Nova Scotia, becoming the new military commander for all of British North America. The absence of a senior officer in Montreal, however, caused nervousness back at the War Office in London. Someone was needed on the spot to ensure there was no backsliding on the implementation of the plan for the evacuation of the garrisons by the end of 1870.

The result was that Lieutenant-General James Lindsay was ordered to Canada. This was not his first time in British North America. Lindsay had been among the reinforcements rushed from Britain at the beginning of the American Civil War and he had subsequently risen to the command of British troops in Canada East. Macdonald

in the language of the day with the emphasis being that the Canadian Government must satisfy the mixed race people at the settlement and not just the Canadians and other English speakers.

13 Pope, *Macdonald*, Macdonald to Sir John Rose, Feb 23, 1870, p128.

14 Agatha Ramm, *The Political Correspondence of Mr. Gladstone and Lord Granville, 1868-1876, Volume 1, 1868-71*, (London: Offices of the Royal Historical Society, 1952), p93.

15 Ramm, *Granville*, p94.

16 Ramm, *Granville*, p94.

17 Stacey, C.P., "MICHEL, Sir JOHN," in Dictionary of Canadian Biography, vol. 11, University of Toronto/Université Laval, 2003–, accessed April 19, 2018.

18 Quoted in Stanley, *Western Canada*, April 27, 1870, p131.

19 Quoted in Stanley, *Western Canada*, April 10, 1870, p130.

responded positively to the news, telling Sir John Rose, "I am exceedingly glad that General Lindsay is coming out. He knows something of the country, and is a good soldier and a frank and ready man of business."[20] He was also remembered enthusiastically by Colonel Garnet Wolseley as "an able, energetic soldier, whose heart was in his work" and "as great a favourite with the Canadians as he was with the troops."[21]

His orders were "to supervise the rundown of the British army in central Canada" and " ... to cooperate with the Canadian government in providing a force to secure the transfer of the Red River colony to the dominion."[22] Superficially, these twin tasks might appear contradictory, but the correspondence between Lindsay and the War Office was very clear that the cooperation with the Canadian Government in sending a force to Fort Garry must under no circumstances get in the way of the primary objective of withdrawing all British forces by the end of the year. On March 24th, the date of his departure from England, Lindsay was informed by the Permanent Under-Secretary at the War Office that the Secretary of State for War, "desires me to request that you will report home your intended arrangements as soon as you are in a position to do so."[23] Time was clearly of the essence and it was additionally made clear that the government in no way contemplated or sanctioned **" ...** the detention of the troops in the Red River Settlement during the winter of 1870-71 ... ."[24]

It is a shame that Lindsay has been largely forgotten today, and it is perhaps his death aged just 58 in 1874 that partially accounts for this. Nevertheless, his energy and quick grasp of detail were essential in dealing with the myriad issues facing him upon his arrival at Montreal on April 4th, 1870. These included not just the Red River Expedition and the evacuation of the garrisons, but also the Fenian threat. The climate of Canada and the HBC lands dictated that the window during which a military expedition could be undertaken to the Red River was a relatively short one. It was imperative that matters progressed quickly and efficiently. With so much to accomplish in such a short space of time, Lindsay's arrival portended a hurricane of activity. His directness would ruffle some Canadian feathers.

20 Pope, *Macdonald*, Macdonald to Sir John Rose, Feb 23, 1870, p128.
21 Morton, Desmond, "LINDSAY, Sir JAMES ALEXANDER," in Dictionary of Canadian Biography, vol. 10, University of Toronto/Université Laval, 2003–, accessed April 29, 2016.
22 See Hitsman, *Safeguarding*, p219 and Morton, Lindsay.
23 Peel's Prairie Provinces 568, "Correspondence Relative to the Recent Expedition to the Red River Settlement with Journal of Operations," Harrison and Sons, London, 1871, No. 1 Lugard to Lindsay, March 24, 1870.
24 PPP 568, "Correspondence and Journal", No. 2 Lugard to Lindsay, March 24, 1870.

8

Lieutenant-General James Lindsay

The approval for the use of Imperial troops was a conditional one and, until Westminster was satisfied that its terms had been met, British soldiers would not be moving west. In the minds of Gladstone and Granville the expedition was to be a peaceful occupation after a negotiated settlement had been achieved, whereas Macdonald had on several occasions written in terms of putting down an insurrection and shelling forts if necessary. As late as April 27th the Canadian prime minister would write to Sir John Young that "We are nearly through our troubles with the delegates, and then *we can take up the military matter*." [Author's emphasis][1] This could be interpreted to mean either that he was still in a bellicose frame of mind or that he had accepted the view of the British Government and it was a case of getting the military force to Red River to peacefully symbolize the Canadian Government's assumption of power in the HBC's lands. Nevertheless, the British were taking no chances in ensuring that Canada fully understood the terms under which its troops would participate. At the beginning of April Lord Granville informed Sir John Young of the pending arrival of Sir Clinton Murdoch, a British civil servant who "is in possession of the views of Her Majesty's Government."[2] As we shall see, though, this did not mean that the British soldiers who would undertake the mission fully endorsed the peaceful nature outlined by Gladstone and Granville.

One area where the British and Canadians were in agreement, albeit for different reasons, was in the need for speed and so planning had to proceed without delay. For Macdonald this was to pre-empt any actions by the Americans. For the British it was to ensure its troops were back in time to leave Canada by the end of the year. For this reason, upon his arrival on April 4th, 1870, Lieutenant-General Lindsay set to work without delay. A series of conferences involving British and Canadian civil and military officials were convened to deal with matters such as the intended route, supply, and transport. It was going to be a difficult and complex task to get a military force from Canada to the Red River Settlement and the success of the mission would be founded on its planning and organization. This did not always proceed free from interruptions and Lindsay was sometimes called away due to the Fenian threat. The expedition was not the only matter that Lindsay had to contend with.[3]

The lieutenant-general was, however, fortunate in that a great deal of preliminary work had already been completed by the time of his arrival. This largely took the form of a document published on March 28th entitled *Memorandum Regarding the Despatch of an Armed Force to the Red River Territory*. It was produced by Colonel Garnet Wolseley, the Deputy Quartermaster-General for the British forces in North America and was a testament to the competence and professionalism of its author.

The memorandum laid out in considerable detail the scope, scale and logistical requirements of the proposed expedition. That such a masterful document, with such detailed grasp of the requirements of the undertaking, was written despite the author's ignorance of the government's intentions, makes it a considerable achievement. That

1 Quoted in Creighton, *Old Chieftain*, p66.

2 The National Archives, CO 143/57.

3 The National Archives, WO 32/7586, Irvine, C.M.G., Assistant Controller M. Bell, "Report on the Red River Expedition of 1870," Harrison and Sons, London, 1871.

Lieutenant-General James Alexander Lindsay in Montreal. (McCord Museum, I-49175.1)

it was waiting for Lindsay when he first set foot in his headquarters, was without doubt a very large contributing factor enabling him to quickly master the complex situation that confronted him.

With considerable foresight, the memorandum outlined the dispatch of one thousand men, one-third of them regulars, "fully equipped for active service, having 210 rounds of ammunition per man, and provisions for 30 days with them."[4] The force " ... will be so constituted that it can overcome all the difficulties to be expected whilst en route between Fort William and the Red River, and that it will be of sufficient strength to destroy any armed force it may have to encounter or even to overawe all options by the moral effect resulting from a well-timed display of strength."[5]

The advance guard of the force, four companies of the 60th Rifles, would embark in the first week of May, as soon as the ice had cleared on the upper Great Lakes. The memorandum spoke to the troops working on road and portage improvements, the establishment of a forward base with a hospital and three months of supplies at Fort Frances, and that the Canadian volunteers would follow along behind the British regulars. It outlined that the first of the Canadians would leave ten days after the British, though, with considerable prescience, the memorandum's author stated that he was unsure if the ten day gap was accurate because "I do not know what state of progress the road may be between Fort William and Shebandowan Lake."[6]

The level of detail was prodigious. Boxes measuring 4' ½" long x 21" wide x 8½" deep would be built to hold 10 rifles each. Each man would have 210 rounds of ammunition. Sixty would be carried in his pouch, with the

4 The National Archives, WO 107/9, Wolseley, Colonel Garnet, "Memorandum Regarding the Despatch of an Armed Force to the Red River Territory."

5 TNA, WO 107/9

6 TNA, WO 107/9

balance being contained in bulk ammunition barrels. There would be three barrels in each boat. Each man would have a water proof and two blankets. During the journey, the force members would wear serge coats and trousers, flannel shirts, 'mocassins' (sic) and forage caps with peaks and white covers. Personal clothing and equipment was detailed and officers would be allowed two waterproof bags the total weight "not, under any circumstances, to exceed 90lbs." Officers were to dress "as much like the privates as possible" and would be on the same rations as the men. Appendices attached to the memorandum spoke to daily rations, the number of axes, picks, rope, spikes, nails, additional blankets, and camp kettles; and detailed the establishment of two hospitals (one at Fort William and one at Fort Frances) together with the make-up and weight of equipment for each. The detail was drilled down to the numbers of men, their equipment and supplies that would be placed in each boat. Lastly, the memorandum spoke to the costs of the expedition. The pay of the British regulars would be made up to that of the Canadian volunteers if there was a difference and a Canadian paymaster would accompany the force. The impetus behind this expedition was Canadian and it was, therefore, clearly laid out that the British would pay the cost of their men only; the Dominion would bear the cost of the rest.[7]

Although Wolseley's appreciation demonstrated that much planning and thought had already taken place, and also provided Lindsay with a solid understanding of the needs and challenges of the proposed expedition, the lieutenant-general also had much broader issues to tackle. The proposed operation would not solely involve British troops and Lindsay knew he would have to contend with some degree of dual control. Indeed, he prefaced an early communication with the phrase, "In the event of the Dominion Government determining to send an expedition to the Red River Settlement," clearly demonstrating his understanding of this duality.[8] However, he also knew that he was dealing with exceedingly tight deadlines and recognized the Canadians lacked the expertise to carry out much of the detailed planning. He wrote, "I felt from the first that the force, though mixed, was an Imperial one, and that I was responsible for everything connected with it. I therefore looked into the details of its organization, supply, equipment and transport, the division expenses and plan of operation."[9] He very quickly made his views clear by unequivocally telling Sir John Young, "It is indispensable that the organization of the Expeditionary Force should be at once entrusted solely to me. I will, in that case, assume all responsibility in the matter."[10]

Drawing heavily on Wolseley's document, within days of reaching Montreal Lindsay sent a comprehensive memorandum to the Governor-General outlining the situation as he found it. He outlined the size of the force he proposed to send; 1000 men of which 250 would be regular infantry, together with a British artillery and engineer component. He nominated the force commander (see the following chapter). He requested that the Canadian Government name the officer who would remain in command once the Imperial troops had left Fort Garry. He detailed his understanding of how the Canadian authorities would form their component. "I am given to understand that it is proposed to select a quota from each Militia District, from those who have volunteered for the expedition."[11] He urged this be undertaken without delay so the men could be brought together and organized into companies, the officers and men acquainted with each other, and discipline created. He made plain his views that the battalion commanders should have prior military experience and the appointment of the field officers and commanders be considered carefully. He asked to be advised as to the method utilized by the Canadian authorities to select the officers for its battalions. His prior service in Canada would have made him amply aware of the patronage endemic within the militia.

Lindsay made clear his intent that the British component of the force would be returning immediately after its mission to the Red River Settlement had been accomplished. His instructions from the War Office in London were clear, as spelled out in a communication received in early May. "I am directed to remind you that so far as the Secretary of State for War is yet informed, there is no intention that part of the Imperial Force shall remain

7 TNA, WO 107/9
8 PPP 568, Correspondence and Journal, No. 8, Inclosure 1, April 11, 1870, Memorandum from Lindsay.
9 PPP 568, Correspondence and Journal, No. 8, May 27, 1870, Lindsay to WO.
10 PPP 568, Correspondence and Journal, No. 8, Inclosure 1, April 11, 1870, Memorandum from Lindsay.
11 PPP 568, Correspondence and Journal, No. 8, Inclosure 1, April 11, 1870, Memorandum from Lindsay.

at Fort Garry during the winter; and he is not prepared to authorize you to hold out any such expectation to the Government of the Dominion."[12] Nevertheless, the risk remained that something might occur that would prevent the return of the British force before the prairie winter set in or the Great Lakes froze over and so Lindsay also sought assurance from the Canadian authorities that his men could be housed and fed if such an eventuality were to occur.

Lindsay next waded into the detail of the logistics. In the interests of time, he instructed that planning undertaken by various Canadian Government departments should cease immediately. He would make application to the Canadian Government should any purchases or actions be deemed by him to fall within Ottawa's purview. He would appoint a Control Officer "to take charge of all duties connected with feeding, and transport of the force."[13] He requested a complete list of what had been purchased or contracted to date, locations where the purchased items were stored and where and when the contracted items were to be delivered. "I will then take steps for having them duly inspected."[14]

One hundred boats had already been ordered for the transport of the force. Lindsay did not feel this number took into account the numbers of men to be carried or possible losses "in consideration of the extremely severe work they will have to endure, and the damage to which they must necessarily be exposed in taking them over the numerous portages and running the many dangerous rapids along the route." He wanted 40 more and, given that the Canadian Public Works Department had already been involved in the procurement of the original one hundred, "these 40 additional boats should be procured by that department."[15]

There was no doubting who was in charge of the preparations for the expedition. Such an approach, though, came at a cost and "the result was friction with the Canadian authorities and complaints from Lindsay of Canadian mismanagement and political interference."[16] Lindsay, however, had a job to do and was not shy about stating his opinion when he saw roadblocks in his way. His choice of expeditionary force commander was a man cut from a similar cloth and, while the end result would be to the benefit of the efficiency and effectiveness of the expeditionary force, in the weeks and months ahead there would be disagreements, particularly with the Canadian Public Works Department. It is time to meet the man who would lead the Red River Expeditionary force.

12 PPP 568, Correspondence and Journal ,No. 7, May 5, 1870, WO to Lindsay.
13 PPP 568, Correspondence and Journal, No. 8, Inclosure 1, April 11, 1870, Memorandum from Lindsay.
14 PPP 568, Correspondence and Journal, No. 8, Inclosure 1, April 11, 1870, Memorandum from Lindsay.
15 PPP 568, Correspondence and Journal, No. 8, Inclosure 1, April 11, 1870, Memorandum from Lindsay.
16 Morton, Lindsay.

9

Colonel Garnet Wolseley

Almost the first decision taken by Lindsay upon his arrival in Canada was to select the man who would lead the expeditionary force should the decision be taken to send it. Given the amount of work that would be required in a short space of time, this is not surprising. What is also not surprising is the man he selected to lead the enterprise was Colonel Garnet Joseph Wolseley, the Deputy Quartermaster-General for the British Army in North America and the author of the *Memorandum Regarding the Despatch of an Armed Force to the Red River Territory* which had so quickly put Lindsay in the frame. Such a prompt decision clearly demonstrates that Lindsay had thought the matter through before reaching Canada and had made up his mind in transit, if not before he had actually sailed from England. He reported that Wolseley "has the full approval of his Excellency the Governor-General and his Government, and I consider it very fortunate that an officer who knows Canada and its Volunteers so well and who has so much ability and experience, should have been available for this service."[1]

Lindsay had known Wolseley during his prior stay in Canada and respected the ability of this ambitious, efficient, and at times egotistical officer. Though opposed to the actual dispatch of an expedition, Sir John Michel also recommended Wolseley to lead it should the final decision to proceed be made. Wolseley was the logical, and indeed the only serious, choice, but at first the appointment was kept secret. Wolseley wrote to his brother Richard that this was because the Canadian Government did not want it to " ... appear they are preparing for war whilst they are professing to treat with Riel"[2]

As an aside, one other name to command the force had been put forward to the British government; Sir William Fenwick Williams. Nova Scotia born and a graduate of the Royal Military Academy at Woolwich, Williams had had a distinguished military career gaining repute during the siege of Kars during the Crimean War. He had been the commander-in-chief of British forces in British North America at the outbreak of the American Civil War and was a former Lieutenant-Governor of Nova Scotia. It was also widely rumoured that he was the illegitimate son of the Duke of Kent and Strathearn, something Williams throughout his long life never denied. This would have made him the half-brother of Queen Victoria. However, Cardwell and Granville both agreed that he would be 'useless' as commander of the expeditionary force. Indeed, almost a decade before, "the young, eager British colonels who came out to Canada ... believed that if war with the United States really came, Williams would have to be replaced."[3] By the time of the Red River troubles he was approaching his 70th year and physically would simply have been unable to withstand the rigours of the journey.

The highly competent Garnet Wolseley, on the other hand, was ambitious, a forward thinker and staunch supporter of army reform. He was also a social climber with an uncanny ability to give offence. In the opinion of the author, this was largely unintentional and, as he was so focused on himself and his own career, he likely did not appreciate the negative impact he could have on people. He would rise to the top of his profession and, as this

1 PPP 568, Correspondence and Journal, No. 8, May 27, 1870, Lindsay to WO.

2 Joseph Lehmann, *All Sir Garnet; A Life of Field-Marshal Lord Wolseley, 1833-1913*, (London: Jonathan Cape, 1964), p137.

3 Waite, P.B., "Williams, Sir William Fenwick," in Dictionary of Canadian Biography, vol. 11, University of Toronto/Université Laval, 2003–, accessed November 22, 2016.

Colonel Garnet Joseph Wolseley, the Red River Expeditionary Force commanding officer in 1873.
(*Illustrated London News*, ILNO-1873-0920-0013-F)

was his first independent command, it is worth taking a look at his career prior to 1870 in some detail to try and determine what set him apart from others as something of a coming man.

By 1870 Wolseley had been in Canada for eight years, serving as Assistant and, after October 1867, Deputy Quartermaster-General. Born in Dublin on June 4, 1833, the eldest in a family of seven children, his family was impoverished by the death of his father when Garnet was seven years old. A deeply religious Protestant with a profound belief in a destiny willed by God, he was nominated by the Duke of Wellington to an ensigncy in March of 1852 on the strength of his deceased father's service following an appeal from his mother. In an era where promotion was normally achieved through purchase, Wolseley lived by the mantra that the only way for a young man with no financial means to make his way in the army was for him to seek to place himself in harm's way.[4] Between 1852 and 1861 he saw active service in the Second Anglo-Burmese War, the Crimean War, the India Mutiny, where he served in the first relief of Lucknow and remained in the besieged town until the second relief, and in China on James Hope Grant's staff during the Second Opium War. In the course of this action packed period, he was badly wounded in his left thigh, leaving him with a permanent injury to his left leg, wounded twice in his right leg, the second time seriously, and lost the sight in his left eye. He also rose in rank from ensign to brevet lieutenant-colonel by the age of twenty-five without purchase and " ... established a reputation for courage and judgement in action and as an able staff officer."[5]

Though given an extended period of leave following his return from China, he was ordered to Canada in the aftermath of the Trent Affair. Wolseley initially viewed his posting to Canada as another 'rung in the ladder' with the distinct possibility of war with the Northern States providing opportunities for further advancement.[6] However, the war scare passed, and with boredom setting in, like many other British officers, he decided to visit the American battlefront; but with a twist. While several of his contemporaries had observed the war on the Union Army's front, Wolseley determined to pass through the lines "into the forbidden land of Dixey."[7] At considerable personal risk, and at one point nearly being taken prisoner by a Union patrol as he attempted to cross the Potomac River, Wolseley entered Confederate territory. Over the next month he went to Richmond,

4 Beckett, Ian F. W., "Wolseley, Garnet Joseph, first Viscount Wolseley (1833–1913)", *Oxford Dictionary of National Biography*, Oxford University Press, 2004; online edn, Jan 2008.

5 Beckett, Wolseley.

6 Lehmann, *Sir Garnet*, p117.

7 Garnet Wolseley, (An English Officer), "A Month's Visit to the Confederate Headquarters," in *Blackwood's Edinburgh Magazine,* Volume 93 No. DLXVII January 1863, p1.

"visiting the scene of several of the battles that took place in the vicinity last June", and met with Stonewall Jackson, James Longstreet, and Robert E. Lee.[8] Upon his return he penned an article for Blackwood's Magazine which argued for British recognition of the Confederacy, referred to the North as a military despotism, and Lincoln as an 'insignificant lawyer'.[9]

Back in Montreal, Wolseley began to believe that his prolonged stay in Canada was depriving him of active service and further promotion. "At times he grew very irritable and depressed."[10] This was about to change. He had gained the attention of both Sir Patrick MacDougall, the Adjutant-General of Canadian Militia, and Sir John Michel, the commander of the British forces in British North America, and both looked favourably upon the ambitious and able young officer.[11] As the Fenian threat began to manifest itself after the North's victory in the Civil War, Wolseley was placed in command of a camp of instruction for Canadian militia officers at La Prairie just outside of Montreal. "The camp was designed to provide practical experience for the graduates of the schools of military instruction operated in Canada by the British army", and though inspired by MacDougall, the day to day operations were left in the competent hands of Wolseley.[12]

"Ignoring time-honoured traditions that were fast becoming obsolete, and placing little stress on the childish parade-ground manoeuvres, Wolseley taught them the practical side of war."[13] James Lindsay, at that time the military commander in Canada East, called out the British garrison at Montreal for the final exercise at the camp's conclusion. Wolseley himself commanded one of the brigades, " ... the first time he had commanded troops above the unit level."[14] Wolseley's view of the camp as a whole was that it was an interesting experiment and a great success.[15] Interest was also taken at a higher level and "Sir John Michel ... sent a favourable report to his superiors, noting, 'it is difficult to speak too highly of this talented, energetic young officer.'"[16]

Following the Battle of Ridgway on June 2nd, 1866, Michel dispatched Wolseley 'hot haste' to 'coach' Major-General George T.C. Napier, the commander of British forces in Canada West, "and prevent him from doing anything very foolish."[17] Wolseley described Napier as being " ... quite useless at all times as a commander" and "a fair specimen of the general then usually selected for colonial commands." He added that Napier "seemed delighted to have someone by him whose advice he might follow."[18] Regardless of the merits of Wolseley's comments regarding Major-General Napier, and they indicate a level of self-belief bordering on arrogance, the fact Wolseley was the man Michel called on in this hour of crisis, exemplifies his rising star status. On the afternoon of the day of his arrival, Wolseley spotted an American cutter mid-stream on the Niagara River with a barge astern loaded with hundreds of Fenians. He rowed out to the American ship, the *USS Michigan*, and on board was received by General Barry, the commander of the Buffalo Military District. Wolseley was informed that the Fenians had been captured re-crossing to the American side and Barry assured him that they would be taken back to the United States.

A command of a mixed force of British regulars and Canadian militiamen at Stratford followed. A few weeks afterwards he was in charge of a camp at Thorold on the Welland Canal, with responsibility for protecting the Niagara frontier and the canal itself. Of arguably greater significance, he was tasked with the training of Canadian

---

8 Wolseley, "Confederate", p11.
9 Wolseley, "Confederate", p29
Wolseley characterized British policy as 'timid' and wrote he was 'frequently sorely puzzled' by questions from those he met during his visit, such as would it not be in Britain's best interest to have 'more than one great republic upon the American continent' and why would Britain run the risk of incurring the misfortune of Northern 'insolence and arrogance' should they be successful in their subjugation of the Confederacy? Wolseley, "Confederate", p25.
10 Lehmann, *Sir Garnet*, p124.
11 Stacey, Michel,
12 Cooke, Wolseley.
13 Lehmann, *Sir Garnet*, p126.
14 Cooke, Wolseley.
15 Field-Marshal Viscount Wolseley, *The Story of a Soldier's Life Volume 2*, (New York: Charles Scribner's Sons, 1904), p150.
16 Cooke, Wolseley.
17 Wolseley, *Soldier's Life*, p169.
18 Wolseley, *Soldier's Life*, p169.

Wolseley in 1882. (Library and Archives Canada, archival reference number R12632-1, e010700647)

militia troops. With a battalion of the Bedfordshire Regiment, together with an artillery component, under his command, Canadians came in batches of four or five battalions for ten days at a time.[19] "Wolseley imparted pragmatic instruction, his aim being 'to afford officers and men instruction in the practical work which real war presents, and to avoid repeating drill-book manoeuvres which never could be required in Canada.'"[20] Each week there were two field days and "one grand one when we have a mimic battle and fire off any amount of H.M. Ammunitions ... It is capital practice for me as I am so little with troops and I now have such opportunities by learning how to handle men", he wrote to his brother Dick.[21] Demonstrating his ever-present ambition and self-belief, he had written in a prior letter, "who knows, but I may be Sir Garnet before another six months."[22]

With the approach of winter, the government decided the crisis had passed and the camp was disbanded. However, in January the Fenian alarm was again raised and Wolseley was ordered to Toronto to organize the Toronto Brigade, with command promised to him should an invasion occur. "In the event it was only another scare, and in the spring his term of office as Assistant Quartermaster-General ended."[23] He left Canada for Ireland fretting that the invasion, and the chance for further advancement, would take place in his absence. He need not have worried about his star waning. The invasion did not take place, but in September he was summoned back and promoted to serve as Deputy Quartermaster-General. At just 34 years of age, he was " ... the youngest officer ever to assume this senior staff post in Canada."[24]

19 Wolseley, *Soldier's Life*, pp162/63.
20 Cooke, Wolseley.
21 Lehmann, *Sir Garnet*, p130.
22 Lehmann, *Sir Garnet*, p130.
23 Halik Kochanski, *Sir Garnet Wolseley; Victorian Hero*, (London: The Hambledon Press, 1999), p41.
24 Cooke, Wolseley.

It was during his time in Canada that the ambitious colonel also began to establish a name for himself as a writer and military thinker. He had penned accounts of the Second Opium War and of his time visiting the Confederate front during the Civil War, though much of the latter had been re-worked by his sister. However, it was with the publication of *The Soldier's Pocket Book for Field Service* in March 1869 that he gained a reputation with the War Office in London as "an advanced forward-thinking young officer."[25] Written at the suggestion of the army's Quartermaster-General, Sir Richard Airey, "it was a guide designed to cover warfare, from the field operations of the various arms to the minutiae of life on campaigns."[26] As Wolseley himself put it, "This Pocket-Book is intended to be a guide to officers from the moment war is declared: it enters into the most minute details with everything connected with the wild life one has to lead in the field when cut adrift, perhaps entirely from civilisation, but at any rate, from cooks, clubs, tailors and bootmakers."[27] Detailed it certainly was and Wolseley covered topics ranging from such high level matters as the organization of the army and civil departments, the importance of intelligence, and the duties of the staff, to the seemingly mundane, though no less important issues, such as tents and camp equipment, rations, ammunition, filters and pumps, building bridges, and even destroying bridges, to list but a few.

The *Soldier's Pocket Book* demonstrated, not only Wolseley's understanding of how to conduct a colonial military campaign, but also advertised his commitment to military reform.[28] In doing so, he risked offending a number of people both inside and outside of the army. Statements such as soldiers 'must be taught to despise those in civil life' and 'like missionaries must be fanatics' were bound to ruffle a few feathers in civilian and religious circles.[29] His comments that spreading false news by using correspondents 'as a medium by which to deceive the enemy' were equally unpopular with 'the gentlemen of the press'.[30] "Perhaps the most startling were his ideas on the relationship between officers and the rank and file."[31] Wolseley urged his readers to realize "the feudal system has passed away." Officers "must make themselves loved as well as respected" and this was most easily achieved by taking an interest in the lives of their men, recognizing their achievements, and ceasing "to treat them as unreasoning children unable to take care of themselves."[32]

> Let us sink as far as possible the respective titles of officers, sergeants and privates, merging them into the one great cognomen of soldier, causing all ranks to feel that it is a noble title of which the general as well as the private may well be proud. Let us give up the phrase 'officer' and 'gentleman,' substituting that of 'soldier' for it; let the word officer be used as seldom as possible, so that the private may really feel that there is no gulf between him and his commander, but that they are merely separated by a ladder, the rungs of which all can equally aspire.[33]

Views such as these, so advanced for the time, would have been seen as radical by some. However, the War Office adopted *The Soldier's Pocket Book* and issued it to all army officers, demonstrating a degree of forward thinking, perhaps unfairly, not always associated with the British Army of this era. The book would subsequently go through five editions.

While in Canada, Wolseley had also fallen in with George T. Denison, the Canada First leader, who he described as "one of the ablest, and professionally one of the best read officers I ever knew ... ."[34] The admiration

25 Kochanski, *Wolseley*, p42.
26 Kochanski, *Wolseley*, p42.
27 Colonel Sir Garnet J. Wolseley, *The Soldier's Pocket-Book for field service*, (London: Macmillan and Co., 1871), ppv/vi.
28 Beckett, "Wolseley".
29 Wolseley, *Pocket Book*, p5.
30 Wolseley, *Pocket Book*, p249.
It is also worth noting that Wolseley put this approach into practice during operations against Arabi Pasha in Egypt in 1882.
31 Kochanski, *Wolseley*, p42.
32 Wolseley, *Pocket Book*, p2.
33 Wolseley, *Pocket Book*, p1.
34 Wolseley, *Soldier's Life*, p148. George Denison was a Canadian politician and influential militia officer who saw active service during the Fenian raids in 1866. He turned against the Conservative Party in Canada firstly after Minister of Militia George-Etienne Cartier failed to appoint him as Assistant Adjutant-General of Cavalry for Canada's militia and secondly due to the

was mutual and Denison, strongly favouring the sending of a punitive expedition to Red River, had throughout the winter of 1869/70 " ... worked very energetically to stir up public opinion in favour of Colonel Wolseley."[35] After the announcement was made, Denison describes being summoned to meet with Wolseley and spending the following week much in his company as the expedition was planned. He also details an episode when Canadian Minister of Militia Cartier arrived at Wolseley's office while Denison was there. Denison and Cartier had fallen out two years previously. Though Denison offered to leave, Wolseley would not hear of it and turned the minister away instead. When Denison warned the expedition commander against making an enemy of Cartier, he replied, "I don't care, I would never let him turn you out of my room."[36] Whether one chooses to take Denison completely at face value in his description of these events, it is clear that the British Army colonel and former Canadian militia officer had become firm friends. As such, the inclination of an ambitious colonel to see some action aside, it is unsurprising that the expeditionary force commander took a decidedly more aggressive view of his mission than his political masters in London.

There is one additional item requiring mention regarding the responsibilities of the expeditionary force commander and this began before Wolseley's appointment. On March 23rd a letter from the Colonial Office to the War Office elevated the status of the pending appointment by stating "the selection of the officer will be still more important if, as is possible, the Canadian Government should desire him to act as the first civil Lieutenant-Governor of the district."[37] This certainly piqued Wolseley's sense of ambition and he left HBC Governor, Sir Stafford Northcote, believing 'he seemed to like the idea.' Northcote was correct in this view and Wolseley was soon writing to his wife about his lobbying to secure 'our governorship.'[38] He wrote again on May 9th telling her that " ... there are no further developments on the governorship," but he hopes that Lindsay " ... may be able to finish our business."[39] It was, however, not to be. On May 14th he wrote "I have just had a telegram from McNeill [the Military Secretary to the Governor-General] in cypher, saying that I cannot be governor ... ."[40] The Canadian Government had opted for the conciliatory Adams G. Archibald.

This then was the outspoken young colonel who would lead the British Army's last military campaign in North America. He had repeatedly shown himself to be fearless in the face of enemy fire, believed in the proper training of troops, including the Canadian volunteers, and held advanced views as regard to officer-enlisted man relations. There was, as well, his eye for detail and organization, qualities that had been admirably demonstrated when he authored *The Soldier's Pocket Book* and the *Memorandum Regarding the Despatch of an Armed Force to the Red River Territory.* Command of the Red River Expeditionary Force was a significant opportunity and he would later write in his memoirs, "This was my first independent command, so I was on my mettle, and felt that if I possessed any genius for such practical work, the time had at last arrived for me to show it."[41]

---

government's handling of the troubles at Red River. Denison was one of the founders of the Canada First movement and had become firm friends with Wolseley even before the latter's appointment to command the expeditionary force. Denison would later write the highly influential book *A History of Cavalry from the Earliest Times with Lessons for the Future*, which was published in London in 1877.

35 Denison, *Soldiering*, p174.

36 Denison, *Soldiering*, p175.

37 Hove Public Library, WP.1/1, Letter from Garnet Wolseley to Lucy Wolseley, May 9, 1870.

38 See Sir Stafford Henry Northcote, *Diaries of the First Earl of Iddesleigh*," (Printed for private circulation 1907), Entry, April 26, 1870 and Hove Public Library, WP.1/1, Letter from Garnet Wolseley to Lucy Wolseley, Undated.

39 Hove Public Library, WP.1/1, Letter from Garnet Wolseley to Lucy Wolseley, May 9, 1870. Wolseley married in June of 1867. His relatively early marriage is interesting in light of the opposition he frequently voiced regarding young officers falling into hasty marriages and having their careers ruined. He was not averse to them being sent home to avoid such an occurrence. Given his impecunious past and his responsibility for looking after his younger siblings, he had always said that he would only marry for money. His marriage to Louisa (Loo) Erskine, after a short home leave, therefore, came as something of a surprise. It appears to have been a happy union, and his frequent (often almost illegible) letters to her contained a wide variety of endearments such as Little Snipe, Periwinkle and Runtyfoozle. See McCourt, *Butler*. p44 for these examples.

40 Hove Public Library, WP.1/1, Letter from Garnet Wolseley to Lucy Wolseley, May 14, 1870.

41 Wolseley, *Soldier's Life*, p179. As he climbed the ladder, some of Wolseley's less flattering characteristics would be noted by the Queen herself. This prompted the response from Lord Beaconsfield, the prime minister of the day. "It is quite true that Wolseley is an egotist and a braggart. So was Nelson ... Men of action when eminently successful in early life are generally boastful and full of themselves." *Beckett, Wolseley*

10

The Route is Chosen

Taking the decision to dispatch an expeditionary force to Red River was one thing, getting it there was quite another. Canada may have been about to assume political control over the Northwest, but there simply was no easy or established route from the Dominion to the HBC lands. The distance from Toronto, where the troops would muster, to Fort Garry was 1228 miles. In between was a labyrinth of mountain passes, swampy valleys, dense insect infested forests, and a multitude of lakes and swift flowing rivers with treacherous rapids. Wherever waterborne navigation was impossible, the men would have to unload the boats and laboriously transport both they and all that was contained in them from one body of water to the next, a task known as portaging.

There were three possible avenues of entry into the Red River territory. The first we can deal with quickly, and that was south of the Great Lakes through American territory. An American railway was already in existence, which, combined with the river boat service in operation on the Red River, could have transported the expedition to their objective with little difficulty. As we have seen, it was the approach of the American settler frontier that had ended the area's isolation, broken the HBC's monopoly and led many in the United States to feel that the destiny of the region lay with them. However, it was quite simply not a viable alternative for the transportation of the expeditionary force. It was a political non-starter for the Canadian Government to request transit through American territory and the American Secretary of State had in November told the British Minister in Washington that, should a request be made, the answer would be no.[1] None of the expedition's planning documents speak to examining this route and so in all likelihood it was never considered as an option.

The other two were the well-established northern HBC route and the largely forgotten southern North West Company canoe highway from Lake Superior. The Hudson's Bay option ran up the Hayes River to Lake Winnipeg and then along the Red River to Fort Garry, a distance of 723 miles. This was the route taken by the military expeditions of 1846 and 1857 and Sir George Simpson had always maintained that it was the better of the two. The problem was that Hudson's Bay was only ice free and open to shipping for a very limited time during the summer, which would make it difficult for the British troops to get to Fort Garry and back again in one season.

Regarding the southern route, by 1870 steamers on the upper Great Lakes had greatly reduced the time and physical effort required to get to the head of Lake Superior. However, the steamers could only begin to operate once the lake ice had broken up at the end of April or the start of May. The freeze up would start again by the beginning of November at the latest, which meant that the southern route still left a limited window of time for the British troops to get to Fort Garry and back again in one season, though in this respect it was certainly a longer window than that offered by Hudson's Bay option.

There had been two different entry points into the interior used by the North West Company; the first when their summer meeting place had been at Grand Portage and second when they moved to Fort William after 1803.[2] After the Canadian expeditions of 1857 and 1858 there had been disagreement between Simon J. Dawson and Henry Hind as to which was the better of the two, with Hind favouring the Grand Portage-Pigeon

1 Bowsfield, *United States*, p11. By all accounts the American authorities did not believe the expedition had any chance of reaching the Red River Settlement without access to their transportation routes.

2 See Chapter 1.

River route and Dawson the Fort William-Kaministiquia River route.[3] In 1859 Dawson had strongly advocated the construction of a road for the influx of settlers to the Northwest from Canada. At that time the Canadian Government was not in a position to assume any responsibility for HBC territory and in any case had shied away from the cost, particularly in light of the disagreement as to the best route.[4] A decade later Canadian intentions were clear. Barring the Americans getting there first, Canada was taking over and a Canadian route was going to be needed. Dawson joined the Department of Public Works and in 1867 set to work on developing the eastern end of the route. This would adopt Dawson's earlier views on the subject and commence at Fort William near the mouth of the Kaministiquia River.

Part of the Canadian Privy Council Memorandum had in February 1870 authorized the construction of boats for the expedition, a task that was also handed over to Simon Dawson, and called for the mustering of the force at Fort William by May 1st.[5] This was a clear indication of the route preferred by the Canadian Government. However, the British did not accept this as a *fait accompli*, and the Topographical Department of the War Office conducted a review of the various route options available. This was undertaken by Captain Charles W. Wilson, R.E. and a comprehensive report under the signature of Colonel Sir Henry James, the Director General of the Ordnance Survey, and according to the Ordnance Survey itself probably the most egotistical man ever to hold the post, was published on March 31st, 1870.[6]

Wilson reviewed the writings of Palliser, Hind, and Dawson, as well Colonel Crofton, who had commanded the expedition in 1846, and the explorers Captains John Henry Lefroy and Thomas Blakiston. Crofton's force had journeyed to Fort Garry from Hudson's Bay, but he departed before the troops were withdrawn, returning via Fort William. He was personally consulted and gave his recollection of this route. The mass of information compiled by Wilson provided detail on climate, soil, rivers, lakes and portages, as well as the ethnic makeup of the community at the Red River Settlement.[7]

Three possible routes were considered: Hudson's Bay and both the Pigeon River and Kaministiquia options from Lake Superior. The report noted that the Pigeon River route was 43 miles shorter and had easier portages. Unfortunately, sections of it fell south of the border with the United States and so it was a non-starter from the outset. This meant that the choice was a simple one between the Hudson's Bay and Thunder Bay-Kaministiquia River routes. As regards the latter option, the report erred in three key areas. First, it spoke of the route going from Fort William to Dog Lake. This had been the route when it had been part of the North West Company canoe highway, but in 1869 Dawson had changed the line of advance to cut out Dog Lake and proceed via Shebandowan Lake. Admittedly, Wilson and James were more removed from the scene of events, but given the comprehensive nature of the rest of the report, this error is somewhat surprising. No mention is made at all of Shebandowan Lake, from where the expedition would first take to the boats on its journey to Fort Garry. Second, it is stated that improvements had been undertaken by the Canadian Government and a road built between Thunder Bay and Dog Lake. Not only was the route not accurate, but the road to Shebandowan Lake, while under construction, had not yet been completed. Third, mention is made of a road having been opened from the Northwest Angle at Lake of the Woods to the Red River Settlement. This was also not the case. As at Thunder Bay, construction had

3 See Chapter 4.

4 *Peel's Prairie Provinces 350*, Henry Youle Hind, George Gladman, Simon James Dawson, W.E. Napier, "Report on the Exploration of the Country between Lake Superior and the Red River Settlement," John Lovell, Printer, Toronto, 1858 & Arthur, Dawson, p10.

5 See Chapter 7.

6 Ordnance Survey History, https://www.ordnancesurvey.co.uk/about/overview/history.html

7 Charles William Wilson served in British North America between 1858 and 1861 as part of the British Boundary Commission mapping the 49th parallel (the border with the United States) between the Rocky Mountains and the Pacific Ocean. In 1882 he served under Wolseley during the expedition in Egypt. He again served under Wolseley during the Gordon Relief Expedition in the Sudan in 1884/85. He took command of the Desert Column after the force commander, Sir Herbert Stewart, was mortally wounded. Wilson led the advance guard in Nile steamers for last part of the journey but arrived at Khartoum too late to save General Gordon.

been started, but was far from complete.[8] It was, incidentally, the work on the western end of the road that had sparked the discontent of the Métis in 1868.

After weighing the pros and cons of the two politically feasible options, Lindsay and Wolseley opted for the southern Lake Superior route. This would necessitate crossing the watershed from the Great Lakes drainage basin over into the Hudson's Bay drainage basin, which " ... are separated by a line of rugged hills which approach to within about 80 miles of Thunder Bay."[9] In all likelihood, two key pieces of information factored into this choice. The first was the limiting timeframe imposed by the ice on Hudson's Bay. The second was the road to Shebandowan Lake. While James and Wilson may not have been aware of Dawson's change in the direction of the road, Wolseley certainly was as is confirmed in his *Memorandum Regarding the Despatch of an Armed Force to the Red River Territory*. He also knew of the difficulties of traversing the Kaministiquia River due to the swift rise in elevation from Thunder Bay to both Dog and Shebandowan Lakes which sit at 710 and 839 feet respectively above the level of Lake Superior. The Shebandowan River, flowing out of the lake of the same name, joins the Matawin River which in turns joins the Kaministiquia River coming down from Dog Lake. From here to its mouth at Thunder Bay, the Kaministiquia is fast flowing with a multitude of rapids; the Kakabeka Falls alone dropping over 130 feet. Dawson himself did not believe it was possible to move the expeditionary force's boats up the Kaministiquia River. The road, so it was envisioned, would allow Wolseley to muster his men at Thunder Bay and move them, their equipment, and the boats quickly to Shebandowan Lake to commence the challenging journey to the interior. As we shall see, matters regarding the road did not work out quite as planned.

The full distance the expedition would have to travel was 1228 miles.[10] This was broken down as follows:

94 miles by rail from Toronto to the port of Collingwood on Lake Huron.
534 miles by steamer from Collingwood to Thunder Bay. The steamers would need to use the canal on the American side of the rapids at Sault Ste. Marie and it was recognized by the expedition's planners that the United States authorities might take exception to this.
50 miles from Thunder Bay to Shebandowan Lake along the Dawson Road.[11]
550 miles from Shebandowan Lake to Fort Garry.

This last part of the journey would take the force from Shebandowan Lake across the height of land into the Hudson's Bay watershed, and then via Lac des Mille Lacs to Fort Frances, named for Frances Simpson, the wife of Sir George Simpson, at the western end of Rainy Lake. From here they would venture down the Rainy River to Lake of the Woods, along which the border with the United States ran, past the Northwest Angle, where the incomplete western end of the road to the Settlement would begin, and then down the Winnipeg River. The last stage would take them across the southern end of Lake Winnipeg and then up the Red River first to Lower and then Upper Fort Garry. All told there would be 47 portages ranging in length from as little as one hundred yards to over a mile.[12] Although the North West Company had used much of this same route with great success prior to 1821, it had never been traversed by such a large body of men, with such a weight of supplies and with boats of a size the expedition would be using. Once moving on from Thunder Bay, they would find little in the way of supplies to sustain them and virtually everything needed would have to be carried.[13] It was a challenging undertaking by any standard.

8 Peel's Prairie Provinces 558, Colonel Sir Henry James R.E., F.R.S., "Notes on the Routes from Lake Superior to the Red River and On The Settlement Itself; Compiled from Reports by Captain Palliser, Professor Hind, and Messrs. Dawson and Napier with Notes Relating to the Transport of Troops &c., by Colonel Crofton and Captain, (Now General) Lefroy, R.A.," Compiled in the Topographical Department of the War Office, March 31st, 1870.

9 Wolseley, *Narrative Part 1*, p716.

10 Hove Public Library, Wolseley Papers, SSL-2/1.1-vi.

11 Actually 48 miles.

12 Charles Rathbone Low, *A Memoir of Lieutenant-General Sir Garnet J. Wolseley In Two Volumes, Volume 2*, (London: Richard Bentley & Son, 1878), p8.

13 Wolseley, *Narrative Part 1*, p718.

Simon J. Dawson of the Canadian Public Works Department and the man charged with the building of the road from Thunder Bay to Shebandowan Lake. (Topley Studio Fonds / Library and Archives Canada / PA-033901)

It was the road from Thunder Bay to Shebandowan Lake, though, that would become one of the major talking points of the campaign, with finger pointing and mutual recrimination between the British military and the Canadian civil authorities. Wolseley would later write that the Canadians had promised that the road would be ready by the end of May and even spoke of a rumour among his troops that delays by the Canadians were part of a conspiracy to try and trap the British into remaining at Red River over the winter.[14] While the Canadians would certainly have viewed the British troops remaining at Fort Garry in a positive light, there is no evidence of conspiracy and Dawson's subsequent writings firmly assert that Lindsay and Wolseley knew full well that the road was not finished before the expeditionary forces left Toronto. Therefore, before we reach this stage in the narrative, it will be advantageous to attempt to disentangle what had taken place and what had been said regarding this contentious topic prior to the expedition's arrival at Thunder Bay.

Dawson had joined the Department of Public Works when the Canadian Government, in anticipation of its takeover of the HBC lands, decided that it was time to finally construct a road that would form part of the settler route to what was soon to become the Canadian west. In other words, the initial work had nothing whatsoever to do with a military expedition to Red River. Dawson was in charge of the building of the eastern end of the road, as well as the improvements to the various water routes and portages. In a report published in May of 1869, he recommended the construction of dams to raise the water levels of the interior lakes and rivers to make them more navigable. It was here that he also proposed an alteration in the direction of the road from Dog Lake to Shebandowan Lake.[15] Dawson argued that the advantages of this change were that the navigable waters of the summit plateau would be reached with one road rather than two roads broken at Dog Lake. He also assured the Canadian authorities that no work had yet been undertaken on the Dog Lake road, so it was not as if construction previously completed was being abandoned. Nevertheless, the additional exploration and surveying required to determine the new route no doubt consumed time and resources that would not have been expended if the original route had been adhered to. With hindsight it could be argued that this did create a delay

14 Wolseley, *Narrative Part 2*, p52.

15 Peel's Prairie Provinces 481, C.E., Simon J Dawson, "Report, the Line of Route Between Lake Superior and the Red River Settlement Printed by Order of the House of Commons, Ottawa, 1869, p9.

in the completion of the road, but it also needs to be pointed out that there was nothing in Dawson's original instructions to indicate that speed was of the essence. He was simply trying to determine and develop the best route for the settlers who would move into the Northwest once Canada had taken control.

In his writings after the expedition, Wolseley appears to have accepted this change of direction without difficulty, though he does mention that it extended the length of the road from 29 to 48 miles.[16] What he apparently misses is that Dawson's report of May 1869 also spoke of a second road of 10 to 12 miles in length on the other side of Dog Lake that, due to the change in route, would no longer be required.[17]

The work that Dawson was overseeing, it also needs to be understood, was taking place in a remote and harsh environment. Once winter closed in, communication and the flow of supplies ceased and it was simply not possible to continue with most of the construction work. Limited communication via the United States was possible, but once crossing into Canadian territory this involved a lengthy journey on foot in exceedingly difficult conditions. This meant that there was no possibility of getting large bodies of men and supplies in or out even using the American route once winter set in, with the consequence that the area of road construction was to all intents and purposes cut off for six months of the year.

What had begun slowly in 1867 was making progress by 1869 and in July Dawson reported that over two hundred men were at work.[18] Late in September he advised the Public Works Department that fair progress was being made despite the exceedingly rainy weather, 'absolutely without precedent', that had caused flooding and had drenched the working parties for the past month. Dawson proposed that one hundred and forty of the men would be discharged and evacuated by the last steamer at the end of October or beginning of November, while the remaining sixty would be retained over the winter to work on bridge building and bring in lumber for the construction of a dock at Thunder Bay.[19]

The mundane nature of the communications between Dawson and the Public Works Department changed suddenly and dramatically in January 1870 when the Canadian Government finally came to the realization that it had a problem on its hands at Fort Garry and needed the road completed without delay. There were essentially three rounds to this correspondence and it is important to closely scrutinize what was said to determine whether there is merit to Wolseley's contention that the promise of a completed road had not been kept.[20]

The first round began on January 12th when Dawson received several pieces of correspondence asking for detail as to the steps required to ensure completion of the road by May 1st[21] and the portages as far as Lake of the Woods by the same date.[22] Somewhat surprisingly in view of the sudden need for urgency in the completion of the route, there was also a reprimand; it being stated that the road was costing $2000 per mile when similar construction was taking place in Ontario for $500 per mile.[23] Dawson replied on January 17th that the portages would be ready by May 1st[24] and regarding the road, that if an 'experienced officer' was sent to Fort William to oversee the resumption of the work as soon as was practicable, this would "ensure the opening of the line by the time stated, in so far that horses with waggons may pass over the greater portion of it (say about twenty-eight miles), and oxen with ox-carts or waggons over the remaining sections. *The line would thus be practicable to the*

16 Wolseley, *Narrative Part 1*, p717.

17 PPP 481, Dawson, "Line of Route", p20.

18 Early Canadiana Online, Canadian Sessional Papers (CSP) No12 1870 No. 7513 Dawson to Braun Dept of Public Works July 21st, 1869.

19 ECO CSP, Braun to Dawson January 12th, 1870 No. 6032.

20 One of the most prolific 'modern' historians to write on the expedition was George F. G. Stanley. His first book, where he relied on the first round of this correspondence, came down on Wolseley's side (see Stanley, *Birth of Western Canada* p135) whereas in his final book, he relied on the third round of the correspondence and was more supportive of Dawson (See Stanley, *Toil and Trouble*, p88).

21 ECO CSP No. 12, 1870, Braun to Dawson January 12th, 1870, 6031

22 ECO CSP No. 12. 1870, Braun to Dawson January 12th, 1870, 6032.

23 ECO CSP No. 12. 1870, Braun to Dawson January 12th, 1870, 6033.

24 ECO CSP No. 12. 1870, January 17th, 1870, Dawson to Braun, 9193.

transport of freight by the time the first steamers can reach Lake Superior, on the opening of navigation." [author's emphasis][25] The break-up of the lake ice normally took place around the last week of April/first week of May.

Confirmation of approval by the minister for the steps recommended by Dawson were forwarded to him on January 21st [26] and the 'experienced officer', Lindsay Russell, was dispatched via Superior, Wisconsin, crossing the final two hundred miles to Thunder Bay on snowshoes. Dawson would later state that Russell carried out his instructions with 'energy and skill'.[27]

The second round of the correspondence occurred on March 26th. Dawson was required to respond to a request from the Canadian House of Commons that he furnish specifics on the road's progress. In light of the fact that he had left the Thunder Bay area on the last steamer the previous November and the ice had not yet cleared to re-open communication, one has to have some sympathy with the Public Works Department official. After all, what new information would he have since his previous replies in January? In fact, much of his response dealt with the history of the road's construction the previous year. He did speak to the construction of six bridges, "four of moderate dimensions and two large ones," of which he stated that three had been constructed, one was under construction and two would be built in the spring. He also stated that twenty-five miles of the road was open, ten was partially open and this took construction to within five miles of the dam site close to Shebandowan Lake. For those keeping track, this adds up to 40 miles, though in fact the road would eventually run for 48 miles. This meant that eight additional miles of road were essentially unaccounted for. Were they still to be constructed or had Dawson simply miscalculated the length?

The report was also less sanguine than the January responses regarding the completion and condition of the road. In January the road would be open if a 'senior officer' was sent to put matters in hand. This had taken place and, as we have seen, Dawson later reported that he had done a good job. Now in March he told the House of Commons that the ten mile partially open section " ... requires a great deal of additional work." Presumably the last few miles from the dam site to the lake itself were as yet not begun.[28]

The third round of communication came on April 25th. In his report on the expedition published in 1871, Dawson wrote that he had been in contact with the military authorities several times through the month of April and " ... was most careful to inform them as to the condition of the Thunder Bay Road ... ."[29] He had in fact provided them with a memorandum on April 25th which stated:

> When the work of road making was brought to a close last fall, a section of 25 miles, reckoning from Thunder Bay, was practicable to waggons, with only one interruption at the Kaministiquia which was then unbridged, and continuing on the line and additional section of ten miles was cut out in such a way as to be practicable to oxen with sleds or carts.
>
> The two large rivers-Kamisitiquia and Matawin-which cross the line, were bridged last winter, and bridges were also built over the more considerable of the smaller streams, so that practically, the work of bridging may be considered completed.
>
> At the same time instructions were sent to the officer in charge, to set all the available force to work on the road as soon as the snow should have so far cleared off, as to admit of operations thereon being resumed, so that eighty men are by this time engaged on the unfinished section of the line.
>
> An additional force of 120 men will be sent to their aid by the first steamer, and a week later, a further number of about fifty will go up.[30]

In light of the controversy, there are two questions that need to be addressed. First, what prompted the subtle, but still substantive, differences in the status of the road as reported by Dawson over the course of these three

25 ECO CSP No. 12. 1870, January 17th, 1870, Dawson to Braun, 9194.
26 ECO CSP No. 12. January 21st, 1870, Braun to Dawson, No. 6121
27 Peel's Prairie Provinces 559, Simon, J. Dawson, C.E., "Report of the Red River Expedition of 1870, and Addenda" Times Printing and Publishing, Ottawa, 1871, p6.
28 CSP No. 12, March 26, 1870, Report on Thunder Bay Road by S.J. Dawson.
29 PPP 559, Dawson, "Report", p6.
30 PPP 559, Dawson, "Report", pp7-9.

sets of communications? Second, did Wolseley have grounds to believe that the road would be ready when the expeditionary force arrived at Thunder Bay or was he making excuses so that he could deflect the blame should the British troops be required to winter at Fort Garry?

Dealing with the first question, after his positive response in January to a completion date of May 1st, as information regarding the state of the road began to trickle out, Dawson appears to have begun to equivocate. The Canadian Government had provided its approval in January for a significant increase in the workforce, but the status of the road at the time of the freeze-up in 1869, combined with the fact that additional workers could not actually arrive at Thunder Bay until the last week of April at the very earliest, meant that it would have been tremendously difficult to complete the road by the beginning of May. It is hard not to sympathize with the Public Works Department man as the government pressed for an early completion date, but Dawson should have been more realistic in January as to what could be delivered. The maxim that it is always better to under-promise and over-deliver, rather than the other way round, springs to mind. Not only would a healthy dose of realism have prevented the backsliding of his subsequent reports, but it would have avoided a lot of acrimony between the British and Canadians in the long-term.

Regarding the second question, Lindsay and Wolseley were aware of Dawson's January response on the road and this probably factored into their decision to opt for the southern route to Fort Garry. It also no doubt influenced Wolseley's thinking on the timetable of the expedition, given the pressure he was under to get the British troops in and out in one season. In all probability Wolseley would not have been aware of Dawson's response to the Canadian House of Commons in March, meaning that he likely first became aware that the road would not be ready at some point in April. Lindsay was certainly complaining as late as April 20th that he lacked 'reliable information' as to the state of the road, however, by April 25th he was in receipt of Dawson's memorandum.[31] This would have been too late to switch to the northern Hudson's Bay route, assuming the short ice free season combined with the pressure to ensure the British troops were gotten to Fort Garry and back again in one season, had ever led to serious consideration of this option. Consequently, while news of the incomplete road might have been a surprise in April, Wolseley would certainly have been aware that it was not complete before he arrived at Thunder Bay in May. Nevertheless, there is a difference in knowing something is not ready and then discovering just how incomplete it actually is. As we shall see, Wolseley was at first fairly optimistic about how quickly the road could be made ready, but in fact there was a great deal to be done and heavy rain combined with forest fires did not speed matters along. But we are getting ahead of ourselves and we will return to the road in a later chapter. The expeditionary force which would traverse this road had not yet been assembled. It was a relatively simple matter to assign British forces already stationed in Canada to the enterprise. The Canadian contingent would prove more problematic.

31 Northcote, *Iddesleigh*, April 20, 1870.

11

The Expeditionary Force is Assembled

On April 2nd Lord Granville informed Governor-General Sir John Young that 200 to 250 British troops could participate in the expedition to the Red River, although he would leave the exact number to Lieutenant-General Lindsay once he had arrived. Granville added, however, that there must be an additional force of five hundred trained Canadian militia volunteers that would accompany the regulars. He also made clear that Gladstone's fiscally responsible government was not going to have the British taxpayer underwrite anything more than the cost of the British component and the Canadians would be expected to pay for their own troops.[1]

The British infantry would come from the 1st battalion of the King's Royal Rifle Corps, the 60th Rifles, commanded by Colonel R. J. Feilden. Their participation had been proposed by Wolseley in his *Memorandum Regarding the Despatch of an Armed Force to the Red River Territory* back in March and, according to one of the expedition's Canadian officers, " ... a finer body of men it was felt by all would be hard to find."[2] The King's Royal Rifle Corps traced its lineage to the French and Indians Wars, having been raised in North America in the aftermath of the disaster that befell Major-General Edward's Braddock's force in 1755. Initially designated the 62nd Royal Americans, it became the 60th Regiment in February 1757. The Royal Americans saw service throughout the Revolutionary War, and it was during this conflict that its battalions began to be raised in Britain. Four line battalions of infantry were raised during the wars against Napoleon, and then in 1797 a fifth rifle battalion was raised with two more following in the coming years. By contrast with the traditional red tunic of the British Army worn by line battalions, the uniform of the riflemen consisted of green jackets with red facings, similar to Austrian Jaeger units.[3] The success of the rifle battalions during the Peninsular War resulted in the 60th being designated a Rifle regiment in May of 1815.[4] In the fifty-five years between the conclusion of hostilities with Napoleonic France and the Red River Expedition, battalions of the regiment served throughout the empire and saw action in the Second Sikh War, the Eighth Xhosa War, the India Mutiny and the Second Opium War. In 1830 the regiment was named the King's Royal Rifle Corps. Henceforth in this narrative it will be referred to as either the KRRC or the 60th Rifles.

Immediately prior to the outbreak of the troubles at the Red River Settlement, there were two battalions of the KRRC in Canada, the 1st and the 4th. The 4th Battalion had arrived shortly before the Trent Incident in 1861 and was commanded by Lieutenant-Colonel Robert Hawley, a soldier renowned for his professionalism and training ability. It was written that "the regiment, both individually and collectively, is deeply indebted to Hawley ... and there are few Riflemen of our generation who achieved distinction who do not directly or indirectly owe their success to his inspiration, and his influence."[5] It is curious that Hawley and Wolseley, both forward thinkers,

1 Peels Prairie Provinces 570, Captain S. Bruce Harman, *T'Was 26 Years Ago; Narrative of the Red River Expedition 1870*, (Toronto, 1896), p9.

2 PPP 570, Harman, *26 Years*, p9.

3 Herbert Fairlie Wood, *The King's Royal Rifle Corps (The 60th Regiment of Foot)*, (London: Hamish Hamilton, 1967), pp32/33.

4 Major R.M. Barnes., *A History of the Regiments & Uniforms of the British Army, 5th Edition*, (Seeley Service & Co. Limited, 1962), p67.

5 Lieutenant-General Sir Edward Hutton K.C.B., K.C.M.G., p.s.c., *A Brief History of the King's Royal Rifle Corps, 1755-1915, (Second Edition)*, (Winchester: Warren and Son Ltd, 1917), p18.

both believing in the efficacy of sound training, and both arriving in Canada at about the same time, did not get along, or in the words of the regimental history, "failed to appreciate one another."[6] One can only speculate on what might have been accomplished if these two reformers, Hawley at the regimental level and Wolseley at the staff level, had worked in tandem. However, it was in all likelihood this difference of regiment versus staff that sparked the difficulty between them in the first place. It seems that Hawley viewed Wolseley as something of an upstart who had not spent enough time soldiering at the regimental level, while "Wolseley failed to appreciate the value of Hawley's 'spade work' or to realize how much his own subsequent success was due thereto."[7]

In any event, the 4th Battalion left Canada at the end of June 1869 and it would fall to the 1st Battalion, which had been in the country since October 1867, to make up the British Army's infantry component of the Red River Expedition. The battalion commander, Randle Feilden, with no active service to his name, had purchased the colonelcy in June of 1866 and so received promotion over four other officers "of proved merit in the field."[8] Nevertheless, as the expeditionary force was preparing to get underway, Lindsay described him as " ... an excellent officer, and his regimental experience has already been brought into play in getting the Militia battalions into shape," though one cannot help but ponder on the effect that Hawley might have had on the forthcoming operation had he and the 4th Battalion still been in the country.[9] As it was, in March of 1870, with the prospect of an expeditionary force being sent to the Northwest, the 1st Battalion was put on notice that it would form the British infantry spearhead. Lindsay's original thoughts were that 200 men would be sufficient.

The raising of the Canadian contribution to the force was more complicated. Ottawa had never shied away from its commitment to provide troops for the expedition, but Canada's most recent Militia Act, like all previous ones, spoke to home defence and the Dominion's existing forces had been raised under these terms and conditions. Given that Ottawa did not yet have jurisdiction over the HBC lands, orders could legally not simply be issued for the militia to deploy to what was *de facto* non-Canadian territory. Legal technicalities in the raising of Ottawa's military contribution notwithstanding, the fact that the impetus to undertake the expedition was being driven by the Canadian Government, other than the vague notion that it would draw volunteers from the Active Militia regiments, little had been done towards raising the Canadian contingent of the expeditionary force until Lindsay pressed for action upon his arrival. Interestingly, Wolseley, so quick to complain if he felt the Canadian authorities were dragging their feet, was surprisingly reticent on the subject. The same cannot be said of Lindsay, and justifiably so.

George F. G. Stanley, an important and influential writer on the history of the Canadian West and the Red River story, wrote that upon his arrival Lindsay suggested to the Canadian Government that "the Royal Canadian Rifles be employed *as the British component* [author's emphasis] of the Red River Force," but that the Canadian Government rejected this.[10] Two points need to be made regarding this comment. First, Lindsay did not need to ask the Canadian Government for approval as to which British regiment would be sent west. This was solely within the purview of the British War Office and the decision had been delegated to Lieutenant-General Lindsay. The decision had been a simple one, made in conjunction with Wolseley, that it would the 1st Battalion of the KRRC. Lindsay never 'suggested' the RCR as the British component of the expeditionary force. Second, Professor Stanley's reading of the document he cites in support of his statement is incorrect. Lindsay was clearly making the case for the RCR to go as the Canadian component of the expedition. With the pending withdrawal of the British garrison, the Royal Canadian Regiment was to be disbanded and Lindsay informed the Governor-General that, if they went as the Canadian component of the force, "there is no doubt that some of the officers, and many

6 Lieutenant-Colonel Lewis Butler, *The Annals of the King's Royal Rifle Corps, Volume 3, The 60th: the K.R.R.C.,* (London: John Murray, 1926), p253.
7 Butler, *Annals*, p253.
8 Butler, *Annals*, p219.
9 PPP 568, Correspondence and Journal, No. 8, Lindsay to WO, May 27, 1870.
10 George F.G. Stanley, *Toil and Trouble; Military Expeditions to Red River* (Toronto & Oxford, Dundurn Press, 1989), p83.

of the rank and file, will be anxious to remain in Canada. Many of the latter will be, doubtless, glad to settle in the country and form a body of loyal settlers."[11]

Providing suitable settler stock for what was to become the Canadian west was not, however, Lindsay's primary motivation in suggesting the involvement of the RCR. His main reason was the lack of action on the part of Canada up to that point in raising its own force. The RCR was trained and ready to move west the moment the order was given. On April 23rd Lindsay wrote to the Governor-General of his 'extreme regret' that the Dominion Government has declined the offer of the soon to be disbanded British unit. The expedition was going to be a hazardous affair due to the challenging 'character of the country' with its 'numerous portages and dangerous rapids'. A trained and cohesive force was needed to overcome the physical obstacles of the journey, as well as any military opposition that might be faced. Not only was there concern of Métis resistance along the route, but there was also the worrying factor that local First Nations people might have been stirred by Riel and his followers to challenge the force's progress. Then there was the potential of Fenian intervention wherever the route passed close to American territory, as it did at Sault Ste. Marie, Thunder Bay and Lake of the Woods. What angered Lindsay most was the lack of preparation on the part of the Canadian Government for what was their initiative. He wrote to Governor-General Young that:

> This expedition has been in the contemplation of the Dominion Government for several months, yet it was only upon the 15th of April, and after my memorandum of the 10th of April, which was sent within a few days of my arrival in this command, that the Adjutant-General of Militia submitted a plan for raising two regiments of Militia for service in the North-West.[12]

Lindsay believed that if the Canadian component had been put together sooner and had been "under arms for a considerable period previous to taking the field", it could form a "valuable and capable force." However, the two Canadian battalions, proposed by the Adjutant-General of Militia on April 15th, were to be drawn from an array of Active Militia units and, in Lindsay's view, this would mean that the officers and men would know nothing of each other resulting in a lack of military cohesion and confidence in one another. There was also the question of training. "These regiments can hardly commence any military training before the end of the first week in May, and only a short time before they should proceed to Fort William, *en route* to the Red River."[13]

On April 19th The Department of Militia officially rejected the use of the RCR, having decided that Lieutenant-Colonel Patrick Robertson-Ross, a British soldier who had arrived in Canada in May of 1869 to take up of the post of Adjutant-General of Militia, would oversee the creation of two new Canadian battalions of riflemen.[14] Lindsay had little positive to report on Robertson-Ross, later stating that if left to him, the expedition would only have been 'half equipped'.[15] Robertson-Ross announced that the two battalions would be drawn from seven of Canada's nine military districts; the two districts in Nova Scotia and New Brunswick were exempted. One battalion was to be raised from Ontario's four districts and one from Quebec's three districts, and it was proposed that each would be comprised of 382 officers and men. The volunteers would wear the same green uniforms and carry the same Short Snider breech loading rifle as the KRRC.[16] The terms of service were for an

11 PPP 568, Correspondence and Journal, No. 8, April 11, 1870, Memorandum from Lindsay.

12 PPP 568, Correspondence and Journal, No. 8 Inclosure 3, April 23, 1870, Memorandum from Lindsay to the Governor-General, Sir John Young.

13 PPP 568, Correspondence and Journal, No. 8 Inclosure 3, April 23, 1870, Memorandum from Lindsay to the Governor-General, Sir John Young.

14 PPP 568, Correspondence and Journal, No. 8 Inclosure 2, April 19, 1870, Deputy Minister of Militia to the Military Secretary.

15 Preston, Richard A., "ROBERTSON-ROSS, PATRICK," in Dictionary of Canadian Biography, vol. 11, University of Toronto/Université Laval, 2003–, accessed April 29, 2016.

16 The .577 Short Snider was a specialist weapon used by the British Army's rifle regiments, as well as sergeants in line infantry regiments and was in service from the mid-1860s until 1874 when it was superseded by the Martini Henry. Barrel length was 30.5 inches, as compared to 36.5 inches for the long version and 19.5 inches for the cavalry carbine version.

engagement of one year or longer if the government required it, but not to exceed two years. Men between the ages of 18 and 45, 'physically fit for service 'and of 'good character and sober habits' would be considered.[17]

There was no shortage of volunteers from amongst the militia units in Ontario. The desire to avenge the killing of Scott remained strong and the ranks of the 1st Ontario Rifles were filled in a very short time.[18] In Toronto the Queens Own Rifles provided their allotted quota of two officers and twelve men and a number of officers chose to 'shoulder rifles in the ranks' rather than miss out.[19] Much the same was occurring among the other Ontario Active Militia battalions. It was, however, a very different story with the 2nd Quebec Rifles.

Wolseley believed this was due to population of Quebec largely being supportive of their French-speaking co-religionists at the Red River Settlement and the Catholic clergy preaching against participation.[20] Captain G. L. Huyshe, a Rifle Brigade officer serving on the staff of the expedition, agreed regarding the clerical influence, but added the additional factor that, as the majority of the officers in the Quebec battalion were French speakers, English-speaking Quebec militiamen were reluctant to serve under them.[21] According to one French language journal, the resentment towards French-speaking officers was a direct result of the killing of Scott and "by May 26 ... complaints in the English-speaking ranks against the preponderance of French officers verged on insubordination."[22]

The French-speaking *Chasseurs Canadiens* in Montreal provided a company of five officers and fifty men, but except for the French-speaking officers in the battalion, with French-Canadian militiamen reluctant to volunteer and English-speaking Quebecers unwilling to serve under French-speaking officers, enlistment in the Quebec Rifles lagged. The battalion commander, Lieutenant-Colonel Louis-Adolfe Casault, had fought in the ranks of the French Foreign Legion during the Crimean War and later against the Berbers in North Africa. After returning to Canada, in 1858 he was commissioned into the 100th Royal Canadian Regiment of Foot, serving in England, Gibraltar and Malta.[23] Unfortunately, even a military pedigree such as his could not incent the English-speaking militiamen to put aside their prejudices and serve under him.

With time pressing, Lindsay, who had been opposed to dividing the Canadian contingent "for sectional and religious reasons," recruited 120 men from the Royal Canadian Rifles, but even this left the battalion with a strength of only 292 volunteers.[24] Matters were finally put in hand when Lindsay and Wolseley found the balance of the required men in Ontario.

The work of organizing and equipping the force began early in May. Before being accepted, volunteers "had to undergo a most rigid medical examination, under the supervision of the Inspector-General of Hospitals" and some 'big strapping fellows' emerged from " ... the Doctor's room looking downcast – some even blubbering because they had been rejected ... ."[25] Upon arrival in Toronto, the men " ... were marched to the old 'Crystal Palace,' which was prepared for their accommodation and which afforded very suitable quarters."[26]

---

17 PPP 568, Correspondence and Journal, No. 8 Inclosure 2A, April 15, 1870, Adjutant –General of Militia to the Minister of Militia.

18 Bugler Joseph F. Tennant, *Rough Times 1870-1920; A Souvenir of the 50th Anniversary of the Red River Expedition and the Formation of Manitoba*, (Winnipeg: Facsimile Publication, Originally self-published, 1920), p24.

19 See Lieutenant Colonel W. T. Barnard E.D. C.D, *The Queen's Own Rifles of Canada 1860-1960; One Hundred Years of Canada,* (Don Mills, Ontario Publishing Company, 1960), Edited excerpts found at: https://qormuseum.org/history/timeline-1856-1899/red-river-rebellion-1870/ and Captain G.L. Huyshe, *The Red River Expedition*, (The Naval & Military Press Ltd, in association with Firepower, The Royal Artillery Museum, Woolwich, first published by Macmillan and Co., London, 1871), p24.

20 Wolseley, *Narrative Part 1*, p714.

21 Huyshe, *Red River*, pp25/26.

22 Elinor Kyte Senior, *The Roots of the Canadian Army: Montreal District 1846-1870*, (Historical Publications; The Society of the Montreal Military & Maritime Museum, 1981), p97.

23 Stanley, George F. G., "CASAULT, LOUIS-ADOLPHE," in Dictionary of Canadian Biography, vol. 10, University of Toronto/Université Laval, 2003–, accessed November 24, 2016.

24 Senior, *Roots*, p98.

25 See Harman, *26 Years*. p7, and Constance Kerr Sissons, *John Kerr*, (Toronto: Oxford University Press, 1946), p24.

26 Harman, *26 Years*, p7.

Colonel Feilden, the commander of the 1st KRRC, was put to work organizing the Canadians and almost immediately had to contend with a brawl between members of the Ontario and Quebec contingents on King Street in Toronto which, before it was over, became a free for all involving civilians as well.[27] The next day Feilden, as quoted in *The Daily Witness*, sought to impress on the Ontario men "the consequences of such broils as had happened the night before."[28] While this apparent antipathy between French and English-speaking members of the force must have been a concern to the expedition's leaders, the episode was in all likelihood blown out of all proportion. In spite of the seeds of dissent that some were trying to sow, Wolseley would later write:

> I had come to know and highly value the Canadian militia, having had the advantage upon several occasions of commanding their camps of exercise. I was fully aware of the splendid material of which that force was constituted. The men are extremely handy and self-reliant; in fact when well trained, they cannot be beaten as fighting soldiers. Their officers, accustomed in civil life to think for themselves, their minds are not dwarfed or trammelled by strict rules and regulations, were men after my own heart, and for the work before us, they were the best possible material.[29]

As the force was being formed and Lindsay began to review the possible challenges it might encounter, he quickly came to realize that there was not sufficient strength to deal with all of its responsibilities. There would need to be garrisons at Thunder Bay and Fort Frances and no allowance had been made for casualties. The expedition after all might have to fight its way through to Fort Garry, and could encounter resistance when it arrived as well. He made two recommendations. First, as a buffer against casualties, the Canadians should form a reserve battalion. He suggested that an existing Ontario Active Militia unit be designated that would be brought up to strength by volunteers from other units in the province.[30] Lindsay clearly was not interested in repeating the problems that were then being encountered in the raising of the 2nd Quebec Rifles. Canada's response was that they would take the matter under advisement, but in fact nothing was done.[31] Second, while the numbers of Canadian volunteers that would go on to Fort Garry would not change, given the requirement to provide men for the two garrisons along the way, Lindsay felt there was a need for an additional 140 militiamen. Alternatively, he proposed that, if the Canadians were in agreement and the British authorities were prepared to approve it, the British contingent from the KRRC could be increased from 200 to 400 men.[32] On April 26th the Deputy Minister of Militia responded positively with Ottawa's agreement to pay for an additional 140 men from the 60th Rifles; the Canadian authorities having apparently combined the two options Lindsay had laid out and settled on an additional 140 British regulars.[33] Lindsay sent his request to London on April 28th and approval was received on May 5th.[34]

As finally constituted, the Red River Expeditionary Force was made up of three battalions of infantry each comprising seven companies. These were the 1st battalion of the KRRC, 26 officers and 350 men, under Colonel R. J. Feilden; the 1st Ontario Rifles, under Lieutenant-Colonel Samuel Peters Jarvis and the 2nd Quebec Rifles, under Lieutenant-Colonel Louis-Adolfe Casault, each of 28 officers and 350 men. In addition, there was a detachment of Royal Artillery under Lieutenant Alleyne, 19 men with a battery of four 7-pounder brass mountain

27 Senior, *Roots*, p98.
28 Senior, *Roots*, p99.
29 Wolseley, *Soldier's Life*, p174.
30 PPP 568, Correspondence and Journal, April 23, 1870, No. 8 Inclosure 3, Lindsay to Governor-General Sir John Young.
31 PPP 568, Correspondence and Journal. April 26, 1870, No. 8 Inclosure 4, Deputy Minister of Militia to Lieutenant-Colonel McNeill V.C.
32 PPP 568, Correspondence and Journal, April 23, 1870, No. 8 Inclosure 3, Lindsay to the Governor-General Sir John Young.
33 PPP 568, Correspondence and Journal, April 26, 1870, No. 8 Inclosure 4, Deputy Minister of Militia to Lieutenant-Colonel McNeill V.C.
34 PPP 568, Correspondence and Journal, April 28, 1870, No. 1 Inclosure No. 4, Telegram from Lindsay and May 5, 1870, No. 7, WO to Lindsay.

Lieutenant Fred Denison, the brother of Canada First leader George Denison and one of the expeditionary force's staff officers. (James Ashfield / Library and Archives Canada / C-009997)

Major James Macleod, future Commissioner of the North-West Mounted Police and brigade major of the expeditionary force. (Topley Studio / Library and Archives Canada)

guns; a detachment of Royal Engineers under Lieutenant Heneage, 19 men; an Army Service Corps detachment, 12 men; and an Army Hospital Corps, 8 men.[35]

While Lindsay had been clear that this was going to be a British run operation, a view certainly shared by Wolseley, the expedition's staff appointments gave recognition to the presence of the Canadian component of the force. There were two staff officers, one from the British Army and one Canadian militiaman. These were Captain G. L. Huyshe, of the Rifle Brigade, and Lieutenant F.C. Denison, the brother of Wolseley's friend George Denison of the Canada First movement. Lieutenant-Colonel Bolton, Royal Artillery, described by Lindsay as 'a man of capacity' who had also passed the Staff College, was promoted Deputy Assistant Adjutant-General.[36] Militia officer Major James Macleod, who would later become Commissioner of the North-West Mounted Police (NWMP), was appointed Brigade Major of Canadian Militia.[37] Lieutenant-Colonel John Carstairs McNeill, V.C., the Military Secretary to the Governor-General, was at his request also attached to the Staff. McNeill had won the Victoria Cross in 1864 in New Zealand for rescuing a private about to be overrun by Maori warriors. In March of 1885 he would command a contingent of the Suakin Field Force in their defeat of the Madhist forces of Osman Digna at the Battle of Tofrek, a few miles from the Red Sea coast.

Other staff officers included Surgeon-Major Young, M.D., the principal medical officer, and Assistant-Controller Matthew Bell Irvine who would act as the expedition's chief control officer. Irvine had been specially

35 PPP 568, Correspondence and Journal, April 15, 1870, No. 8 Inclosure 2A, Adjutant–General of Militia to the Minister of Militia. The number of men reported by Low as embarking is four fewer in each Canadian battalion than outlined in the Robertson-Ross document found in the Correspondence of the Expeditionary Force. Low, Wolseley, op. cit. p12. For a breakdown of the force composition see also Appendix 1

36 Correspondence and Journal, op. cit. May 27, 1870, No. 8 Lindsay to the WO.

37 See: Sherrill MacLaren, *Braehead; Three Founding Families of Nineteenth Century Canada*, (Toronto: McClelland and Stewart, 1986) & Macleod, R. C., "MACLEOD, JAMES FARQUHARSON," in Dictionary of Canadian Biography, vol. 12, University of Toronto/Université Laval, 2003–, accessed May 10, 2016.

Assistant-Controller Matthew Bell Irvine, chief control officer of the expedition. (Library and Archives Canada, *Canadian Illustrated News)*

sent from England by the War Office due to his Canadian connections and " ... was eminently qualified to direct a Department which threw him so much into personal contact with the civilian element."[38] Under Irvine were six commissaries, together with three officers of the Royal Canadian Rifles and one from the militia, who were attached for transport duties.[39]

There were two late arrivals to the expeditionary force's staff. The first was William Francis Butler, later a traveller, explorer and writer on the Canadian west, and commander of British forces in South Africa immediately prior to the Second Boer War. Here he would clash with the aggressive policies of the High Commissioner, Sir Alfred Milner, causing his resignation shortly before the outbreak of hostilities.[40] Butler would play an interesting role in the Red River Expedition.

He was born into an impoverished family of Irish gentry and joined the 69th Regiment in September of 1858. Butler's impecunious status meant that he was unable to afford promotion and for a time he considered leaving the army. While his regiment was stationed in Canada he had met Wolseley, but at the beginning of 1870 had returned to Ireland hoping to raise money for a business venture. It was while here that he first heard of the expedition to the Red River. He sent an immediate telegram to Wolseley simply stating "Please Remember Me."[41] Wolseley would later write that the communication read 'Remember Butler 69th Regiment'.[42] The precise words are unimportant, and whichever version one chooses to accept, Butler said that it was short and to the point because words cost money.[43] He rushed back to Canada by way of Boston and met up with Wolseley in Toronto where he was informed that the expeditionary force was full; " ... there's not a vacant berth for you. I got your

38 Low, *Wolseley*, p12.

39 Low, *Wolseley*, p13.

40 Ian F.W. Beckett, "Butler, Sir William Francis (1838-1910)", Oxford Dictionary of National Biography, Oxford University Press, 2004; online edn, Jan 2008, http://www.oxforddnb.com/view/article/32219, accessed 25 Nov 2016, p4.

41 William Francis Butler, *The Great Lone Land; A Narrative of Travel and Adventure in the North-West of America*," (Edmonton: M.G. Hurtig Ltd., 1968, First Published 1872), p8.

42 Wolseley, *Soldier's Life*, p200.

43 Butler, *Lone Land*, p8.

telegram, but the whole army in Canada wanted to get on the Expedition."[44] Butler brashly replied that there remained one important unfilled position. "You will want to know what they are doing in Minnesota and along the flank of your march, and you have no one to tell you."[45] Wolseley would later claim the idea of using Butler as a special intelligence officer as his own.[46] Regardless of which of the two devised the idea, approval for a special intelligence officer still had to come first from Lindsay and then the Canadian Government, and by the time his orders finally did arrive on June 8th, for the first time in his military career Butler had come under hostile fire. His regiment was still in Canada and he had rejoined them when they were dispatched to the border following reports of a Fenian incursion. While on patrol, he almost rode into a concentration of three hundred of the Irish insurgents, only managing to escape " ... with bullets rattling the bushes on either side of the trail along which he galloped."[47] Shortly after this close shave, he finally received the approval he had been waiting so impatiently for and was soon on his way. His journey would take him through the United States to the Red River and a meeting with none other than Louis Riel himself.

The second of the late arrivals was Captain Hugh McCalmont of the 9th Lancers. He later served in the Second Afghan War in 1879, the Anglo-Egyptian War in 1882 and the Nile Expedition of 1884. Stationed in England in 1870, his regiment had been reduced by one troop and, as the junior troop commander, "I was therefore at the moment a supernumerary, out of a job, and more or less a fifth wheel to the coach."[48] During an inspection visit by General Sir James Hope Grant, lacking a troop to command and with nothing else to do, McCalmont was made the general's orderly for the day. Hope Grant knew Wolseley well, the colonel having been on his staff during the India Mutiny, and " ... a particularly warm friendship had existed between the two soldiers."[49] The general gave McCalmont a letter of introduction to the Red River Expeditionary Force commander and leave was approved for the young captain to go to Canada to try to have himself attached to the force, though it was only granted by the War Office on the understanding he kept his intentions quiet until he arrived.

Like Butler, upon reaching Montreal he was informed that nothing was available for him. However, as he was on leave and in his words 'my own master,' he determined to go to Thunder Bay. By chance, also on board the steamer he travelled on was Wolseley's wife, " ... on her way to see her husband and to bid him good-bye before he disappeared with his troops into the wilderness."[50] Delayed due to fog, he and Mrs. Wolseley " ... were a good deal thrown together during the two or three days on board."[51] Arriving in late June, at first Wolseley told him that there was simply nothing for him and even Hope Grant's letter did no good. He remained at the camp however and within a day or so was approached by Wolseley who asked him if he knew anything about boats. He had been a rower at Eton and he was immediately put to work with the militia moving boats up the Kaministiquia River.

Among the officers of the KRRC was Captain Redvers Buller in command of C Company. At the time he was regarded as an officer of exceptional talent. In the various contemporary descriptions of him he comes across as reckless, bumptious, and a blusterer, albeit one who did more than his fair share of the heavy lifting. He had served in the 4th battalion and prospered under Hawley's tutelage. Returning to England, he had reluctantly returned to Canada to serve with the expeditionary force. He would later win a Victoria Cross during the Zulu War in 1879, rise to the rank of General and command the army corps sent to South Africa at the start of the Second Boer War. His performance during the attempts to relieve Ladysmith were pilloried at the time and he was later unceremoniously removed from his command, though today he has his defenders.[52]

---

44 Butler, *Lone Land*, p27.
45 Butler, *Lone Land*, p27.
46 Wolseley, *Soldier's Life*, p201.
47 McCourt, *Butler*, p45.
48 Major-General Sir C.E. K.C.B. Callwell (Editor), *The Memoirs of Major-General Sir Hugh McCalmont K.C.B., C.V.O.*, (London: Hutchinson & Co., 1924), p45.
49 Callwell, *McCalmont*, p46.
50 Callwell, *McCalmont*, p47.
51 Callwell, *McCalmont*, p47.
52 See Geoffrey Powell, *Buller: A Scapegoat? A Life of General Sir Redvers Buller, 1839-1908*, (Pen and Sword Books, 2005) and Thomas Pakenham, *The Boer War*, (Weidenfeld and Nicholson, 1979).

Captain Redvers Buller of the 60th Rifles in 1886. (*Illustrated London News*, ILNO-1886-1106-0005-F)

Hugh Macdonald, the son of Prime Minister Sir John A. Macdonald. (Topley Studio / Library and Archives Canada / PA-025742)

Sam Steele of the Ontario Rifles ca. 1874. (Library and Archives Canada / e008128843)

Serving as an ensign in the 1st Ontario Rifles was Hugh John Macdonald, the son of the Canadian prime minister. In the same company was his namesake Captain Alexander R. Macdonald. A medical man, Captain Macdonald would venture west after the expedition to provide aid to victims of a smallpox epidemic.[53] Then there was Private Sam Steele who held a commission in the militia. He was offered a non-commissioned rank in the 1st Ontario Rifles, but chose to serve as a private, writing " ... as far as experience went, I was better off without

53 For pen portraits of a great many of the Canadian members of the expeditionary force, see Tennant, *Rough Times*.

chevrons and learned how to appreciate the trials of other men to an extent that I should never have been able to do had I been promoted."[54]

In addition to the soldiers, Simon Dawson had hired approximately 400 *'voyageurs'* to navigate the boats through the treacherous rapids and across portages of the interior waterways, and one hundred teamsters to convey the supply waggons along the road from Thunder Bay to Shebandowan Lake. Wolseley was highly critical of a large portion of these boatmen who he felt bore little connection with the *voyageurs* during the heyday of the North West Company, and were " ... utterly ignorant of the management of boats."[55] Around one hundred were, however, Iroquois from villages near Montreal, who were "fully capable of navigating boats in rapid water, and indeed without their services, the expedition could not have been conducted."[56]

Regarding the boats, early in 1870 the ubiquitous Simon Dawson had again been called upon and he had a conundrum to wrestle with. For the expeditionary force the *Canot du Nord*, the traditional canoe used so successfully by the North West Company, was clearly impractical as far too many would have been required to carry such a large body of men together with their supplies.[57] The HBC used the larger and heavier York Boats along many of their routes, however, Dawson also recognized that the lakes and rivers of the route from Thunder Bay to Fort Garry had never before been 'traversed by any vessel larger than a canoe.'[58] In his report on the expedition published in 1871 he wrote:

> When it was first anticipated that a Military Expedition might become necessary, I had under the instructions of the Government, ordered and superintended their construction, in which the just medium suited to the occasion had to be observed between two opposite principles-strength, on the one hand, to endure the severe trials to which they had to be subjected on their long voyage, and lightness on the other to admit of their being taken by waggon to Shebandowan Lake, and transported by the men over the numerous but short portages of the interior.[59]

$12,000 was made available for the purchase of the boats by an Order in Council on January 18th and contracts were tendered shortly thereafter.[60] The boats were smaller than the HBC's York Boats, and, while fairly standard, varied in size from 25 to 33 feet long, 6 ½ to 7 ½ feet wide and 30 to 35 inches deep, with a carrying capacity of between 2 ½ and 4 tons. They were constructed by a variety of companies, mostly in Ontario, though sixteen were built in Quebec.[61] One hundred and two boats were already completed or under construction when Lindsay arrived and he very quickly determined that this was likely not enough. One hundred boats, he calculated, would just about get 1000 men to Fort Garry, but no allowance had been made for losses and damages.[62] Credit is due to Dawson in that within days of reading Lindsay's views on the need for additional boats, he was able to report that thirty-three more had been ordered and, together with two first class 'North Canoes', they would be completed by the time the expeditionary force was ready to move.[63] The canoes were for the use of the commanding officer. The expedition would not be travelling as a composite force and would in fact be strung out along the route. They would provide Wolseley with a swift conveyance to move back and forth to ensure all was well with the extended

54 Sam Steele, *Forty Years in Canada; Reminiscences of the Great North-West with Some Account of His Service in South Africa*, (Toronto: Prospero Books, 2000, originally published 1915), p12.
55 Low, *Wolseley*, p13.
56 Low, *Wolseley*, p13.
57 The *Canot du Nord* was a birch bark canoe of twenty to twenty-five feet in length and capable of carrying a ton and a half of goods. In translates into English as North Canoe and both terms are used in the text.
58 Arthur, *Dawson*, p14.
59 PPP 559 Dawson, "Report", p53.
60 ECO, Correspondence and Papers Connected with the Recent Occurrences in the North-West Territories I. B Taylor Ottawa 1870, Report of a Committee of the Honorable the Privy Council, approved by His Excellency the Governor-General in Council on the 18th January, 1870.
61 PPP 568, Correspondence and Journal, April 14 1870 , No. 8 Inclosure 2B, Memorandum by Dawson in reference to Lindsay's Report of April 11, 1870.
62 PPP 568, Correspondence and Journal, April 11, 1870, No. 8 Inclosure 1, Memorandum by Lindsay.
63 PPP 568, Correspondence and Journal, April 14 1870 , No. 8 Inclosure 2B, Memorandum by Dawson in reference to Lindsay's Report of April 11, 1870.

boat brigades, though in practice during the expedition's journey the colonel was always to be found with the leading elements of his force.

Planning continued apace as Wolseley and his staff continued to work through the minutiae of detail necessary to ensure the success of the operation. The purchase and requisitioning of equipment and supplies was underway, and despite delays in the raising of the Canadian component of the force, matters were beginning to fall into place, though it would take time before the volunteers were ready to move. Before it could embark on its hazardous journey into the wilderness, however, the expeditionary force, together with all of its equipment and supplies, had to be transported across Lakes Huron and Superior to Thunder Bay and this necessitated the hiring of steamers. This would cause the next round of Anglo-Canadian controversy in the story of the Red River Expeditionary Force.

12

The Lake Steamers

The success of almost any military operation is founded on the efficiency of its supply chain, and even when the military force in question is embarking on a journey that will take it several hundred miles into the wilderness with almost no opportunity for re-supply along the way, its line of communication remains of primary importance. The first order of business in creating the Red River Expedition's supply chain was to organize the flow of men and supplies across the Great Lakes. On the face of it, it might seem a relatively simple process to hire a few steamers for this purpose, but for a number of reasons it became so much more complicated.

Not all the battalions of the expeditionary force would be moving from Toronto at the same time. The 60th Rifles would be the first to proceed to Thunder Bay, followed by the 1st Ontario Rifles, and finally the 2nd Quebec Rifles. Then there were the *voyageurs*, teamsters, road workers, transport horses for the waggons, the expedition's boats, and all the other supplies and accoutrements necessary to give the expedition a reasonable chance of success. As the expedition readied itself at Thunder Bay, additional supplies might be identified that would need to be brought in, and after the force had moved on there would still be a fortified base camp that would need to be supported. There were all manner of details that would require a line of supply and communication, not least of which were the despatches and mail to and from the expeditionary force. Consequently, a stream of vessels would be required to operate between Collingwood and Thunder Bay. The numbers of these ships and the amount of cargo would peak as the expeditionary force built up its men and supplies prior to setting out, but it would never cease. There was also the complication of the American response at the Sault Ste. Marie canal, which we will deal with in the next chapter.

It is difficult to comprehend exactly why the chartering of the lake steamers became so complicated. It appears there were two major factors. The first resulted from a lack of communication on the part of the Canadian Government as to exactly what agreements it had previously entered into, though this may have been more due to secretiveness than the incompetence the British suspected. The second was an apparent lack of understanding, again by the Canadians, as to the scale of the supply chain that would be necessary to support the force.

When Lindsay arrived in Canada at the beginning of April, he quickly initiated a series of conferences dealing with supply, transport, and the general situation involving the speedy onward movement of the force to Fort Garry.[1] To ensure matters were in hand, on April 22nd Assistant-Controller Matthew Bell Irvine, who had been brought out from England, was dispatched to Toronto and Collingwood to investigate whether any of the lake steamers had been chartered. He reported that they had not. Lindsay later wrote:

> I early directed the attention of the Dominion Government to the necessity of control over steamers in both lakes [Lakes Huron and Superior], informing them that I considered it their duty to furnish the necessary transport; and on the 28th of April, I applied for a permanent steamer to be stationed on Lake Superior. Having proceeded to Collingwood on 5th May, with my Controller, I ascertained that no arrangement had been made.[2]

1 TNA, WO 32/7586, Irvine "Report on Red River", p1.
2 PPP 568. Correspondence and Journal, May 27, 1870, No. 8, Lindsay to WO.

The former Confederate blockade runner, the Chicora. Chartered for the use of the expeditionary force, she would be refused entry by American authorities into the Sault Ste. Marie canal. (Hime, W. / Library and Archives Canada / C-003947)

Given the time constraints under which Lindsay was operating, combined with this not being the only piece of business with which he was dealing, he was unsurprisingly perturbed by the news. We need to dig a little deeper, however, into exactly what had transpired.

As mentioned in the communication quoted above, on May 5th, accompanied by Wolseley and his staff, Lindsay travelled overnight from Montreal and, along with Simon Dawson, caught a special train to Collingwood on Georgian Bay.[3] Together with Lieutenant-Colonel B. A. Martindale, the British Army's Acting Deputy-Controller in Canada, he inspected the steamers *Chicora* and *Frances Smith*, spoke with their owners and "arrived at satisfactory arrangements with them for the use of these vessels."[4] They also spoke with the agent for the steamer *Algoma* which had already left for its first run of the season to Lake Superior, carrying 140 *voyageurs* and road workers bound for Thunder Bay.[5] According to Wolseley, Lindsay had demonstrated the "thoroughness and energy for which he is celebrated" and in "one day by dint of hard work [he] inspected the steamers, decided on their different capabilities for the conveyance of troops, and actually concluded a bargain on very favourable terms with their owners."[6] However, when Lindsay telegraphed to Ottawa for permission to finalize the arrangements, he was told to do nothing and that the lake transportation was to be arranged by the Canadian Post-Master General.[7] Wolseley put this decision by the Canadian authorities down to political jobbery. The "arrangement did not suit their political ends. A large outlay of money was to be made, and they wished to spend it as much as possible amongst their political supporters."[8]

3 PPP 568. Correspondence and Journal, Appendix, p54.
4 TNA, WO 32/7586, Irvine "Report on Red River", p11.
5 PPP 559, Dawson, "Report", p14.
6 See Wolseley, *Narrative Part 2*, p50 and Huyshe, *Red River*, pp30/31.
7 TNA, WO 32/7586, Irvine "Report on Red River", p1.
8 Wolseley, *Narrative Part 2*, p50.

By May 11th, according to all contemporary British reports, no deal had yet been struck between the Canadian government and the owners of the lake steamers. Lindsay, believing that time was slipping away from him, dispatched Lieutenant-Colonel Martindale to negotiate an agreement and arrangements were immediately concluded with the owners of the five available ships "at 15% under ordinary tariff."[9] The five ships were the *Algoma, Chicora, Waubuno, Shickluna and Frances Smith.* There is some contention that this action was taken by the Canadian Government rather than the British, but most contemporary sources say it was Lindsay who was responsible for the chartering of the steamers, though it was of course the Canadians who would ultimately foot the bill.[10]

Wolseley would later write, "the original plan of the military operation was based upon the belief that the regular troops (more than one-third of the whole force), were to have left Collingwood for Thunder Bay in the first week of May, whereas they did not leave that port until the 21st, 25th, and 26th of that month."[11] He alleged that part of this delay was the fault of the Canadian Government for failing to provide the shipping for the transportation of troops and supplies across the lakes.[12] Wolseley believed that delay was also caused by the American action at the Sault Ste. Marie canal, but blamed the Canadians here as well for failing to foresee this and for not taking steps to get a steamer onto Lake Superior at an earlier date. However, we are getting ahead of ourselves and will deal with the events at Sault Ste. Marie in the next chapter.[13]

The Canadian Government at this time had no experience in the planning or implementation of military operations, whereas the British Army conducted campaigns like this throughout the empire on a regular basis. This lack of experience on Canada's part is after all one of the reasons Prime Minister Macdonald was so insistent on British participation. It is highly unlikely, therefore, that the Canadian authorities had any real conception of the number of ships that would be required to support the expeditionary force. That being said, Lindsay and Wolseley were wrong in their views that Canada had done nothing. The problem was that Canadian authorities neglected to inform the British of the steps they had taken.

In his report published the following year, Dawson wrote that the Canadian Government had chartered the *Algoma* and *Chicora* and, as we have seen, when Lindsay and Wolseley visited Collingwood on May 5th, the *Algoma* was already making its way to Thunder Bay with 140 *voyageurs* and road workers on board.[14] Given that Dawson was with the two British officers on the day of the visit, and met with them repeatedly during this time, it is difficult to fathom that he would not have told them of the Canadian Government's actions. This of course assumes that Dawson knew, and perhaps at that time he did not. What is certain is that on January 26th,1870 Sir John Young the Governor-General had passed in Council an agreement between the Post-Master General and the owners of the *Chicora* for weekly round trips between Collingwood and Fort William during the navigation season. In addition to the mail, the steamer would convey " ... such men and stores as the Government may desire to send ... ." The fee for this service was $4,900, an unheard of sum for a normal mail contract.[15] No mention is made of the *Algoma* in this document, though one source refers to the steamer as operating under an 'initial contract' during its first trip of the season to Thunder Bay.[16]

The Canadian Government appears to have gone to great lengths to hide, presumably from the Americans, the true purpose of the *Chicora's* 'mail contract', which was in reality to move men and material for the expedition. As the steamer would have to transit the American canal at Sault Ste. Marie, the need for security was understandable. However, did this also mean that Lindsay and Wolseley were to be kept in the dark? Did Dawson know, was he

---

9 TNA, WO 32/7586, Irvine "Report on Red River", p1.

10 See Stanley, *Toil*, p101 and TNA, WO 32/7586, Irvine "Report on Red River", p1.

11 PPP 568, Correspondence and Journal, July 16, 1870, No. 21 Inclosure 2, Wolseley to the Military Secretary in Montreal.

12 PPP 568, Correspondence and Journal, July 16, 1870, No. 21 Inclosure 2, Wolseley to the Military Secretary in Montreal.

13 See Huyshe, *Red River*, pp30/31 and Low, *Wolseley*, p11 regarding the allegation that delays in the hiring of the lake steamers resulted in the delay in the departure of the force.

14 PPP 559, Dawson, "Report", p14.

15 ECO, Correspondence and Papers, Report of a Committee of the Honorable the Privy Council, approved by His Excellency the Governor-General in Council on the 28th January, 1870.

16 Scott L. Cameron, *The Frances Smith; Palace Steamer of the Upper Great Lakes, 1867-96*, (Toronto: Natural Heritage Books, 2005), p62.

sworn to secrecy, or was this just a bureaucratic oversight? At this juncture it is impossible to say, but the fact that no one in the British military hierarchy appears to have known what the Canadian authorities had done, resulted in a great deal of wasted effort to secure shipping, not to mention unnecessary rancour.

But did the muddle around the steamers result in a delay to the expedition setting forth from Collingwood? Wolseley believed two weeks had been lost and Captain Huyshe "a week or ten days."[17] On the other side of the debate, Dawson asserted that there was no impact and, "when the *Algoma* set out from Collingwood, on the 3rd of May, it was not even known that she would get through on account of the ice which generally remains in the straits, above Sault Ste. Marie".[18] Wolseley himself conceded that the ice on Lake Superior would typically not clear until "about the 8th or 10th of May."[19] In fact, the *Algoma* had no difficulty in making the passage to Fort William and arrived without incident. This means that had there not been so much confusion over the status of the steamers, by May 6th, a number of them could have been made available and ice would not have prevented their movement across Lake Superior. So were Wolseley and Huyshe correct in their allegations of delay?

According to the expedition's Official Journal, between May 6th and 12th Wolseley was "busily engaged at Toronto in organizing the Expedition ... and completing the two battalions of Militia."[20] In addition, Wolseley would write, "it was not until late at night on the 12th of May, that I received instructions from Ottawa authorising me to send forward troops."[21] He issued his Standing Orders on May 14th and the same day moved the first of his troops, two companies of the 1st Ontario Rifles, to Collingwood. He did not begin to move the KRRC forward until May 21st!

One must therefore conclude that, while the muddle surrounding the Canadian Government's chartering of the *Chicora*, and possibly the *Algoma*, could certainly have been avoided, and the dates of the chartering of the additional three steamers could have been brought forward and handled more efficiently, neither of these appear to have delayed the expedition's departure. Wolseley was simply too busy with a myriad of details that needed to be worked through before embarking the force for Thunder Bay; not the least of which was the militia battalions were not yet ready. He also did not have authority to move until late in the day on May 12th and did not circulate the expeditionary force's Standing Orders until May 14th. The first troops began to move the same day, but as we shall see, these were to protect his supplies at Sault Ste. Marie rather than to begin the general movement forward of the force to Thunder Bay. It would be another week before the troops of the KRRC were dispatched to Collingwood. If Wolseley truly believed that he was only held back from moving his regulars forward "in the first week of May," as he wrote on July 16th, because the shipping was not then available, would it not have made sense that he would have them ready to go as soon as authorization was received and not eight days later? In the meantime, however, a new issue had reared its head with the potential to slow the expedition's forward deployment. The Americans were looking to exercise their influence on the Wolseley's progress at Sault Ste. Marie.

17 See Wolseley, *Narrative Part 2*, p50 and Huyshe, *Red River*, p31.
18 PPP 559, Dawson, "Report", p15.
19 Wolseley, *Narrative Part 2*, p48.
20 PPP 568, Correspondence and Journal, Appendix p54.
21 PPP 568, July 16, 1870, No. 21 Inclosure 2, Wolseley to Military Secretary in Montreal.

13

The Sault Ste. Marie Canal

Wolseley's intent was to use Thunder Bay as his base of operations for the expedition's push into the interior. The troops would muster at Toronto and proceed by train to the port of Collingwood on Georgian Bay. From there they would be transported by steamer across Lakes Huron and Superior to Thunder Bay, a journey of 534 miles through waters peppered with a multitude of islands, islets and rocks. This was a hazardous journey as the shores of Georgian Bay were at this time sparsely populated, there was little in the way of navigational aids, and charts were often incomplete or outdated.

Lake Superior drains into Lake Huron through the 75 mile long St. Marys River, with the twin towns of Sault Ste. Marie, one in Michigan and one in Ontario, at the western end. They had once been a single community but were divided when the border was established after the War of 1812. Here there is a drop of 23 feet and the Americans had constructed a canal with locks on their side in 1855. The canal was the only way for ships to transit between the two lakes.

In many respects Lake Superior was an even more perilous prospect than Lake Huron. Given the relatively recent construction of the canal, steamers on the upper lake were a new phenomenon and there were even fewer navigational aids than there were on Lake Huron. Superior's "rugged shores were treacherous under the best of conditions, with boulders, shoals, islands and points of land thrown in the path of whatever watercraft dared trespass its waters."[1] Depths could range from hundreds of feet to mere inches over very short distances and, to make matters worse, "its waters were swept by impenetrable fogs in the spring and summer, by powerful gales in the fall and by thick floes of ice in the winter and early spring."[2]

However, as large as the factors of weather and geography were in the journey across the lakes, the big question in May of 1870 was what would the reaction of American authorities be to the use of their canal by a military force engaged on an expedition to an area coveted by many powerful men in Washington and St. Paul, Minnesota?

As we saw in the previous chapter, the first steamer of the season to leave Collingwood was the *Algoma* on May 3rd. She is referred to by one historian as a troopship.[3] This was not technically the case, though she was certainly carrying *voyageurs*, road workers and supplies for the expedition. Simon Dawson was onboard as well, making his way to Thunder Bay at last to check on the progress of the road and oversee its completion. So too was a man who would play an important, but largely forgotten, role in the story of the expedition. Eton College old boy Wemyss Mackenzie Simpson had been in North America since 1841. A former employee of the HBC, by 1870 he was the Conservative MP for Algoma in western Ontario. As Dawson reported:

> It was at this time apprehended that the insurgents at Red River might endeavour to tamper with the Salteaux Indians, a tribe which occupies the country about Fort Frances and Lake of the Woods in formidable number, and in order

1 Cameron, *Frances*, Foreword pXII.
2 Cameron, *Frances*, pp XII/XIII.
3 Stanley, *Toil*, p96.

> to establish and keep up friendly relations with these Indians, by direction of the Government, I sent instructions to a trusty agent at Fort William, [Wemyss Simpson] to proceed to Fort Frances, where he had long resided, and enter into communication with the chiefs and leading men of the tribe.[4]

There was fear of native unrest closer to the Red River Settlement as well. The presence of Sioux warriors in the Red River region had been known in Ottawa for some time and it was the rumour that Lieutenant-Colonel Dennis had been parleying with them that had led to the stinging rebuke that McDougall had received from Howe back in January. On April 22nd it was reported that there were still several hundred Sioux in the region of the Forks and they were being given gifts to stay away from the settlement after they had announced that they were going to Winnipeg to kill the Americans there. The local Cree aboriginal peoples were reported as being angered by these gifts for the Sioux as 'they are the true owners of the soil', and had been loyal yet received nothing.[5] Simpson would not be travelling this far west, and if trouble did break out here, it would be up to the expeditionary force to deal with it once it arrived.

The *Algoma* had an uneventful voyage passing quietly through the canal on May 5th, arriving at Fort William the following day. The same could not be said for the former American Civil War blockade runner, the *Chicora,* a "fine steamer which has recently been overhauled and repainted white, with red stripes to water line."[6] Departing Collingwood on May 7th, she was loaded with military stores and 120 road workers, *voyageurs*, and a small number of soldiers from the military advance party.[7] Perhaps it was due to her past in the service of the Confederate cause, but despite the unloading of the steamer's military cargo and passengers on the Canadian side of the river before moving up to the canal, an inspection by American officers resulted in the canal master determining that the *Chicora* " ... was 'obviously' carrying military supplies."[8] She was turned back from the canal and, leaving her passengers and supplies on the Canadian side, made her way back to Collingwood.

Lindsay, Wolseley and the Canadian Government must have realized that such an action was a distinct possibility, although why the *Algoma* was allowed through remains unclear. United States aspirations towards the HBC lands, not to mention Canada itself, were also well known in both Ottawa and London and the Americans knew that many within the British establishment would have viewed a severing of their country's North American commitments favourably. Secretary of State Hamilton Fish kept Sir Edward Thornton, the British Minister in Washington, fully apprised of American views on the matter, though Great Britain's man in Washington was equally clear that, if either Canadian independence from Britain or annexation to the United States were to proceed, the initiative must come from Canada itself. Britain would on no account take the lead to promote either scenario.[9]

Fish came to know quite early on that the Canadians were considering sending an expedition to the Red River Settlement. He also received advice from Oscar Malmros, the American Consul at Fort Garry, that this could only be successfully carried through if the force was to travel through the United States. There simply was no viable route through Canadian territory. Consequently, the annexationists believed the best way to expedite an American takeover of the Northwest was to reject any Canadian overture for assistance. As we have already seen, seeking permission from the United States to allow the expedition's troops to pass through its territory was never considered as an option by the British and Canadian planners. If they had, Grant's cabinet had already discussed the matter and determined that the request would be denied. When the Americans realized that the expedition, now supported by the British, would be travelling via Lake Superior to Thunder Bay, it was immediately recognized that they would need to make use of the Sault Ste. Marie canal. After further cabinet discussions, President Grant determined that, should a request for its use be made, it was to be denied by the local authorities and then referred

4 PPP 559, Dawson, "Report", p6.

5 TNA, PRO CO 42/686, Report from Jas J. Hill, April 22, 1870.

6 Maritime History of the Great Lakes, described in the Owen Sound Advertiser, April 28, 1870. http://images.maritimehistoryofthegreatlakes.ca/6873/data?n=44

7 Stanley, *Toil*, p96.

8 Stanley, *Toil*, p98.

9 Bowsfield, *United States*, p10.

to Washington for further direction. At least twice at the beginning of April this news was communicated by Fish to Thornton.[10]

Thornton, however, did not let the matter rest. He argued on April 14th that Canada had allowed the use of the Welland Canal by Northern forces during the Civil War. The Secretary of State did not see a parallel, stating, somewhat dubiously, "that munitions carried through the Welland Canal had been articles of merchandise and not part of the supplies of a military expedition."[11] The matter was again broached on April 28th, when Thornton suggested a variety of scenarios by which the canal could be used. These ranged from the full use by vessels carrying troops and military supplies, to vessels with the troops disembarked, to vessels without men or military supplies aboard. All were rebuffed. Fish would make no concessions for ships being emptied of men and stores prior to passing through the canal. All vessels associated with an expeditionary force would be refused access. He added that he hoped the British would not make a formal request for the use of the canal, as he "should not wish to refuse it."[12]

Early in May American plans were formalized and Fish instructed Governor H.P. Baldwin of Michigan that the decision as to whether or not a foreign power would be allowed to use the canal was a matter for the Federal rather than the State Government. No military expedition from any foreign power was to " ... be allowed to pass through the Sault Ste. Marie canal without express instructions to that effect from the Government at Washington."[13]

Given the Thornton-Fish conversations, it is difficult to believe that Lindsay, Wolseley and the Canadian Government were not fully aware of what was likely to happen once the first elements of the expedition arrived at the canal. Lindsay would later write to the War Office in London on May 27th outlining his criticism of the Canadian Government for being unprepared when the *Chicora* was denied passage. He cited that the effects of this could have been minimized if the Canadians had done as he had 'specially begged' on April 28th for a permanently based steamer on Lake Superior.[14] It could be argued that this request on Lindsay's part, occurring the same day that Thornton's latest proposal had been categorically rejected by Fish, is proof that Lindsay at the very least, knew of the American attitude. However, it is highly unlikely that the news would have reached Lindsay so promptly and, as late as April 20th, he was telling Sir Stafford Northcote that "he anticipated no objection on the part of the United States to our passing through the canal at Sault Ste. Marie."[15]

Assuming Thornton actually passed information regarding the American attitude along (and we will broach that issue in a moment), it would most likely have been sent to the Foreign Office, and perhaps the Governor-General, before Lieutenant-General Lindsay. It would probably have gone by diplomatic courier, although there is always the possibility it could have been sent by cyphered telegram. Even then it is unlikely that it would have reached Lindsay at military headquarters in Montreal in such a short space of time. It also needs to be said that the author has uncovered no record in the British or Canadian archives to confirm that Thornton passed along the substance of his conversations with Fish. The only reason we know so much about these discussion is because the details are found in Fish's diary. Rather incredibly, it seems likely that the British Minister in Washington kept the information to himself.

In support of the contention that the American position had not been communicated are the two responses to the canal closure, the local one at Sault Ste. Marie and the higher level one from Ottawa. The local one clearly shows that the British were in the dark as to where the decision to deny them access had come from. Did it come from the Americans at Sault Ste. Marie or from a higher authority? Brevet Lieutenant-Colonel Bolton R.A., the senior British officer at the scene, was dispatched to pay a tactful visit on the brigadier in command of the garrison on the American side of the river. Of course this had no effect as the decision had nothing to do with the local

10 Bowsfield, *United States*, p11.
11 Bowsfield, *United States*, p11.
12 Bowsfield, *United States*, p11.
13 Bowsfield, *United States*, p12.
14 PPP 568, Correspondence and Journal, May 27, 1870, No. 8, Lindsay to WO.
15 Northcote, *Iddesleigh*, Entry for April 20, 1870.

American commander. The order had come from Washington and, if the substance of Thornton's discussions with Fish had been forwarded, this would have been known to the British and Canadians.

The initial response in Ottawa was also one of surprise and indignation. It was a full week before Governor-General Sir John Young requested that Thornton make a personal appeal to President Grant. Young spoke of 'great surprise' on the part of the Canadian Government upon learning the canal had been closed to them. One can only speculate as to Thornton's thoughts when he read this communication, given that he had known of the American attitude for weeks. The Governor-General instructed Thornton to request that the United States Government intervene "and let Ste. Marie canal remain on same footing as regards Canadian vessels as Welland is as regards United States vessels."[16] Here was a definite threat of retaliation. If the canal was not made available to the expedition's ships, Canadian waterways, specifically the important Welland Canal, could be closed to the Americans. There was, however, conciliation too. An assurance was given that "no munitions of war will be sent through the canal in any event, not even tents."[17]

Sir Edward made the appeal to Grant on May 16th. He informed him that delegates had been received from Red River in Ottawa and with their assistance an Act of Parliament had been passed establishing the new province of Manitoba. "The expedition, therefore, which is now being sent to that Settlement is in no way to bear a hostile character. It will be a peaceful expedition, with the object of maintaining good order in that district and of insuring the regular and harmonious establishment of the new Government."[18]

Whether it was the threat of retaliation, the reasoned approach from Thornton, or the simple realization that the canal closure alone was not going to stop the expedition, instructions were issued by Washington the same day to lift the embargo. Canadian ships, were now free to proceed as long as troops and supplies were unloaded prior to passing through the canal. This was certainly an inconvenience, but a condition the British and Canadians were happy to accept in return for the free movement of their supply vessels through the canal. In any case, Wolseley maintained "it had never been contemplated to send soldiers through that canal. They were to be landed on our side of the Ste. Marie River, below the rapids, to march up the bank about three miles, and then embark again in the same steamers in which they had sailed from Collingwood,"[19]

Despite his successful diplomatic handling of the situation, the *Globe* vented its anger on Thornton accusing him of "' ... humiliating himself and his country' by offering a 'pitiful explanation' ... " to the American president, though he was only carrying out the direction of the Governor-General.[20] It is difficult to feel sympathy towards Thornton in light of his prior handling of events, however, it is not clear what alternative solution the *Globe* thought was appropriate. The minister had made no concessions to the Americans that the Canadian Government, Lindsay, or Wolseley would not have willingly made, and he had effectively negotiated a quick end to a difficult situation.

While the American action had clearly been intended to stop the expedition in its tracks, by May 17th the canal was open. Wolseley succinctly summed up the situation when he said that if the American authorities "had but reflected for a moment" they would have realized there was no way to stop the expedition short of "actual war." For while they could deny the use of the canal, they could not prevent the British from portaging their men and supplies up to Lake Superior on the Canadian side of Sault Ste. Marie and then sending them on their way to Thunder Bay, in chartered American vessels if necessary.[21]

As with the lake steamers, Wolseley would later claim that the American action delayed the expedition's departure, but had there been a delay?[22] There were three ways the closing of the canal could hinder the progress of the expedition. The first was the inability to get the expedition's steamers from Lake Huron onto Lake Superior. As we have seen, Lindsay had in late April been concerned enough about this to argue the need for a

16 Stanley, *Western Canada*, p134.
17 Stanley, *Western Canada*, p134.
18 Stanley, *Toil*, p100.
19 Wolseley, *Narrative Part 2*, p48.
20 Stanley, *Toil*, p101.
21 Wolseley, *Narrative Part 2*, p49.
22 PPP 568, Correspondence and Journal, July 16, 1870, No. 21 Enclosure 2, Wolseley to the Military Secretary, Montreal.

'permanent steamer' to be immediately stationed there and criticized the Canadian Government for not acting more decisively.[23] Once again Lindsay had demonstrated his astute assessment of events, however, his criticism of the Canadian Government is overly harsh. The *Algoma* was the first steamer of the season and she sailed on May 3rd, just five days after Lindsay's request of April 28th. By May 5th she was on the upper lake. Whether it would have been possible to get another steamer onto Superior at an earlier date is a question difficult to answer this far removed from the events. Ice was always a concern this early in the year and just because the *Algoma* had gotten through on May 5th, did not mean that even just a few days prior the way would have been clear. Regardless, once the presence of the *Algoma* on Lake Superior was an accomplished fact, the Americans could not stop the expedition or even seriously delay it. The *Algoma* was ordered to remain there and, even before Grant ordered the opening of the canal for the expedition's use, an American ship chartered at Sarnia, the *Brooklyn*, had also passed unmolested onto Lake Superior, its master having assured the United States authorities that he had not been hired by the Canadian Government and had nothing whatsoever to do with the Red River Expedition.[24] Wolseley himself was quite clear that, "having even one steamer on that lake would render us independent" and, if more ships were needed, these could be chartered from American owners.[25]

The second potential for delay was the state of the road on the Canadian side at Sault Ste. Marie. The plan had always been to disembark the troops below the canal and have them re-embark once their ship had navigated the canal. That the road between the two lakes on the Canadian shore would need some work had been recognized and, according to Simon Dawson's report written the following year, "men had been set to work on the Portage road, on the British side at the earliest possible moment." The earliest possible moment was apparently May 5th because his report also explains that, as the *Algoma* passed Sault Ste. Marie on its journey to Fort William, "an agent was at the same time despatched ... for the purpose of organizing a force to improve the Portage road on the British side, and to provide means of embarkation at the head of the rapids."[26] It is highly unlikely that work could have been commenced earlier; the *Algoma* was after all the first steamer of the season and it was not possible to have gotten someone into Sault Ste. Marie to organize the work at an earlier date. When the *Chicora* was turned back, the *voyageurs* and workmen aboard her were put ashore and immediately set to work to assist the locals organized by the agent. The result of all this was that the road was quickly put in order.

The third potential delay stemmed from the necessity to unload the expedition's supplies from the ships at the eastern end of the portage road and then reload them onto ships at the western end. While it might have always been intended that the troops would disembark below the rapids at Sault Ste. Marie, this does not appear to have been the case regarding the cargo and the enforced change of plan was a serious logistical and administrative headache.[27] Stores and supplies continually being unloaded, moved, stored, and then reloaded risked damage and loss. Irvine wrote that this unwelcome turn of events resulted in "claims for wharfage and storage, and damaged the stores by crowding and transhipment, to the great increase of delay, confusion and expense."[28] There was also the ever present concern of a Fenian incursion, and so Wolseley ordered forward four companies of the 1st Ontario Rifles; the first of the expedition's infantry to move west from Toronto. Two companies left Collingwood on May 14th (the 1st and 4th under Captain Cook) and two more on May 16th (the 2nd and 3rd under Major Wainwright). Their role was to form a garrison and superintend "the passage of the troops and the transport of the stores across the portage."[29]

The officer in charge at Sault Ste. Marie was Lieutenant-Colonel Bolton R.A., the Deputy-Assistant Adjutant-General and Senior Staff Officer of the expedition. Wolseley dispatched him to the Sault Ste. Marie when problems

23 PPP 568, Correspondence and Journal, May 27, 1870, No. 8, Lindsay to WO.

24 Wolseley, *Narrative Part 2*, p49.

25 Wolseley, *Narrative Part 2*, pp48/49.

26 PPP 559, Dawson, "Report", pp 14/15.

27 TNA, WO 32/7586, Irvine "Report on Red River" p2.

Martindale and Irvine in their detailed report make no mention of an intent to unload the expedition's supplies at the lower end of the falls and move them by road to the upper end.

28 TNA, WO 32/7586, Irvine "Report on Red River", p2.

29 Huyshe, *Red River*, p33.

The camp of the Ontario Rifles at Sault Ste. Marie. (Toronto Public Library, JRR2421. Artist: William Armstrong)

there arose and it was he who paid the informal visit on the commander of the American garrison. A staff college graduate, he was highly regarded by all who came into contact with him. Lindsay described him as "a man of capacity."[30] Dawson said he was "a most able and energetic officer" and that his " ... kind and considerate bearing to the voyageurs and all with whom he came in contact, made him a general favorite with the civilian portion of the Red River expeditionary force."[31] Even the *Globe* reported favourably on him stating that he was "courteous and affable and while possessing nothing of the martinet, still holds his troops well in hand. He is generally liked."[32]

Lieutenant-Colonel Bolton left Collingwood on May 14th and probably arrived at Sault Ste. Marie on the 16th, meaning that his informal visit to the American brigadier did not take place until several days after access to the canal had been denied. It also means that work on the road would already have been underway for about 10 days and the movement of men and supplies for about a week prior to his arrival. Bolton's significance is that, while he was there, the road was put into a much improved state and an effective system was established by which the men and supplies were transported along the road and re-embarked for transport to Thunder Bay. Perhaps most importantly, his tactfulness in man management when it came to his handling of the Canadian volunteer troops and the civilian workers ensured that the work was conducted smoothly and efficiently. The Sault Ste. Marie road had only been intended as a quick land transportation link on the road to Thunder Bay. Out of necessity the area became an important military base and supply compound as well. This had never been part of the plan, but it worked effectively for as long as was required until the force and all its supplies had passed through. The credit for this to a large extent belongs to Lieutenant-Colonel Bolton.

The canal closure was incontrovertibly an inconvenience for the expedition. So too was the necessity of offloading men and supplies at the lower end of the portage road and then re-embarking and reloading them at the upper end, though this would continue even after the American climb down. It had never been anticipated that such a large body of men would remain ashore for such a prolonged period; or that the transhipment of the

30 PPP 586, Correspondence and Journal, May 27, 1870, No. 8, Lindsay to WO.
31 PPP 559, Dawson, "Report", p15.
32 Stanley, *Toil*, p276.

stores and supplies would, in effect, turn the area into a forward base. The last detachment of troops and supplies would not leave until June 19th. Nevertheless, " ... a camp was soon pitched and the stores were placed under shelter, some in HBC buildings, and the remainder under tarpaulins."[33]

But what about the question of delay? Wolseley would later claim that "this affair of the canal had the effect of retarding for some time the departure of the expedition."[34] As with the colonel's allegations regarding the lake steamers discussed in the previous chapter, it is difficult to reconcile this with the timeline of actual events. Regardless of any remedial steps that could have been taken to rectify the canal's closure, it was in fact open by May 17th and, as we have seen, the 60th Rifles did not begin their move forward from Toronto until May 21st. Getting to Fort Garry was going to be a complex and difficult operation. While the events at the canal were underway, Wolseley and his staff remained immersed in the finer details of planning. As Captain Huyshe would write, "After a stay of seventeen days in Toronto, *every hour of which had been busily spent in the multitudinous details of preparation,* [Author's emphasis] matters were at length in a sufficiently forward state to enable the first start to be made."[35] This was the real cause behind the timing of the expedition's departure, not the American canal closure or even the delay in hiring the steamers.

33 TNA, WO 32/7586, Irvine "Report on Red River" p2.
34 Wolseley, *Narrative Part 2*, p49.
35 Huyshe, *Red River*, p37.

14

Toronto to Prince Arthur's Landing

The British Government's conditions for the participation of its troops in the Red River Expedition were outlined in a telegram from the Foreign Office in London to Sir John Young in Ottawa on April 23rd.

> Troops may advance on the following conditions:
>
> First If Rose [Sir John Rose, Macdonald's man in London] is authorized to pay £300,000 at once and Her Majesty's government is at liberty to make the transfer before the end of June.
>
> Second If Her Majesty's Government pays only the expense of British Troops not exceeding 250 and Canadian Government the rest, sending not less than 500 trained men.
>
> Third Canada to accept the decision of Her Majesty's Government on disputed points of Settlers Bill of Rights.
>
> Fourth General Lindsay to be satisfied with military arrangements.[1]

On May 5th, with the all the details from the April 23rd telegram settled, Young sent the following message to Granville: "I presume I am now at liberty to issue final orders for the troops to proceed to Red River – General Lindsay asks for such orders from me."[2] By the following day Young was able to inform Lindsay, "Troops may proceed."[3] Lindsay's *Instructions for the guidance of Colonel Wolseley* are undated, but must have been issued around the time of the General Orders on May 10th. Wolseley says he was authorized to begin moving the force forward late on the night of May 12th and the *Standing Orders for the Red River Expeditionary Force* were published on May 14th.[4] The path was, therefore, clear for Wolseley to proceed, but despite all of his subsequent complaints about delays, the first troops bound for Thunder Bay did not set out from Toronto until May 21st. Young reported to Granville on May 19th, "All the Regular Troops will be at Fort William on the 26th of May ... .It is hoped that all the Volunteers and their stores will have reached Fort William by the 10th of June."[5] It seems these dates were received with some consternation in London, because on June 9th Granville expressed his surprise " ... that the whole body of troops will not have reached Fort William until the 10th of this month. I trust they will be pushed forward without delay and that Her Majesty's Regular Troops will reach Toronto at the time fixed by Colonel Wolseley."[6] In fact, the last of the troops would not arrive at Thunder Bay until June 21st.

The ambitious colonel was anxious to make a good impression on this, his first independent command, and so cement his reputation. The expedition was a complex undertaking, both politically and militarily, and Wolseley and his staff had been working flat out for weeks to complete the preparations. It was the detailed planning, for which most of the credit is due to Wolseley, that would contribute so significantly to the success of the operation. Nevertheless, word of Granville's 'surprise' would undoubtedly have become known to the expeditionary force

1 TNA PRO CO 43/157 Holland on behalf of Granville to Young April 23, 1870.
2 TNA PRO CO 43/157 Young to Granville May 5, 1870.
3 TNA PRO CO 43/157 Young to Lindsay May 6, 1870.
4 PPP 568, Correspondence and Journal, July 16, 1870, No. 21 Enclosure 2, Wolseley to the Military Secretary.
5 TNA, PRO CO42/686 Young to Granville May 19, 1870.
6 TNA, PRO CO143/57 Granville to Young June 9, 1870.

commander and it is highly likely that his subsequent allegations of the incompetence of others leading to delays not of his making originated here.

Before beginning the narrative of the expeditionary force's move towards Thunder Bay, it is worth taking a few moments to review Lindsay's instructional document to Wolseley, as well as Wolseley's Standing Orders for the expeditionary force. There are some interesting points contained therein providing insights into how the two officers envisaged the operation would run.

Lindsay was emphatic that Wolseley was to take orders from no one but himself. He provided a general overview of the purpose of the expedition, speaking to such matters as the composition of the force, the transit at Sault Ste. Marie, precautions to guard against Fenian raids whenever close to American territory, and ensuring a contingency plan was in place should any part of the British force be compelled to spend the winter at Fort Garry. He warned against camping on American territory, stressed the importance of maintaining communication with Canada, and outlined the procedure for handing over British stores and supplies to the Canadian battalions when the Imperial force withdrew. This would ensure that the accounts could be balanced. A team of workers was to follow in the wake of the force to complete the road from the Northwest Angle to the Red River Settlement. This would more effectively open up communication and speed up the return journey of the British troops. There was to be respectful treatment from the troops towards the *voyageurs* and "Indians should be ceremoniously treated." Finally:

> It is most important that none of the persons who had during the last winter taken part in the troubles at Red River should accompany the Expedition, you will do all that lays in your power to prevent them doing so. I have to recall to your memory that both in public and in private certain of those gentlemen have expressed themselves anxious to take the opportunity of the advance of the Expedition to pay off their scores. You will therefore discountenance them in a public manner should they attempt to fasten themselves upon you.[7]

This final statement reflects credit on Lindsay, however, the Ontario battalion, as well as a sizeable proportion of the Quebec battalion, were made up of men who, while having no direct connection with the events of the previous winter, had enthusiastically volunteered due to their anger over the killing of Scott. If Lindsay was looking for a detached perspective from the members of the expeditionary force, he was not going to receive it from the Canadian component.

Wolseley's Standing Orders unsurprisingly were even more detailed and specific. They dealt with how the force would be structured once it got underway. "It will move by detachments, consisting of one or more companies. To each company a brigade of 5 boats will be attached."[8] It detailed precisely the tools, equipment and rations each boat would contain, the numbers of men, including *voyageurs*, even going so far to state that no one would be allowed to sit on the boat's gunwale. Under no circumstances would unauthorized personnel be allowed to accompany the expedition and each company's officers would be responsible for enforcing this. Before setting forth on Shebandowan Lake, stores would be moved up the Dawson Road and Lieutenant-Colonel McNeill would be stationed at the lake end. Once the force was on its way, detachments would be posted at portages along the route as required. The steps as to what would happen if men fell sick or were injured were outlined. If a man was unfit to continue, he was to be left behind, preferably in the care of a medical officer until he could be removed back to Thunder Bay. Precautions to prevent forest fires were emphasized, as was the daily schedule of operations; reveille at 3:00 a.m. (the accounts by expeditionary force members typically speak to it actually being 4:30 a.m.),

7 PPP 568, Correspondence and Journal, No. 9 Inclosure 1

8 The expeditionary force travelled from Shebandowan Lake to Fort Garry divided into boat brigades and some explanation of this term is required. These are not brigades in the same sense with which many military historians are familiar; i.e. of a certain number of battalions being grouped into a brigade. The term as used here is a carryover from the days of the fur trade when groups of canoes moved together and were referred to as brigades. A modification from the Standing Orders resulted in the boat brigades of the expeditionary force containing between 5 and 7 boats per brigade. See Appendix 2 for additional detail.

commencement of the journey shortly afterwards, boats to keep together, halts of one hour for breakfast at 8:00 a.m. and dinner at 1:00 p.m., cease of operations at the end of the day to occur at least one hour before dark. In keeping with Lindsay's direction:

> All officers belonging to this Force will be most careful in impressing upon those under their command the great necessity there is for cultivating the good will of the Indians and others employed as voyageurs. Colonel Wolseley will punish with the utmost severity anyone who ill treats them. The same rule applies to all Indians who may be met on the line of the route.[9]

Wolseley's plan was to concentrate the expedition at Thunder Bay. A fortified camp would be established to ensure communications with Canada were maintained and to protect his supply depot on which the force "could fall back in the event of any untoward disaster."[10] One company of the 2nd Quebec Rifles would remain here to protect the base once the rest of the force moved on.

The expedition would not be travelling as a compact unit. Once the van had commenced to move, the following units would embark at intervals that would leave the boat brigades ahead of them reasonable time to maintain their positions in the line of advance. This would avoid traffic jams at the portages, but would mean the force would be strung out along the route. The KRRC would be in the lead, followed by the 1st Ontario Rifles and then the 2nd Quebec Rifle. Of course, this also meant that the forward elements would reach the Red River Settlement first and at that time Wolseley would have to decide whether he needed to wait for the Canadian battalions to catch up before moving on to Fort Garry.

Once the rearmost elements had set off, other than the sending and receiving of written communications (official communiques and personal mail), the expeditionary force would be isolated from the outside world and self-sufficiency was critical. Ration requirements had been carefully calculated and would be carried in the boats along with all the rest of the force's needs, though Wolseley did arrange with Dawson for the transport of 20,000 complete rations to Fort Frances.[11] Supplies of fresh meat would cease once the boat journey began and a daily diet consisting predominantly of biscuit, salt pork, and beans or preserved potatoes would become monotonous very quickly. Any supplemental supplies of non-preserved protein would have to be sourced along the way, and as this was a journey across lakes and rivers, this was largely going to consist of fish.

Wolseley intended to establish an advanced depot at Fort Frances prior to his final move on Fort Garry. A rather complex plan for moving surplus supplies, as outlined in the Standing Orders, was scrapped when it was discovered that the boats could carry sixty days of supplies. All brigades were then simply ordered to make their way to Fort Frances and it was arranged for the additional supplies remaining at Shebandowan Lake to be brought forward to this point by Dawson's *voyageurs* using the additional boats.[12] Wolseley, travelling in his North Canoe, would be constantly on the move along the axis of advance, urging his men forward and ensuring that all was running smoothly.

One item that was not included in the Standing Orders concerned the consumption of alcoholic spirits. There would be none accompanying the expedition. Wolseley was adamant that for the health of the troops, not to mention the maintenance of discipline during the long and arduous trek to Fort Garry, spirits would not be allowed. Instead a large daily ration of tea was to be issued. "It was an experiment based upon the practice common in Canada, where lumbermen, who spend the whole winter in the backwoods, employed upon the hardest labour, and exposed to freezing temperatures, are allowed no spirits, but have an unlimited quantity of tea."[13] The results of this decision were, in the colonel's view, remarkable. The men performed their unceasing hard

9 PPP 568, Correspondence and Journal, No 9 Inclosure 2
10 Wolseley, *Narrative Part 2*, p51.
11 Low, *Wolseley*, p35.
12 TNA, WO 32/7586, Irvine "Report on Red River", p10.
13 Wolseley, *Narrative Part 2*, p64.

work effectively and without complaint. There was no crime and the troops remained healthy from the beginning to the end of the expedition.

On the morning of May 21st Wolseley and the advance guard of the expedition left Toronto for Collingwood and passage to Thunder Bay on the *Chicora*. The Red River Expedition was finally properly on the move. Colonel Wolseley was accompanied by Assistant-Controller Irvine, Captain Huyshe, Lieutenant Denison, Surgeon-Major Young, Assistant Surgeon-Major Robertson and G Company of the KRRC under Captain Ward. It had rained incessantly all day, but as their train arrived at Collingwood the sun came out. "It was a moment of magic. Smart-looking officers, their brass buttons shining, marshalled onto the platform. After them, the soldiers fell into formation. Each soldier carried a bedroll over one shoulder and a rifle over the other."[14]

Later that same day, as Wolseley and his men were departing aboard the *Chicora,* a second troop train steamed into the Collingwood Railway Station. Aboard were the headquarters and four more companies of the 60th Rifles, three from Ottawa and one from Toronto, under the command of Assistant Surgeon-Major Robertson with orders to proceed to Fort William aboard the *Frances Smith*.[15]

According to the reporter for the *Owen Sound Advertiser*, Collingwood had become a town "filled with unwonted life and activity. The noise of preparation for the outgoing expedition, resounds through her usually quiet streets."[16] Perhaps with some intended hyperbole, the *Globe* reported on May 23rd that Collingwood had changed from a 'dreamy quiet town' into a 'miniature Chicago'. Special freight trains arrived day and night and locals and visitors alike "swarmed around the wharf hoping to get a glimpse of the soldiers." [17] Freight was stowed in the holds and crammed on the decks of the *Chicora* and *Frances Smith*.

> Between 8:00 a.m., Saturday May 21, and early evening, the *Frances Smith* was loaded with 200 half barrels of pork, 300 barrels of biscuits, 100 barrels of sugar, 300 half barrels of flour, enough tents for a battalion of 350 men, camp equipment, 300 bags of oats, 40 horses with their teamsters and tons of pressed hay. There were caskets of tobacco, bags of beans, and chests of tea crowded into the main deck. The *Chicora* tied up a few metres away was similarly loaded.[18]

While the troops waited to board a heavy fog rolled in, but by 5:30 p.m. it began to lift and the *Chicora* took advantage of the improved conditions, slipped her moorings and headed out onto the lake. Arriving at Sault Ste. Marie early on the morning of May 23rd, Lieutenant-Colonel Bolton and Weymss M. Simpson came aboard to report that all was well on the American side and that 'very cordial relations' now existed with the American garrison commander.[19]

The men and military supplies were offloaded and the *Chicora* uneventfully passed through the canal. The troops were marched along the portage road for 1¾ miles and temporarily put up in one of the HBC barns. The road "was found to be in good order, a great deal of work having been done to it since the arrival of Colonel [sic] Bolton."[20] The troops were re-embarked above the rapids and Captain Huyshe remarked on the 'bustle of activity'. "The river was full of ships engaged in the work of transport, and the picturesque beauty of the scenery was much enhanced by the white tents and open-air gipsy-looking fires of the camps of the Iroquois and Canadian voyageurs."[21]

14 Cameron, *Frances*, p67.
15 PPP 568, Correspondence and Journal, Appendix, p54.
16 Maritime History of the Great Lakes, described in the Owen Sound Advertiser, May 26, 1870. http://images.maritimehistoryofthegreatlakes.ca/6882/data
17 Cameron, *Frances*, p236 and p66.
18 Cameron, *Frances,* p67.
19 PPP 568, Correspondence and Journal, Appendix, p55.
20 PPP 568, Correspondence and Journal, Appendix, p55.
21 Huyshe, *Red River*, p44.

At Sault Ste. Marie Wolseley found the schooners *Pandora* and *Orion* at the wharf loaded with boats for the expedition and stores for Simon Dawson's men. The *Schickluna* towed the schooners through the canal and then took onboard No.1 Company of the 1st Ontario Rifles, who were to provide protection against any Fenian raiders during the journey. [22] While he had been angered by the Americans closing of the canal, Colonel Wolseley was satisfied with the steps that had been taken to ameliorate their action. This stage of the journey to Fort Garry, at least, seemed to be falling into place nicely. However, there was one wrinkle of which Wolseley was not yet aware. While his journey on the *Chicora* had proceeded smoothly, the voyage of the *Frances Smith* had been a different story and she did not finally arrive at the Sault Ste. Marie until two days after Wolseley.

Launched in 1867, the *Frances Smith* was a wooden side wheel steamer, "the first steam passenger ship to be built in Owen Sound on Georgian Bay."[23] Upon arrival, Assistant Surgeon-Major Robertson, the senior officer aboard her, reported to Lieutenant-Colonel Bolton that the ship had no working compasses, no lifebelts, and only two boats, neither of which had any way of lowering them in the event of an emergency. Most seriously, the captain had been drunk the whole way from Collingwood. Bolton interviewed W.H. Smith, the steamer's master, and instructed him to move his vessel through the canal up onto Lake Superior. Smith refused to comply without a guarantee of $65,000, claiming he had received no instruction that he would be travelling beyond Sault Ste. Marie and so had not provided his vessel with insurance for such a journey.[24] By this stage the men had been disembarked and most of the supplies had been removed as well, though some were still on board. Smith told Bolton that if his demand was not met within two hours he would begin charging $500 for every twenty-four hour period after 10:00 p.m. that night.[25] The ever efficient Bolton was by this stage, no doubt, becoming angry and frustrated with the uncooperative and truculent Smith. It was also apparent that Smith had made up his mind that he would not be proceeding to Thunder Bay. Bolton said he would not sign the manifest once all of the supplies had been unloaded, to which Smith replied that he would immediately weigh anchor and sail back to Collingwood with whatever stores remained on board.

Short of boarding the *Frances Smith* with an armed party and seizing control of the wayward captain's vessel, a step, assuming he even considered it, he probably would have decided was not worth the effort, Bolton had little choice but to give way. The last of the stores and supplies were unloaded and, along with the troops, were transferred to the *Algoma* and the *Brooklyn* on Lake Superior. Captain Smith and the *Frances Smith's* association with the Red River Expedition was at an end.[26]

The *Chicora* set sail from the Sault Ste. Marie bound for Thunder Bay on May 24th. The steamer was " ... soon out of sight of land, and pitching and rolling with a fresh north-east breeze and a heavy swell."[27] Land was sighted early the following morning and the imposing headland of Thunder Cape was passed about 7:45am. "We passed on our left the mouth of the Kaministiquia River, with the clean white building of the Hudson's Bay Company's post of Fort William shining clearly out against the dark-green background of foliage, and with the heavy folds of a huge Union Jack floating lazily in the light summer air. Almost four miles further on a small clearing, with three or four wooden houses and a few tents marked the beginning of Mr. Dawson's road."[28] By 10:00 a.m. they had anchored and the work of getting the men and supplies ashore was begun. Wolseley named the point of

22 In the Journal of Operations the ship is referred to as the Chickland, but this is certainly incorrect.

23 Cameron, *Frances*, p5.

24 PPP 568, Correspondence and Journal, No. 17, Inclosures 4, 5, & 6 and Appendix, p55.

25 PPP 568, May 24, 1870, No. 17 Inclosure 6, Captain of Francis (sic) Smith to Bolton.

26 This sort of behaviour does not appear to have been uncommon with Captain Smith. In 1873 when the North-West Mounted Police were moving from Ottawa to the Canadian West, it was reported that "Three officers and 53 men ('C' Division) left Collingwood onboard the steamer Frances Smith. As they crossed Lake Superior, the latter group of men and 28 Canadian militiamen narrowly escaped a watery disaster brought upon them by a ferocious storm and a frequently inebriated captain." See: Merv Ahrens, "The First NWMP Trek: From Ottawa to the Stone Fort, 1873," *The Beaver, Canada's National History Society*, Winnipeg June/July 1998 p5. However there seems to have been another side to the man. He is also described as "handsome, congenial and generous" and a local hero in his home port of Owen Sound where he served on the municipal council in 1859 and 1860. "Tales of his efforts to put Owen Sound on the map are the stuff of local folklore." Cameron, *Frances*, p16.

27 Huyshe, *Red River*, p45.

28 Huyshe, *Red River*, pp47/48

The camp of the expeditionary force at McVicar's Creek on Thunder Bay. The tent in the centre of the picture is the expeditionary force commander's. The woman is Mrs. Wolseley who had come to say goodbye to Colonel Wolseley prior to the expeditionary force embarking on its journey to Fort Garry. (The Toronto Public Library JRR2429, Artist: William Armstrong)

disembarkation at the beginning of the Dawson Road Prince Arthur's Landing, in honour of the twenty year old Prince Arthur, the seventh child and third son of Queen Victoria, who was then serving in Canada with the Rifle Brigade.[29]

The first step was to get a camp in order, but the sight that greeted the men from the *Chicora* was depressing. A fire had raged through the area about ten days prior to their arrival, "devastating the country for hundreds of square miles and doing much damage to the road."[30] Wolseley described the scene as 'extremely desolate', but placed a positive spin on it by saying that at least the fire had reduced the number of insects. Insects, along with the weather, would cause constant discomfort and difficulties for the men of the expedition during the next few months. One officer wrote that "a forest through which a fire has passed presents a melancholy spectacle. Half-burnt trunks of trees here and there stand erect, shorn of branches, waiting for another conflagration or a strong wind to prostrate them to the ground."[31]

29 While stationed in Canada Prince Arthur was feted by Canadian society and went to garden parties and balls. He took his ceremonial and soldiering duties seriously attending the opening of Canadian Parliament and visiting President Grant in Washington. While concerns were raised for his safety during the Fenian troubles, on May 25, 1870, the day Wolseley named his camp on Lake Superior after him, the prince participated in the Battle of Eccles Hill, for which he received the Fenian Medal. Prince Arthur attained the rank of Field Marshal and aspired to succeed the Duke of Cambridge as Commander-in-Chief when the latter retired in 1895. He was disappointed to be denied this and Garnet Wolseley was appointed in his stead. He returned to Canada as Governor-General between 1911 and 1916. He was hard working and popular but, when he donned his field marshal's uniform and attended military camps to address the troops without ministerial advice after the outbreak of the First World War, he was seen by Prime Minister Robert Borden as overstepping his responsibilities.

30 Huyshe, *Red River*, p49.

31 Peel's Prairie Provinces 589, Lieutenant H.S.H. Riddell, "60th Rifles, The Red River Expedition of 1870", Transactions of the Literary and Historical Society of Quebec, Session of 1870-71, Printed by Middleton & Dawson, at the "Gazette," p103.

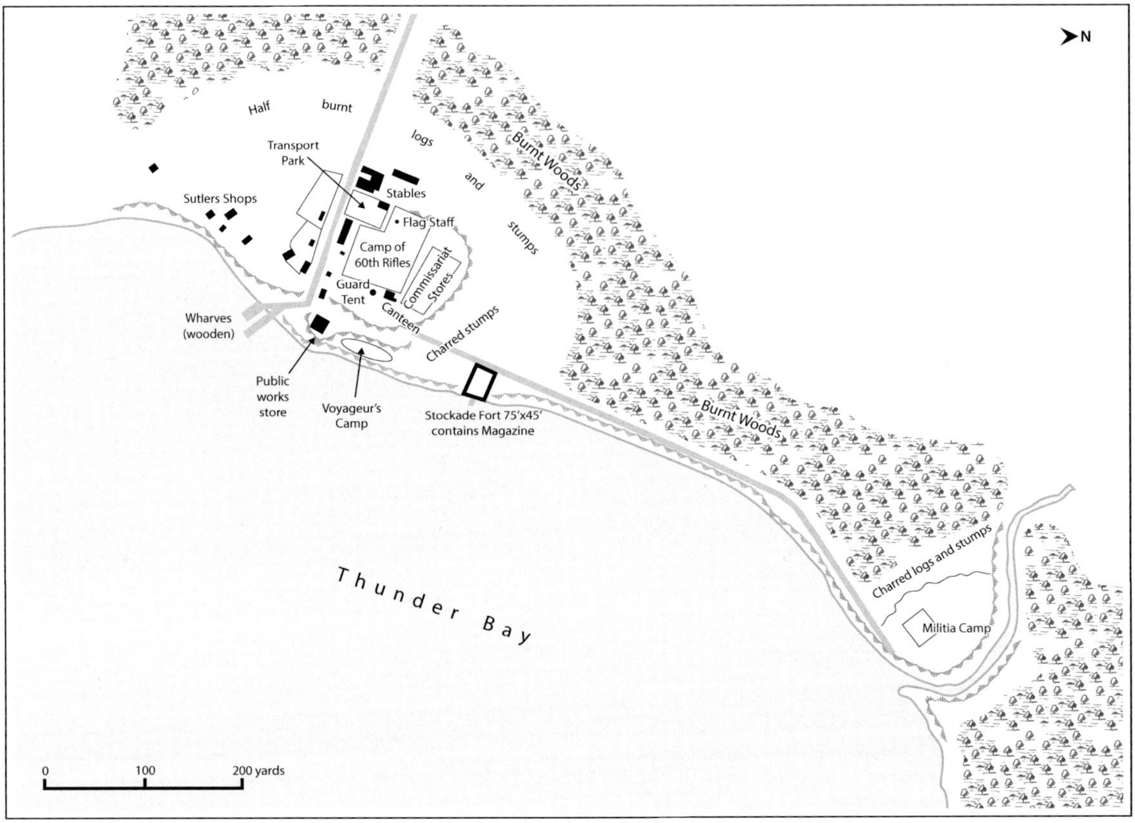

The Camp at Prince Arthur's Landing.

The camp was pitched on a hill not far from the lake and, according to Lieutenant Riddell, the fire made the labour of clearing the ground less arduous. However, "hard work, of every description, went on day after day, commencing at sunrise, and everybody seems to work with a will."[32] There was an immediate minor challenge confronting the troops on their first day when it was found that, while the tents and other camp equipment had arrived safely, all the tent poles were missing. The constant packing and re-packing of the stores due to the canal closure had claimed its first casualty. With the considerable stress Wolseley had been under for the past several weeks, it would have been understandable if he had received this information with something less than equanimity. "The chief Control Officer had expected an explosion of ill-humour," but his response was simply to question whether the expedition's axes had been left behind as well. When advised they had not, he pointed to the forest and, with a laugh, said "then you can help yourselves to as many tent-poles as you require."[33] It was instances such as this that inspired confidence amongst the men in the leader of the expeditionary force, though his behaviour is perhaps unsurprising considering his comments on man-management found in *The Soldier's Pocket Book*.

Over the next few weeks a steady stream of steamers and other support vessels carried the rest of the force with all of its stores, supplies, boats, waggons and livestock to the camp at Prince Arthur's Landing. On May 27th 18 officers and 213 KRRC men arrived, together with a company of the 1st Ontario Rifles, consisting of 3 officers and 50 men. The latter laid out their camp 600 yards NNE of the Headquarters Camp in a small clearing.[34] On June 1st a further 25 officers and 79 men of the 60th were disembarked, followed by the headquarters and four companies of the 1st Ontario Rifles, comprising 17 officers and 213 other ranks on the evening of June 3rd. The

32 PPP 589, Riddell, *60th*, p105.
33 Low, *Wolseley*, p17.
34 Huyshe, *Red River*, p53.

Canadian troops were accompanied by Lieutenant-Colonel John McNeill VC. The last of the Ontario battalion, 6 officers and 102 men, reached Thunder Bay on June 13th followed by the first batch of the 2nd Quebec Rifles, 9 officers and 151 men, on June 15th[35] The final detachment arrived on June 21st.[36]

Assistant-Controller Irvine hired a small tug to assist in the unloading of the transports and "the Bay assumed an unwonted appearance of life and bustle."[37] A 90 foot long pier was constructed extending into the shallow waters of the bay and stores were unloaded using a large shallow draught wooden scow, 55 feet long by 15 feet wide, with a carrying capacity of 500 barrels and drawing only about 18 inches of water when loaded. When the bay was calm, the transports could anchor within 300 yards of the beach, and, by running a cable from ship to pier, the scow was quickly hauled backwards and forwards between the two. However, when the wind was blowing from the east or south-east, a not uncommon occurrence, a heavy surf prevented vessels from coming nearer than half a mile or more from the shore. At such times the tug was put to work towing the scow with its loads of supplies from ship to the pier head.[38]

An officer of the Control Department by the name of Mellish was charged with the loading and unloading of the scow. "Being so constantly on board ... he acquired the sobriquet of the 'Admiral.' An expedition wag christened the scow the *Water Lilly* and 'Admiral' Mellish and his flag-ship "were well known to every soul in the camp."[39] The efficient unloading of the expedition's supplies was important work, but it appears the 'Admiral' began to take his role aboard the *Water Lily* a little too seriously.

> On one occasion, some individual having presumed to give an order about the working of the scow, Mellish called to him indignantly, hold your tongue, sir; do you command this ship, or do I? The roar of laughter elicited by this question awoke him to the absurdity of the situation, but it was too late; the joke was too good to be lost, and went the round of the whole camp.[40]

With each arrival at the pier, a strong fatigue party was ready and waiting. The scow's cargo was quickly removed, placed in waggons and then moved to the camp's growing supply dump where it was stored under the hospital marquees. The *Globe* reported that in short order the camp was turned into 'an orderly and systematized station' with streets laid out and marked with signposts.[41] No time was lost on starting the building of the fort, an earth redoubt 75 feet long by 45 feet wide surrounding the magazine, which was constructed under the command of Lieutenant Heneage. The artillery for the entire force consisted of four bronze 7 pounder cannons. They weighed two hundred pounds, fifty pounds more than the same calibre steel gun. However, they required lighter carriages than the steel equivalent and, being made from older bronze guns, were much cheaper to produce. Two of these would remain at the fort and two would accompany the expedition to Fort Garry.[42]

During the first ten days the weather at Prince Arthur's Landing was fine with the warmth of the day tempered by an onshore lake breeze, though it was cool enough at night " ... to induce one to pile on the blankets."[43] The change was sudden, violent and relentless. From June 1st to July 16th it rained on twenty-three days.[44] Thunder Bay came by its name honestly.

> Many officers who had been 'all over the world' admitted they had never heard such appalling claps of thunder before. On some occasions trees were blown down, on others they were split into shreds. At times, especially at night, the

35 PPP 568, Correspondence and Journal, Appendix pp55-63.
36 TNA, WO 32/7586, Irvine "Report on Red River", p3.
37 Huyshe, *Red River*, p53.
38 Huyshe, *Red River*, p54.
39 Huyshe, *Red River*, p55.
40 Huyshe, *Red River*, p55.
41 Globe July 1, 1870 quoted in Stanley, *Toil*, p113.
42 Huyshe, *Red River*, pp57/58.
43 Huyshe, *Red River*, p50
44 Wolseley, *Narrative Part 2*, p64.

Designed to shield the men from the hordes of tormenting insects, the mesh veils were found to be impractical to wear while at work. (Library and Archives Canada, Acc. No. R9266-3428)

> noise was such that the ground seemed to shake, and it sounded so close that one expected to see the tent – pole riven in two. Now and then these storms were accompanied by rain of quite a tropical character, after which the numerous streams became so swollen that bridges were swept away, and long portions of the road, which had been constructed with infinite toil, were completely destroyed.[45]

On June 6th twelve of the expedition's boats broke from their moorings on the bay and were washed ashore. One was badly damaged.[46]

If the weather wasn't bad enough, black flies and sand flies tormented the men by day and mosquitos at night. Veils made from netting to be worn about the head had been issued, but quickly were found to be too restrictive when working. A use was later found for them when the force reached Lake of the Woods. Here the lake was green, "almost opaque from vegetable matter," and the netting was used as a water strainer.[47] Mosquito oil was also provided. Made from creosote and pennyroyal, according to Wolseley, this 'disgusting' concoction prevented torment by mosquitos and other winged creatures if it was liberally applied and was fresh. By the end of the journey it was used as fuel for the lamps when the oil supply had been exhausted.[48] One dark night Captain McCalmont, the officer of the 9th Lancers who had travelled to Thunder Bay and prevailed on Wolseley to let him join the force, tormented by mosquitos doused himself with what he thought was a bottle of the repellant. In the morning he discovered that he had actually used a bottle of Harvey's Sauce.[49] In the evenings it "was desirable to have as much smoke as possible round where you sat ... to keep them at a distance."[50] At the entrance to each tent, and sometimes actually in the tent, smudges "of damp moss or wet rotten wood or bark" were lit and once

45 Wolseley, *Narrative Part 2,* p51.

Dawson disputed the level of destruction, along with a great many other assertions made by Wolseley in his "Narrative" articles. He maintained that one small bridge had been washed away and a culvert loosened, and portions of the road with clayey soil had been made soft and mushy. PPP 559, Dawson, "Report", Addenda p 45. Captain Huyshe described the thunderstorms as being of "extraordinary severity." Huyshe, *Red* River, p68.

46 PPP 568, Correspondence and Journal, June 29, 1870, No. 18 Inclosure, Military Secretary W. M. Earle to Governor-General Sir John Young.

47 Wolseley, *Narrative Part 2,* p59.

48 Wolseley, *Narrative Part 2,* p59.

49 Hampshire Archives, 170A12W/D/0438, Captain N. Willoughby Wallace, "The Rebellion in the Red River Settlement; Its causes and suppression, A Lecture." Delivered at Clifton October 25th, 1871, (Barnstaple: Henry T. Cook, 1872), p27.

50 Wolseley, *Narrative Part 2,* p60.

A camp scene around the fire in the evening. (Library and Archives Canada, Acc. No. R9266-3428)

the tent was sufficiently filled with smoke and the annoying insects had hopefully flown out, the tent would be fastened up tight for the night."[51]

Recreation was limited to bathing and fishing, though given the hard physical labour being endured on a daily basis, it is hard to imagine men would have had the time or energy for much more. As Wolseley would later write, men working in the boats, spent more than enough time in the water, but for those moving stores or working on the road, "a swim after the day's work was over was most enjoyable. The water in Lake Superior is always very cold; but that in some of the rivers – the Matawan [sic], for instance – was positively tepid, so that the men would roll about in it for a length of time without feeling any ill effects."[52]

But as the troops arrived and the organization of the camp, the unloading of supplies, and the construction of the fort were put in order, the state of readiness of the road from Thunder Bay to Shebandowan Lake became the issue of the moment. A great deal of time would subsequently be expended on allegations of who or what was responsible for the condition of the road and this is where we must now direct our attention.[53]

51 Wolseley, *Narrative Part 2*, p60.
52 Wolseley, *Narrative Part 2*, p60.
53 For the road controversy, readers may wish to reacquaint themselves with background detail provided in Chapter 10.

15

The Road to Shebandowan Lake

As we saw in Chapter 10, the early promises by Dawson in January that the road would be useable by May 1st had been eroded in subsequent communications with the Canadian Government. There is no question that Lindsay and Wolseley knew that the road would be incomplete when the expeditionary force arrived, although, as has been mentioned previously, recognizing its incomplete state and realizing just how much was still required to be done are two very different matters. Dawson was adamant that his numerous meetings with Lindsay and Wolseley throughout the month of April, combined with his memorandum of April 25th, would have left the British military authorities in no doubt as to the road's state of readiness. Wolseley in his subsequent reports on the expedition was equally adamant that he had been told the road would be ready *by the end of May* (author's emphasis).[1] It is interesting to note as well that the condition of the road was already a talking point even before the first steamer of the season had arrived at Thunder Bay. As the *Algoma* sailed from Collingwood on May 3rd, it was reported in the *Globe* that the French-Canadian workers on board were singing a song that spoke of them giving their lives '*pour la patrie*'. The story went on, "the singers, it is hoped, will not die for their country, but live to complete the Dawson Road, the greater part of which, from all I can learn, has yet to be built."[2]

In late 1870 and early 1871 Blackwood's Magazine published in three instalments *Narrative of the Red River Expedition* by "An Officer of the Expeditionary Force." Just why he chose to style himself this way is not known, but everybody knew that the author was Wolseley. In it he was highly critical of the Canadian authorities over much of their handling of the expedition, including the non-completion of the Dawson Road to Lake Shebandowan. He was adamant that Ottawa had been clear that the road would be finished by the end of May, " ... whereas by that date not more than thirty miles of it were finished, and many miles were still uncut through the primeval forest."[3] He postulated the conspiracies that members of the Canadian Government were trying to trap the British troops into spending the winter at Fort Garry and, rather contradictorily, that the minister responsible for the Public Works Department, Hector-Louis Langevin, was trying to block the expedition altogether because of his sympathies with the French-speaking Louis Riel.[4] He stated categorically that the lack of a completed road " ... retarded our progress to an extent which had not been anticipated."[5] His memoirs written many years later, were almost as inflammatory and the message remained the same; the road had been promised and it was not ready. He was complimentary regarding Simon Dawson himself, describing him as " ... an able and hardworking public servant, who ... did all in his power to help forward the expedition."[6] However, he was extremely critical of Dawson's political masters and those working for him. "I often pitied him for his work was constant and the assistants sent to him by the Minister responsible for the department in the Canadian Cabinet were only too

1 It is in the *Narrative of the Red River Expedition*, published at the end of 1870 and in 1871 that we first read of Wolseley's assertion that the end of May was the promised date of the road's completion. The date is not mentioned in the expedition's official records.

2 From the Globe May 14, 1870. Quoted in Stanley, *Toil*, p96.

3 Wolseley, *Narrative Part 2*, p52.

4 Wolseley, *Narrative Part 2*, p52.

5 Wolseley, *Narrative Part 2*, p56.

6 Wolseley, *Soldier's Life*, p192.

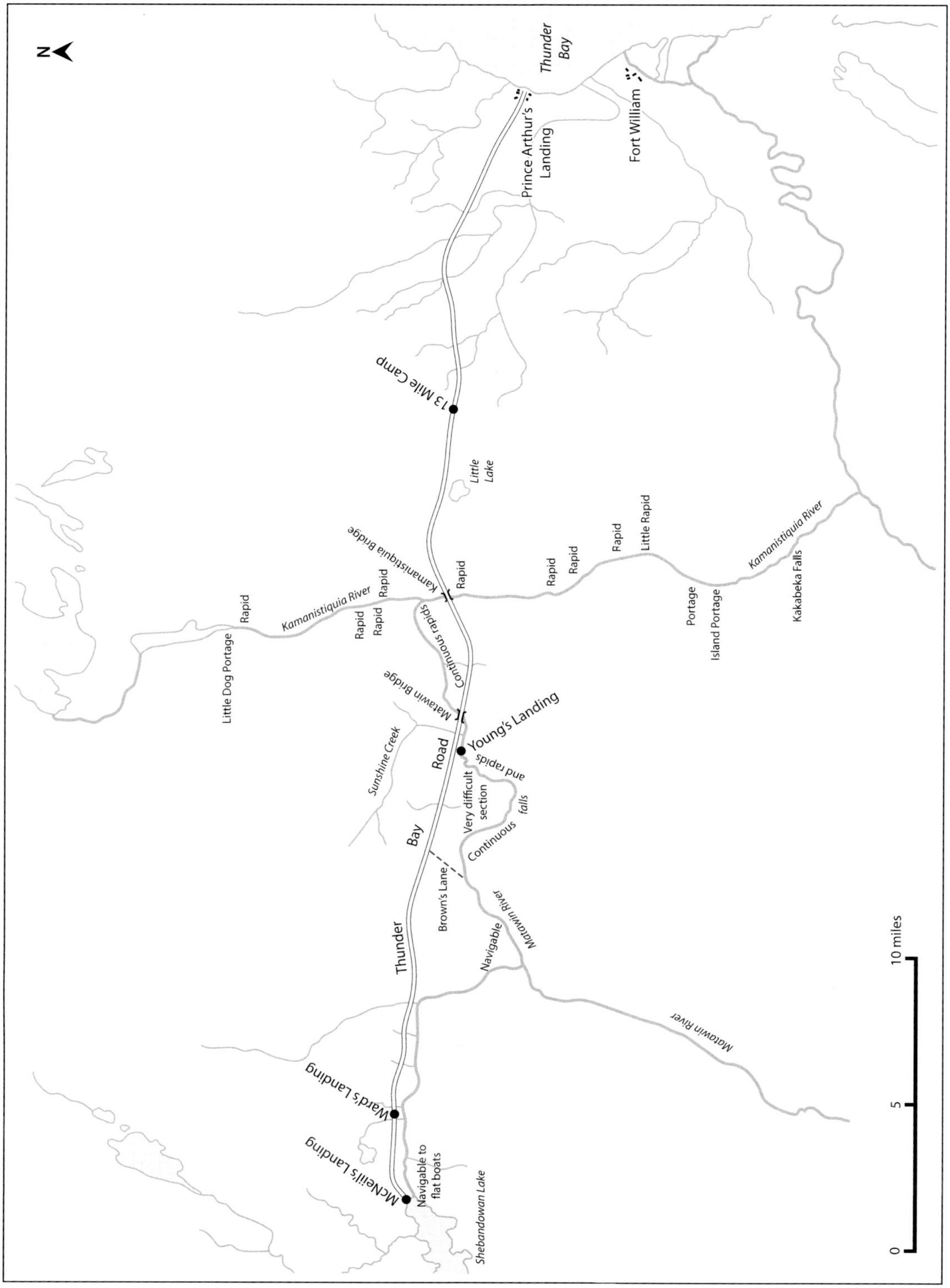

The road from Prince Arthur's Landing to Shebandowan Lake.

often drunkards or incapables."[7] In some cases he asserted that they were 'ne'er-do-well' friends of politicians. He cited one case where one of these 'loafers' admitted to having no actual job with the expedition, but " ... his uncle had merely given him his billet in order that he might be taken at Government expense to Manitoba, where he had a brother he wanted to join."[8] Contemporary British accounts generally mirror Wolseley's view of the road's overall state of readiness and the abilities of most of those involved in its construction, as do his later biographers, which of course just touch on the Red River Expedition as the first independent command of a man who rose to the top of his profession.[9]

In spite of the positive comments regarding Dawson personally, needless to say the Canadian Public Works Department official took grave exception to Wolseley's assessment of events in *Narrative of the Red River Expedition* and wrote a very detailed and tetchy response to all of the many points of criticism in the addenda to his report published in 1871.[10] Dawson's anger went so far as to minimize the impact of work by the troops on the road and he even tried to claim credit for Wolseley's policy of no alcohol. He wrote that it was already his policy regarding his own workers so they could not have been drunk as Wolseley had alleged, and it was in fact he who 'induced' the colonel to implement it for the rest of the expedition.[11] A letter was attached to the addenda adding that the only reason alcohol was not taken was due to the " ... difficulty in transporting so bulky and weighty an article ... along so difficult a line of march ... ."[12]

One could devote a great deal of space to the allegations made by both Wolseley and Dawson shortly after the fact regarding the state of the road, the best way to move men and equipment along it, and the impact of it not being completed, real or imagined, on the forward progress of the expedition. However, to understand Wolseley's views at the time the road was actually under construction, rather than a few months after the fact when he wrote *Narrative of the Red River Expedition,* it is necessary, first, to review the correspondence of the expeditionary force and, second, take note of the actions the colonel took in the face of the delays he was encountering. The expeditionary force's correspondence encapsulates Wolseley's perspective of events as they were unfolding, at least insofar as he was prepared to officially go 'on the record.' His actions at the time speak for themselves.

The day after his arrival at the newly named Prince Arthur's Landing, along with Lindsay Russell, the member of the Canadian Department of Public Works who had laboriously made his way to Thunder Bay during the previous winter, Wolseley set off up the Dawson Road to determine just how ready it was for the transportation of the force and its equipment. He identified a stretch with a bad gradient just a mile from the bay, but a new section that bypassed the troublesome hill was already under construction and the colonel stated that this was the " ... only really bad patch" in the 31 miles that the two men rode.[13] From Thunder Bay to where it crossed the Kaministiquia River, a distance he reckoned to be 23 miles rather than the 21 ½ miles it had been surveyed at, he described as 'very fair,' though the fire that had recently burned through had done a fair degree of damage. The bridge over the Kaministiquia was a 'very good one' of about 360 feet in length. From here to the next bridge over the Matawin River (about 5 miles further on) "the road is of a different character" and only wide enough for one waggon. Still, while it was rough in places, Wolseley believed it was passable for waggon traffic. For the next five or six miles the road was not good, but work was underway on it and in places it had been corduroyed.[14] Although it does not appear he personally conducted the reconnaissance along the final stretch, Wolseley reported that ox waggons currently could go to within four miles of where the boats could be launched, though a 'creek' (presumably the Oskondagee River) still required bridging. Most significantly for his initial view

7 Wolseley, *Soldier's Life*, p192.

8 Wolseley, *Soldier's Life*, p192.

9 Low says in April while in Ottawa, Wolseley had been promised the road would be ready for traffic by May 25. Low, *Wolseley*, p19.

10 PPP 559, Dawson, "Report", Addenda, pp43-57.

11 PPP 559, Dawson, "Report", Addenda, pp48/49.

12 PPP 559, Dawson, "Report", Addenda, p55.

13 PPP 568, Correspondence and Journal, May 27, 1870, No 17, Inclosure 2, Memorandum from Wolseley.

14 A corduroyed road is one where logs have been laid across it to create a road surface.

of how matters stood, he stated that "Altogether the road is better than I expected, although somewhat longer, for instead of being 40 it is certainly 45 or 46 miles long."[15]

To assist the road builders, most of whom would only have recently arrived on the *Algoma*, and whose numbers had been reduced by the need for those on *Chicora* to remain for a period of time at Sault Ste. Marie to work on the portage road improvements, Wolseley ordered two companies of the KRRC up to the Matawin Bridge.[16] A third was dispatched on June 2nd and on the 16th one of these three was pushed along to the Oskondagee Bridge.[17] As they arrived at Prince Arthur's Landing, other units were moved up the road to work on its construction as well. No doubt there were many grumblings among the troops, but one will have to speak for the multitude. "Nothing but work, work upon the roads ... the disappointment was great, and with some cause as the men would say: It was only as a volunteer that I left my abode, I never thought of coming here to work on a road."[18] By the time the expedition was finally ready to set out across Shebandowan Lake, 5,433 days of military labour, in addition to those of the labourers and *voyageurs*, had been provided to get the road to a suitable condition for the force's use.[19]

Wolseley conducted a second reconnaissance in company with Assistant-Controller Irvine beginning on June 6th. This time he rode further along and reported that the road seemed to end at 'Oskondigee Creek' [sic] which was still unbridged. He did not believe that the bridge construction would take long, though the lumber that had been prepared over the course of the winter and all of the large trees in the vicinity had been destroyed by the recent forest fire. For eight or nine miles prior to reaching the Oskondagee River the road was only a track that was impassable for loaded waggons in wet weather. Wolseley reported that men were working on it and he expected that it would be 'open for traffic' by June 25th. The two men camped on the banks of the Oskondagee, Wolseley writing that it was surveyed at 37 miles, but he believed it to be 'a good 40.' A satellite map today places it at 39. The colonel crossed the river by raft the following morning, but after about a mile it was no more than 'an execrable track'. Irvine continued for another 2 ½ to 3 miles and then had to turn back. The satellite map shows Ward's Landing, where the boats would eventually enter the Shebandowan River before navigating the last few miles onto Shebandowan Lake, as being 5 ½ miles beyond the Oskondagee Bridge.[20]

The next officer to survey the status of the road was Lieutenant-Colonel McNeill beginning on June 14th. He reported on the 16th that he had walked from the Oskondagee up to the dam site and then poled a canoe up five short rapids, 'tracked' up one more, and reached the area of the lake " ... to which the road will eventually be brought ... ." Of the 5½ miles from Oskondagee Bridge to the dam site, he reckoned that 4 miles had been cleared and a rough waggon road had been created.[21] This is a slight improvement over what Wolseley had found on his previous reconnaissance, though McNeill reported that after the four miles of rough track, nothing further had been done and from the dam site to the lake was three miles, which had not been touched either. He believed it would take 'a good week' to put the road from the Oskondagee to the dam site into good condition and, to make matters worse, on his return journey to Thunder Bay he noted that the heavy rains had badly damaged sections of the road. He noted two stretches, one two miles in length and the other a mile, where it was impassable.[22]

On June 21st Wolseley made yet another reconnaissance of the road, going as far as half way between the Oskondagee River and the dam site. He found the road between the Matawin and Oskondagee Rivers 'practically impassable for waggons'. A few bullock carts navigated the road daily, but it was not suitable for regular organized

15 PPP 568, Correspondence and Journal, May 27, 1870, No 17, Inclosure 2, Memorandum from Wolseley
16 PPP 568, Correspondence and Journal, May 27, 1870, No 17, Inclosure 2, Memorandum from Wolseley
17 PPP 568, Correspondence and Journal, June 29, 1870, No 18, Inclosure, Military Secretary W. M. Earle to Governor-General Sir John Young.
18 Harman, *26 Years*, p13.
19 PPP 568, Correspondence and Journal, July 16, 1870, No.21 Enclosure 2, Wolseley to the Military Secretary.
20 PPP 568, Correspondence and Journal, June 29, 1870, No. 18 Inclosure 1 Military Secretary W. M. Earle to Governor-General Sir John Young.
21 PPP 568, Correspondence and Journal, June 29, 1870, No. 18 Inclosure 1 Military Secretary W. M. Earle to Governor-General Sir John Young.
22 PPP 568, Correspondence and Journal, June 29, 1870, No. 18 Inclosure 1 Military Secretary W. M. Earle to Governor-General Sir John Young.

transport with ordinary loads. "There were several places that on horseback were only passed with difficulty." Beyond the Oskondagee the road was still not cut all the way through to the lake.[23]

One more assessment of the road was made this time on July 1st in company with Lieutenant-General Lindsay himself. There was still much to be done and Wolseley commented that "he [Lindsay] saw for himself... the hopeless condition which it was in, and as his horse struggled through the swamps between the Matawin and Oskondagee Rivers, he could well appreciate the difficulties of my position."[24]

After his first two journeys along the road, Wolseley's comments had been fairly optimistic. One senses his frustration beginning to set in by the time of his two later visits on June 21st and July 1st. When he wrote up his report on the latter two, they formed part of a longer memorandum to the Military Secretary in Montreal. This was on July 16th. Wolseley was clearly beginning to feel the mounting pressure due to the expedition having not yet gotten beyond Thunder Bay more than six weeks after its forward elements had arrived there. It was in this memorandum that he made his first allegations of delays caused by the failure of the Canadian Government to secure the lake steamers more expeditiously and the action by the Americans at Sault Ste. Marie. These have been dealt with in previous chapters, but the fact that they receive their first mention at this time, speaks volumes to the colonel's assertions having much more to do with the pressure he was beginning to feel with the progress of the Shebandowan Lake road rather than any real delays caused by these events on his departure from Toronto. However, regarding the road, while he certainly voiced his frustration – it was still three miles short of the lake and in places from Young's Landing (just beyond the Matawin Bridge) to the Oskondagee River was " ... still practically useless as a highway for constant and heavy traffic," – unlike his subsequent writing, he did not apportion blame.[25] In fact, his comments at the time were quite the opposite:

> I have no intention of imputing to anyone a want of zeal or energy in pushing it forward. Mr. Dawson, of the Public Work Department, as well as the engineers working under his orders, have been untiring in their exertions to get the road in a working order. He has had to contest with great difficulties. Fires have raged twice over considerable portions of it, consuming culverts and cribwork, retaining walls, and corduroy work. Heavy rains have swamped it at other times, carrying away bridges and rendering it impassable for days.[26]

Wolseley was well-aware of the weather conditions that were hampering the road's completion and, regarding the rain, wrote:

> I may here add that the rain seems to be the rule and fine weather the exception in this portion of Her Majesty's dominions. It rained upon 15 days in June and of the 16 days that are already passed in July it has rained upon eight of them. It pours at times in a manner I have seldom seen equalled even in the tropics.[27]

As a result, only the corduroyed portion could take continuous traffic, " ... for although they are rough and only suitable for slow draught, still they are passable in all weather."[28]

On June 3rd the first four boats were transported up the road, a feat achieved by detaching the wheels from the waggons and then joining them together with longer sturdy timbers, " ... so as to leave the fore and hind wheels some distance apart."[29]

23 PPP 568, Correspondence and Journal, July 16, 1870. No.21 Enclosure 2 Wolseley to the Military Secretary.
24 PPP 568, Correspondence and Journal, July 16, 1870. No.21 Enclosure 2 Wolseley to the Military Secretary.
25 PPP 568, Correspondence and Journal, July 16, 1870. No.21 Enclosure 2 Wolseley to the Military Secretary.
26 PPP 568, Correspondence and Journal, July 16, 1870. No.21 Enclosure 2 Wolseley to the Military Secretary.
27 PPP 568, Correspondence and Journal, July 16, 1870. No.21 Enclosure 2 Wolseley to the Military Secretary.
28 PPP 568, Correspondence and Journal, July 16, 1870. No.21 Enclosure 2 Wolseley to the Military Secretary.
29 Huyshe, *Red River*, p59.

The expeditionary force camp at Matawin Bridge. (*Illustrated London News*, 1871-1028-0008-F)

A platform was then constructed with the boats hoisted aboard keel up. Given that Dawson had overseen the construction of the boats and provided the waggons, the need to reconstruct the latter in this manner seems to be something of an oversight. Nevertheless, the boats were launched just above the Matawin Bridge and moored midstream to prevent their loss should a forest fire again sweep through the area. This was fortuitous as there was another fire in which hay stores and the dwellings of some of the road workers were lost. The boats, anchored far enough from the river's edge, were undamaged. It had taken three days to get the boats to their destination and the waggons back to Thunder Bay and, in spite of the road conditions, 28 boats were moved in this manner in fairly short order. In Dawson's view this method of transportation was working 'admirably'. [30]

Wolseley's actions show his view was somewhat different and, regardless of what he would write in his memorandum of July 16th, almost six weeks earlier he was already losing patience with the lack of progress being made on completing the road. It should be noted that this is before even his second road reconnaissance, for which his official comments were not particularly unfavourable.

In the opinion of the expedition commander, the road was simply not suitable for carrying heavy loads due to its 'incompleteness' and the heavy rain that was washing parts of it away and churning large sections into a muddy morass. These conditions meant that the waggons could carry loads of only 1000 pounds and the horses were starting to suffer as well. Captain Huyshe reported as many as 35% of the 150 animals fell ill due to careless driving by the waggoneers, ill-fitting harnesses and the overall severity of the work on the difficult road.[31] Wolseley and some of his staff seriously questioned the abilities of many of the teamsters hired by Dawson; another issue for the Public Works Department man to take exception to in his later report.

Wolseley determined that the solution was to lighten the load of the waggons on the road and try moving the boats from Thunder Bay to the Matawin Bridge using the Kaministiquia River. Dawson was adamant that the

30 PPP 559, Dawson, "Report", p17.

31 Huyshe, *Red River*, p66.

The arrival of troops at the Matawin Bridge. (Library and Archives Canada, Acc. No. R9266-3428)

river's many rapids made it unsuitable for such a purpose. Wolseley, however, consulted with the HBC officer at Fort William and he advised that it was feasible.[32] The movement of the boats in this manner began as an 'experiment,' and, despite Dawson's opposition, the force commander, " ... doubting the possibility of the road being finished in sufficient time to fulfil our requirements ... considered it worth while [sic] to risk a few men and boats in determining the point."[33] Every boat that could be transported in this manner meant another waggon that could be used for the transport of stores.[34] This was the real beginning of the rift with Simon Dawson.

Captain Young, with a company of the 60th Rifles and a force of *voyageurs*, was given the task of getting the boats moving up river. They started on June 4th with six boats and over the next seven days with grit and determination, and no doubt bloody mindedness, succeeded in hauling the craft up the river. It was no insignificant feat as Sam Steele of the Ontario Rifles reported:

> From the mouth of the Kaminsitiquia to the Matawin bridge are 12 miles of quiet water and 33 miles of rapids, with now and then short navigable sections. Boulders of all shapes and sizes and sharp rocks set on edge were encountered along that part of the stream, which could be traversed with little or no risk to men, but which was very dangerous for boats. Great care had to be taken to prevent damage to keels and bottoms, and the labour of getting the boats safely over the portages and tracking up the stream was exceedingly trying.[35]

When Young and his party set out, the rain was falling heavily and the river, fed by many smaller streams, was becoming a torrent. In one night its level rose by six feet. Seven new portage roads were constructed including one

32 PPP 568, Correspondence and Journal, op. cit., July 16, 1870. No.21 Enclosure 2 Wolseley to the Military Secretary.
33 PPP 568, Correspondence and Journal, op. cit., July 16, 1870. No.21 Enclosure 2 Wolseley to the Military Secretary.
34 Huyshe, *Red River*, p66.
35 Steele, *Forty Years*, p16.

a mile long at the more than 130 foot high Kakabeka Falls. The boats had to be dragged over the portages using skids laid across the road at intervals of a few feet with the man at the bow having to lift it over any obstacles in its path. "This was hard work, but drawing the boats across was mere child's play compared to the labour of carrying the stores and tracking or poling up the torrent."[36]

It took seven days for Young and his party to make it as far the Matawin Bridge and they arrived on June 12th. "The men had been almost constantly wet through – drenched to the skin by rain, and wading up to their waists in the river. They had also suffered severely from flies ... ."[37] Young was told that it was not possible to continue beyond the Matawin Bridge and the *voyageurs* returned from here back to Thunder Bay. The following day, however, he decided to press on with one boat, but found a rough and rocky route that he was unable to navigate. The perpendicular sides of a steep gorge meant that a portage road could not be constructed. With this intelligence, according to the official correspondence of the expedition, Wolseley decided to collect the boats at the Matawin Bridge and then transport them by road to a point on the river five miles below the dam site.[38] By June 19th 50 boats had reached the Matawin Bridge. Ten more were to commence the journey that day with twelve more following shortly afterwards.[39]

Unsurprisingly, Simon Dawson's opinion on the movement of the boats by this method did not concur with that of Colonel Wolseley. In his mind the road as far as the Matawin Bridge was suitable and he could not understand why a seven day one way 45 mile river journey, with the resulting damage he claimed that was being inflicted on the boats, was preferable to a three day road roundtrip to the same destination. Dawson believed that if there were insufficient waggons, then Wolseley should order more.[40] As to the advice received by Wolseley on the navigability of the Kaministiquia River, Dawson referred to this as coming from " ... inexperienced persons, who, although living in the vicinity, had never been over the country through which the road passes, or had ever so much as seen Shebandowan Lake ... ."[41] Despite his opposition to hauling the boats up the Kaministiquia, Dawson would later write " ... that there was nothing for it but the river. I sent *voyageurs* to improve the portages, and endeavoured to organize some system by which the boats might be in as far as possible saved from damage." By the time all was said and done, a total of 101 boats were hauled, manoeuvered and manhandled up the Kaministiquia River.[42]

Nevertheless, in spite of his compliance, his perspective had not changed. Dawson strongly opined that, not only did the backbreaking effort of moving the boats up the river cause a number of his men to quit, but also:

> ... I was deprived of the services ... of about five hundred of the very best of the voyageurs, who were relied upon for work on the road, but were put instead to the profitless ... heart-breaking task of dragging the boats up the river. Had these men been left at road work, I have no hesitation in saying that a great deal of time would have been saved in the progress of the Expedition.[43]

This was a point of view with which Wolseley did not agree and, as the road inched closer to Shebandowan Lake, his lack of confidence in its ability to meet his needs continued. However, he also saw parts of the river as presenting problems and cast his gaze on a stretch between the Matawin and Oskondagee Bridges. He had Captain Young establish a supply post approximately two miles upstream from the Matawin Bridge where the river and the road came together. This would come to be called Young's Landing. Approximately four miles

36 Steele, *Forty Years*, pp17/18.
37 Huyshe, *Red River*, p69.
38 PPP 568, Correspondence and Journal, June 29, 1870, No 18, Inclosure, Military Secretary W. M. Earle to Governor-General Sir John Young.
39 PPP 568, Correspondence and Journal, June 29, 1870, No 18, Inclosure, Military Secretary W. M. Earle to Governor-General Sir John Young.
40 PPP 559, Dawson, "Report", p18.
41 PPP 559, Dawson, "Report", p40.
42 PPP 559, Dawson, "Report", pp18/19. Dawson put the poor fitness of the horses down to their military rations rather than the poor handling, badly fitting harnesses and overwork that Captain Huyshe alleged.
43 PPP 559, Dawson, "Report", Addenda, p53.

further along the road was Brown's Corner and Wolseley had Dawson's men cut a track from here down to the river to create another landing place. This would be called Calderon's Landing after Captain Calderon of the 60th Rifles. Between Young's and Calderon's Landings was the stretch of river which Captain Young had deemed to be unnavigable after he had arrived at the Matawin Bridge with the first batch of boats on June 12th.[44] The colonel's idea was that supplies would be taken from the depot at Young's Landing, transported by way of the Dawson Road, and then the new track, to Calderon's Landing. From here they would be moved further up the river by boat. Inevitably Dawson saw the building of the track from Brown's Corner and the creation of Calderon's Landing as so much wasted effort. His view remained that the road was the better route, although Huyshe reported there were many places that were virtually impassable, describing it as a 'so-called "road"'.[45]

To add even more complexity to this matter, it appears that Young's unnavigable section of the river was in fact put to use under Dawson's direction. The Public Works Department man mentions this almost in passing, saying that, after he took over the job of 'tediously' dragging the boats " ... over the rocks of the Kaministaquia [sic] and Matawin Rivers," 120 of his men were occupied for the better part of a month moving the boats up to the Oskondagee River.[46] An account has been provided in greater detail by Sam Steele who explained that Dawson called upon the local knowledge of a Scots resident of Fort William by the name of Donald McKellar. McKellar selected " ... ten Fort William Indians, ten Iroquois, and ten Sault St.[sic] Marie Indians."[47] McKellar set out from Young's Landing with three boats, ten men in each boat, and successfully navigated the gorge that Young had found to be impassable.

From Calderon's Landing the river was navigable for 'lightly laden boats', but it was hard going with a swift flowing current, " ... the men having to track along the high rocks sometimes poling or wading the swift and shallow water up to the armpits."[48] Once beyond the Oskondagee Bridge, the river was too difficult and the boats would have to be transported the last four miles to Ward's Landing by road. From Ward's Landing they travelled the last three miles to Shebandowan Lake, and the starting point for the expedition, by river.

Wolseley made no mention of McKellar and his men in either the official correspondence or in his later *Narrative of the Red River Expedition*. Whether this possibly resulted from 'jealously or annoyance' on Wolseley's part, as one prominent historian speculated in the 1980s, is impossible to say.[49] Captain Huyshe, who goes into some detail in explaining the transportation methods on this stretch of river, makes no mention of it either.[50] Even Dawson, who like Wolseley did not shy away from sharing an opinion, does not go into any great detail and does not mention McKellar by name either. Perhaps it is simply best to conclude that beyond the Matawin Bridge, the boats were sent partly by road and partly by river.[51]

By the middle of July, nearly two months after Wolseley had left Toronto, the boats and the supplies had all been moved to the Shebandowan Lake end of the Dawson Road. Here Lieutenant-Colonel McNeill had been overseeing their organization and stockpiling, along with the construction of a small wharf on the lake. On July 13th Wolseley moved his headquarters from the Matawin Bridge to Ward's Landing. The expedition was finally about to get properly underway.

It remains only to assess the debate on the contentious issue of the road. Unquestionably its lack of readiness delayed Wolseley's ability to get the expeditionary force on the move at an earlier date, but was anybody at fault for this? Dawson certainly over promised in January and then spent the next few months drawing back from a May 1st completion date. It is easy to have sympathy with him. His role of builder of the eastern end of the settler

44 Huyshe, *Red River*, p74.
45 PPP 559, Dawson, "Report", p24 and Huyshe, *Red River*, p91.
46 PPP 559, Dawson, "Report", pp 20/21.
47 Steele, *Forty Years*, p19.
48 Steele, *Forty Years*, p16.
49 Stanley, *Toil*, pp125/126.
50 Huyshe, *Red River*, p74.
51 Butler, *Annals*, p269.

The camp of the expeditionary force near Shebandowan Lake. (*Illustrated London News*, 1871-1028-0005-F)

road to the nascent Canadian West was overnight transformed into a demand from the Canadian Government to complete the road without delay. This transition occurred in the midst of winter when the isolation of the Thunder Bay region meant communication was essentially closed down. Dawson was clearly highly competent and a great deal, probably too much, had landed on his plate once the Canadian authorities came to realize the seriousness of the problem confronting their plans to take over the HBC lands. The Public Works Department man accomplished the vast majority of his tasks with great skill, though it is difficult to comprehend why he initially took such an optimistic view of the road's completion date. He also appears to have been prone to defensiveness when challenged. We do not have a record of Dawson's thoughts during the expedition itself. The addenda to his report was written the following year in response to Wolseley's comments in *Narrative of the Red River Expedition*. However, if it is an accurate representation of his views during the time of the expedition itself, rather than an angry retort to Wolseley's article, it would appear that he and the force commander were frequently at loggerheads. It should be noted that Colonel Wolseley never alleged this. The force commander had a job to do and was under great pressure, but in his addenda Dawson depicts himself as being less than supportive as the weeks dragged on with the road unfinished and the expedition commander searching for solutions to get his force moving. Ultimately he did as Wolseley instructed, but apparently grudgingly; always seemingly carrying the view that he was right and the colonel wrong. The motivation behind Wolseley's inflammatory comments in *Narrative of the Red River Expedition* will be considered shortly. However, Dawson's rejoinder to the criticisms leveled by Wolseley towards his department and his political masters, though not to him personally, went too far. Without question, Wolseley's three instalment article was a provocation, but the Public Works Department man's reply was over the top and he comes across as overly sensitive, petulant and whinging.

As for Wolseley, he clearly knew the road would not be ready before he arrived, but likely did not realize just how much work was required. Matters were not helped by the delay of some of the road's workforce at Sault Ste. Marie, though forest fires and torrential rains appear to have been the cause of the worst of the problems.

Given his propensity to over promise, it is possible that during the April meetings Dawson conceded a late May completion. There is nothing in the expeditionary force's documents to state this with certainty, though in his writings after the expedition's return, Wolseley certainly maintained that it was the case. And who knows, if not for the fires and rains at Thunder Bay, perhaps late May would have been a realistic completion date.

On his first two reconnaissances, Wolseley seemed quite optimistic regarding the road's progress and there is no talk of missed promises by Dawson. Even once the pressure began to build on him and he started to justify the reasons for his lack of movement towards Fort Garry, his ire was directed at the Canadian Government for the perceived delay over the lake steamers and the American Government for its actions at the Sault canal. While the road is certainly mentioned as a delaying factor, it is not the fault of Dawson or his men, rather it is external factors which seem to be conspiring against the expedition. However, as the work on the road's completion progressed, a fundamental difference of opinion developed between the two men. Dawson recognized that ongoing work was necessary to construct and improve the road, but saw it as essentially usable while construction carried on. If transport was limited due to a lack of waggons and horses, then the goal should be to get more waggons and horses. Wolseley had, however, drawn a different conclusion. He had decided that the road could not by itself meet the needs of the expedition. Progress was being made too slowly to put it in a usable condition. The road was simply not going to be able to withstand the impact of the heavy traffic travelling on it. In all likelihood, Wolseley's view was the more accurate; the road was simply not getting the job done. Given the wide variance of the views between the two men, there was never going to be a meeting of the minds.

What truly converts the delay on the road into the controversial topic that it became, though, is Wolseley's *Narrative of the Red River Expedition*, published at the end of 1870 and the beginning of 1871. What possessed Wolseley to write such an inflammatory document is difficult to say. After all, the pressure was off. He had completed the task of getting his command to Fort Garry and returning with the British component before the winter set in. He had made his name. Perhaps it was hubris in the aftermath of his success. Perhaps he had been frustrated by Dawson's contrary views during the road construction and believed it was time to set the record straight. Perhaps he was trying to cement his reputation by overstating the odds it had been necessary to overcome to accomplish his mission. Whatever the colonel's motivation, Dawson, who had not yet completed his report on the expedition, responded with broadsides. Whether Wolseley ever became aware of the hornets' nest that he had stirred up is unknown. It is, however, doubtful. After all, following his success at Red River he was 'the coming man.' He was now looking ahead to new projects, not behind to consider feathers he might have ruffled on the road to Shebandowan Lake.

16

Shebandowan Lake to Fort Frances

After all of the problems and delays with the road, the day of departure was finally in sight. Lieutenant-Colonel McNeill had been working tirelessly on the organization of men, boats and supplies at the lake and had overseen the construction of a wharf at the place of departure, which had been named McNeill's Bay. However, another controversy had arisen. Colonel Wolseley and his staff were dissatisfied with the quality of the *voyageurs* hired by the Canadian Public Works Department. The British found that many had little in the way of boating skills. "The object of having voyageurs was not to pull an oar, a duty which the soldiers were quite competent to perform, but to take the management of the boats in rapid water, and to instruct the soldiers."[1] The original intent was to have three of Dawson's men in each boat, although, given the volume of equipment and stores to be carried, each of the boat brigades was increased from five to six boats with two *voyageurs* in each, plus one pilot for the brigade as a whole.[2] Many were rejected before departure and Wolseley gave orders that any who demonstrated a lack of skill during the journey were to be put ashore at the first portage. This was merely one more issue for Dawson to take umbrage with in his post-expedition report.[3]

Such criticisms were not, however, levelled at the Iroquois boatmen. Their leader 'old Ignace', " ... was a fine old fellow, one of Nature's noblemen; most dignified, quiet, and gentlemanly, and a splendid man to steer a boat down a rapid. He had been one of Sir George Simpson's men ... .His men obeyed him readily, and when any little thing was wanted from them, a word from Ignace was sufficient."[4] It was Ignace's men who moved the boats and supplies from Ward's Landing to McNeill's Bay, a difficult stretch of river only three miles long but containing no fewer than six rapids.

Between July 5th and 10th, the men of the expeditionary force were still spread out all the way back to Prince Arthur's Landing with units working on the road, taking boats up the river to the Matawin Bridge, or transporting stores either to Young's Landing or from Calderon's Landing to Ward's Landing.[5] Wolseley was determined that the expeditionary force would set off on July 16th. However, in the days leading up to the planned departure a strong westerly wind continued to blow off Shebandowan Lake " ... so that upon some days such a sea came rolling in and breaking upon the shore that it was impossible to load boats, or to get them off had we even succeeded in equipping them."[6] Then on the night of July 15th the most violent thunderstorm of the entire expedition blew in and the rain during the night came down in 'sheets of water'. On the 16th it was fine and sunny, but again with a strong westerly wind and a heavy surf breaking on the beach at McNeill's Bay.

As difficult as the conditions were, once the lake calmed sufficiently, a mad scramble began to ensure that the boats were ready to leave.

---

1 Huyshe, *Red River*, p95.

2 PPP 559, Dawson, "Report", pp23/24

3 PPP 559, Dawson, "Report", p6 & Addenda p48.

4 Huyshe, *Red River*, p96. Ignace was certainly an experienced boatman. Sir George Simpson had been the HBC's governor-in-chief in North America. He had died in 1860.

5 Huyshe, *Red* River, p92

6 Wolseley, *Narrative Part 2*, p62.

> Officers and non-commissioned officers were running about in all directions, some searching for oars, others missing sails, etc. Here a sergeant came to say the spare rowlocks issued his boat would not fit; another reported that although he had been given a lamp, he had not received any oil for it, – and so on; staff officers running about in all directions, endeavouring to rectify mistakes and smooth down difficulties.[7]

Wolseley commented that such a scene must have looked like 'pandemonium' to a civilian.

It was late in the day before all final repairs had been made and all equipment, together with sixty days of supplies, stowed aboard. The rations were stored in barrels or half barrels. Salted pork half barrels weighed in at 200 lbs, flour barrels 120 lbs, and biscuit barrels at 100 lbs.[8] Captain Willoughby Wallace, in command of G Brigade which would depart on July 19th, noted the total cargo of the seven boats in his brigade amounted to:

> 40 barrels of biscuit, 42 barrels of flour, 50 barrels of pork, 7 barrels of sugar, 7 cans of tea, 13 sacks of beans, 8 boxes of preserved potatoes, 9 tins of pepper, 19 axes, 11 picks, 22 hatchets, 13 kettles, 1 oven, 18 frying pans, 13 shovels, 13 spades, 11 tents, 7 tins of mosquito oil, 13 boxes of medical comforts, boxes containing our rifles, and 6000 rounds of ammunition.[9]

The total cargo in each boat weighed in at three to four thousand pounds.[10]

The day was wearing on, but Wolseley was determined that a start would be made no matter how late the hour. "It was an evening of surpassing loveliness; the wind, which had been blowing fresh all day from the west, had gone down and the lake lay calm and smooth as a mirror ... ."[11] Three brigades, A, B, and C comprising seventeen boats, were launched and, despite the lateness of the day, the men were delighted to be finally getting underway. They carried Colonel Feilden, the battalion commander, two companies of the KRRC under Captains Young and Ward, together with the force's Royal Artillery and Royal Engineer components under Lieutenants Alleyne and Heneage, the former later described by Wolseley as " ... the best artillery officer then in Canada ... [and] one of the best men I have ever known in the Army."[12]

Typically there was a captain in command of each brigade and he was found in the lead boat. An ensign commanded the centre boat and a lieutenant the last. NCOs were spread through the other boats of the brigade.[13] D and E Brigades followed on July 17th, F on the 18th and G on the 19th. Wednesday July 20th was cloudy with drizzling rain in the morning. This turned to heavy showers and thunder in the afternoon with an onshore gale. As a result it was quite impossible to load the boats and no brigades were launched, though there was a shortage of rowlocks that would have prevented the departure of more than a few boats in any case.[14]

The lack of rowlocks was proving to be a problem. They had been expected on the *Algoma*, but had not arrived. "Mr. Dawson says they will certainly come by *Chicora*, which is expected at Prince Arthur's Landing on Sunday [July 24th] morning."[15] In the meantime Wolseley set all of Dawson's carpenters to work making thole pins. Not only would this solve the problem of the missing rowlocks, but it was also felt that, being made of wood, they would be easier to replace if they broke after the force had set off on its journey.[16]

---

7 Wolseley, *Narrative Part 2*,pp62/63.

8 Huyshe, *Red River*, p106.

9 HA, 170A12W/D/0438, Wallace, "Rebellion", p9.

10 Harman, *26 Years*, p18.

11 Huyshe, *Red River*, p99.

12 Wolseley, *Soldier's Life*, p175. For those looking for greater deal on the composition of the expeditionary force's boat brigades, please see appendix two. It should be noted that there is very little information available on the composition of the brigades of the Quebec Rifles, or indeed documentation of their journey to the Red River Settlement.

13 PPP 570, Harman, *26 Years*. p18.

14 PPP 568 Correspondence and Journal, Appendix, p79.

15 PPP 568 Correspondence and Journal, Appendix, p80.

16 A rowlock is the pivoting bracket that is set into the top of a boat's gunwale, anchors the oar and acts as a fulcrum when the boat is being rowed. A tholepin is an alternative to the rowlock. It is a wooden pin also set in the gunwale that also acts as a fulcrum for the rowing of a boat.

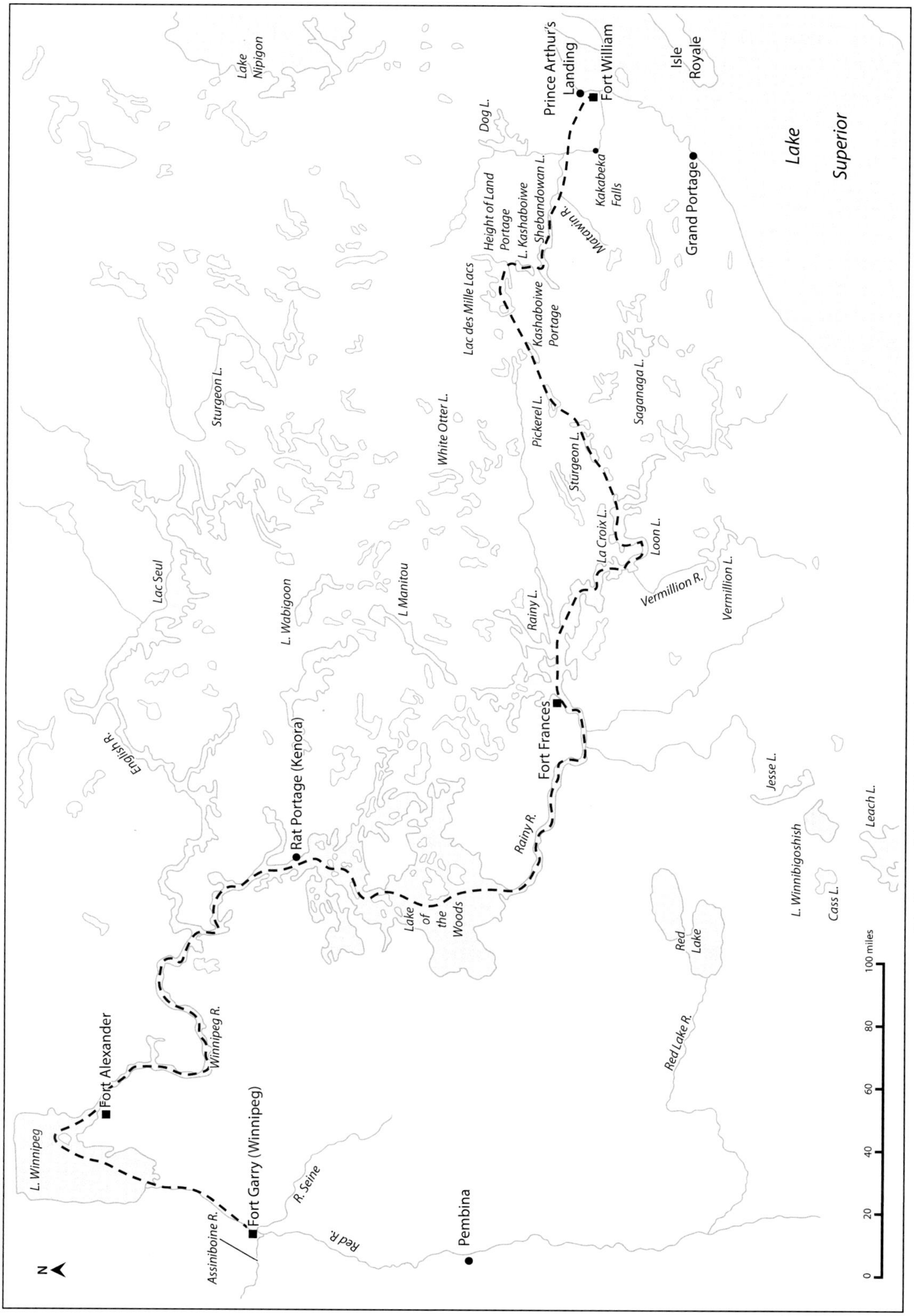

The Route of the Red River Expeditionary Force from Thunder Bay to Fort Garry.

The first of the Ontario Rifles in H Brigade and the Headquarters staff in I Brigade set out on the 21st, the Ontario men in boats named *Leaky Sallie*, *Shoo Fly*, *Dreadnought*, *Fanny Latimer*, *Fairy Belle*, and *D.A.K.*, named after Lieutenant D.A.K. Macdonald of No. 7 Company.[17] The naming of the boats was common throughout the expedition. Sam Steele travelled in the *Flying Dutchman*, replaced at Fort Frances by a lighter boat which they named *The Girl of the Period,* and James Macleod in *La Belle Manitoba*.[18] Behind the Ontario battalion came the 2nd Quebec Rifles and by August 2nd all twenty-one brigades of the expedition were on the way. Wolseley, accompanied by Assistant-Controller Irvine had set off by canoe on July 23rd, the same day as M and N Brigades of the 1st Ontario Rifles. By the time of McNeill's departure, after all of the 2nd Quebec Rifles had embarked, the forward units of the expeditionary force were 150 miles ahead.

Despite Dawson's views regarding bringing the boats up the Kaministiquia River, many of the troops had gained invaluable experience in their handling as a consequence. Nevertheless, rowing the boats was going to be difficult due to the weight and space taken up by the cargo. In the early stages they were so laden down with supplies that there was " ... no space whatever for the men's feet on the floor, they, therefore, had to stretch them out on the top of the load, and make footholds as best they could."[19]

A number of the expedition's members left written records, although, given their staggered departures, they frequently had different experiences at the various points they described along the way. For example, it may have been raining at a particular portage or stormy on a stretch of lake for one writer, and sunny and calm at the same location for another. One common theme, though, is how easy it was to lose one's way along the journey. Observing a general physical map of the region through which the expedition was travelling makes this readily apparent. It is a labyrinth of lakes and rivers and, while the route to be taken had been mapped out, there were still a multitude of channels where it was easy to become lost. "It is most disheartening for the men to find, when they get to the end of one of these bays, that they have come eight or ten miles out of the way and have all that distance to row back again."[20] One can only imagine the annoyance if they found that another member of their own brigade had failed to relay to them intelligence as to the correct route, as in the case of Captain Redvers Buller in the lead boat of E Brigade.

> Noticing one night that the water ahead – which shone clear in the moonlight – was dead calm for some miles, while rippled water could be seen through an opening between the island, he [Buller] instantly judged that the latter must be the true course, and turning sharp to the right gained the proper channel, while every other boat's crew, accompanied by a less competent guide, going straight on, found itself headed off by the shore and had a five mile row round shore.[21]

When Wolseley caught up with the forward elements of the expeditionary force, it was decided that he would travel ahead wherever possible and make axe cuts into trees clearly visible so as to mark out the route to those following.[22]

Mention has already been made regarding Wolseley's opinion of the quality of some of the *voyageurs*, but it was now the lack of availability of guides that drew his ire. According to the *Annals of the King's Royal Rifle Corps*, Shebandowan Lake was " ... a beautiful sheet of water, comparatively narrow, but about 20 miles in length ... ."[23] In fact it is a series of three lakes and Captain Huyshe, travelling by canoe without a guide, lost his way twice. The expeditionary force commander would write that "we had been promised an ample supply of guides, but only very few were forthcoming when required. The officer representing the Canadian Government ... , whose duty it was to have furnished them, found at the last minute that the Indians he had depended upon to act in this capacity

17 Sissons, *Kerr*, p32.
18 Steele, *Forty Years*, p24.
19 PPP 570, Harman, *26 Years*, p19.
20 Huyshe, *Red River*, p126.
21 Lewis William George Butler, *Sir Redvers Buller*, (Delhi: Facsimile Publisher, 2013, First published 1909), p22.
22 Huyshe, *Red River*, p127
23 Butler, *Annals*, pp270/271.

held back, and refused the 'job' upon all sorts of excuses."[24] Dawson put this down to a number of them quitting because " ... the work of dragging boats [up the river] had become so distasteful to them ... ," though he still felt there were sufficient numbers.[25]

When on June 17th Buller's brigade was forced to set off without *voyageurs* or guides, Wolseley sent a note to Dawson, who was away overseeing work on the portages. "This is only the second day of the operation," wrote Wolseley, "and yet neither [*voyageurs* nor guides] are ready."[26] It transpired that the Iroquois did not feel they were required to work on a Sunday, a state of affairs resolved when adjustments to their rates of pay were made. Dawson sought to excuse himself in his report by claiming that there were plenty of men involved in dragging boats or moving stores up the river "within easy reach of Shebandowan Lake ... ."[27] Was he implying that Wolseley should have sought out these men himself, or was it a dig at Wolseley due to their disagreement on the manner in which the boats were transported to Shebandowan Lake? Dawson added that there was no difficulty reaching the Height of Land Portage without a map, though as we have seen, Huyshe lost his way twice on Shebandowan Lake.

It is hard to defend Dawson in this particular matter. Despite his protestations, there is really no way around the conclusion that there was an oversight on his part. He may simply have had too much on his plate, but it was his responsibility to ensure there were sufficient guides and *voyageurs* available when and where they were needed. There is no escaping the fact that Dawson failed in this regard during the early stages of the expedition's departure. But it was also the competence of those guides that were available that was called into question and Dawson admitted as much in his report when he wrote, that " ... even among the Indians, there were few really well acquainted with the route. It had been long abandoned as a line of traffic ... ."[28] He would have gotten no argument on this point from Captain Wallace when he listed the men under his command in G Brigade as five officers, fifty-eight men, fourteen voyageurs, " ... and a guide, who did not know the way ... ."[29]

At the end of Shebandowan Lake is Kashabowie[30] Lake which drains into Shebandowan and is 29 feet higher. When Captain Huyshe arrived at the portage, there was a backlog of the three lead brigades. As we have seen, these included the artillery component of the force with their two brass 7-pounder guns and ammunition " ... which occupied much time in portaging."[31] Wolseley had intentionally increased the weight of firepower in the force's forward elements to project an impression of power. He did not yet know that the work carried out by Weymss Simpson had removed any threat of First Nations opposition to the expedition as it transited through their lands. He was also concerned that word of their progress would make its way to Red River, with the possibility that he might encounter Métis opposition along the way. The colonel wanted there to be no doubt that the expedition was a military force to be reckoned with.

The Kashabowie Portage was about 1500 yards long. Dawson's men had done some preliminary work, but it was expected that each brigade passing through would make improvements. This included felling trees to be used as skids to drag the boats over to the next river or lake. The work was carried out by the troops and *voyageurs*, and when the latter knew their business, it was noted that "it is perfectly astonishing to see the way in which trees of large dimensions fall before the axe of the backwoodsman; they appear to be swept away like corn before the reaper; anything under 18 inches in diameter stands but a very few blows from the heavy chopping-axe."[32] Invariably, the first-hand accounts left by the officers and men of the expedition speak of the extreme physicality of the work at the portages. Hauling the boats and supplies required backbreaking effort, though Captain McCalmont would write that " ... the navigation along the waterways joining the various lakes ... proved to be considerably easier than

24 Wolseley, *Narrative Part 2*, p65.
25 PPP 559, Dawson, "Report", p20.
26 PPP 559, Dawson, "Report", pp24/25.
27 PPP 559, Dawson, "Report", p25.
28 PPP 559, Dawson, "Report", p25.
29 Wallace, *Rebellion*, p9.
30 Spelled 'Kashaboiwe' in contemporary writings,
31 Huyshe, *Red River*, p105.
32 Huyshe, *Red River*, p129.

Troops crossing a portage. (*Illustrated London News*, ILNO-1871-1028-0008-F)

it had been between Lake Superior and Lake Shebandawan [sic]"[33] The cavalryman, who had inveigled himself onto the expedition, had been involved in bringing the boats up the Kaministiquia.

Ideally the portage road was 8 to 12 feet wide and the best trees for use as rollers were American Poplars. When wet, the bark acted as a lubricant and the boats could be dragged as if they were on 'greased rollers'.[34] When the grade was particularly steep, pegs were hammered into the rocky ground so that the rollers did not slide backwards. However, as necessary as the rollers were for moving the boats, they were a hindrance to the men toiling with their heavy loads of supplies across the uneven and frequently steep ground of the portage. A plan to remove the rollers while the carrying was underway and then to re-lay them once the work was done was discarded as being too time consuming.[35]

Despite sometimes having to wait in line for access to the portage while those ahead of them manhandled their boats and stores across, the troops were under orders not to pass the brigade ahead of them. Once the way was clear, the officers and men working side by side, immediately began the laborious task of getting the supplies across. Each boat crew was responsible for its own cargo and everybody had to do his fair share. However, one soldier, John Kerr, did find a way to avoid the toil. When the cook in his boat was found to be unsatisfactory, Kerr agreed to assume his duties, but only on the condition that he was allowed to relinquish his share of carrying.

33 Callwell, *McCalmont*, p50.

34 Huyshe, *Red River*, p110.

35 PPP 570, Harman, *26 Years*, p19.

It seems he considered this a fair bargain despite his new work meaning that he had to be up and working well before reveille in order to prepare the breakfast.[36]

There are stories of men carrying loads of 300 to 400 pounds and making as many as ten trips depending on the length and the difficulty of the portage.[37] One officer recorded:

> I myself have carried from 200 to 250 lbs. An Indian can carry 300 to 400 lbs; and this, remember, not only on a level, or merely for a yard or two, but over rocky, hilly, and slippery ground, and for distances of up to 2000 yards; each man having to make from four to five journeys over every portage, and sometimes encountering six or seven portages a day.[38]

These are certainly heavy weights, but one force member later urged caution against unquestioning acceptance of exaggerated claims.

> Some authentic stories are told of the heavy packs carried occasionally by a strong man over a portage, but most of the stories related should be taken with a grain of salt. Harness a 200-lb. barrel of pork, or an arm[s] chest of the same weight, to a man's back and forehead with a tump strap, [and this] ... leaves little room to add to the burden. This, too, over rough ground, with climbing and mudholes en route.[39]

Perhaps a more realistic record is provided by Captain Buller. Writing in a private letter, and comparing the Kashabowie Portage with later experiences on the Winnipeg River, he said:

> The portage was about three-quarters of a mile long. Over it we had to carry on our backs all our loads, consisting of about twenty-eight barrels a boat, and then to drag the boats over. This took us just a day, and we camped the other end ... .I carried five loads over. I thought them heavy then; they averaged about 100 lb. [sic] a piece. To show how practice improves one at this work, I should say that, coming down the Winnipeg, my load over twenty-seven portages seldom averaged less than 180 lb. [sic], and I carried through without putting down or resting, which at first I had to do every 150 yards or so.[40]

The heavy weights were managed by using either a portage strap or portage poles, and sometimes a combination of both. The first was:

> ... a broad thick band of ox-hide leather, 26 inches long and 3¼ inches broad, tapering off at both ends to one inch in breadth. To each of these ends is sewn a long leather strap about one inch wide and five to seven feet long, the whole forming one long strap ... .The long ends are tied firmly round the barrel or package to be carried ... .The barrel is then hoisted on to the back, and the broad part of the strap rests against the forehead. In this way almost the whole strain bears on the backbone and vertebrae of the neck. An Indian usually clasps his hands round the back of his head to help the 'leverage', and in this manner will carry an immense weight. Our men at first were rather awkward at it, and could not carry a great weight, but they got into the way of it very quickly, and before they got to Fort Garry would think nothing of a weight which at first they would have been physically unable to stagger under.[41]

The portage poles were two poles of roughly two inch circumference joined together by two slings. The load to be carried was placed on the centre of the slings with a man at each end holding the poles, very much in the

---

36 Sissons, *Kerr*, p34.
37 PPP 570, Harman, *26 Years*, p19.
38 Wallace, *Rebellion*, p10.
39 Tennant, *Rough Times*, p37.
40 Butler, *Buller*, p23.
41 Huyshe, *Red River*, pp105/106.

manner of carrying a stretcher. To ease the weight on their arms, the men would " ... fasten their portage straps to the poles, letting the broad part rest across their shoulders."[42]

John Kerr described portaging as 'horrible work'. He added that, as bad as the pork barrels were to carry, it was the boxes of rifles that he detested the most because the sharp edges cut into the carrier's flesh.[43] Once across, " ... campfires were lit and pannicans of black hot tea served out with the grub. The men, nothing daunted, would quickly revive to launch their boats, and with a laugh and song rush each other for the lead on the lake or river, to get to the next portage."[44]

It took Captain Huyshe's party a full day to get across the Kashabowie Portage. They were new to the work and the day was a hot one. Kashabowie Lake itself was " ... about nine miles long, and studded with beautifully-wooded islands."[45] There was not a sound to break the 'perfect stillness' but 'the measured dip of the oars'.[46] At the end was Height of Land Portage, about one thousand feet above Lake Superior and the watershed for the Great Lakes and Hudson's Bay drainage basins. By all accounts it was also one of the most challenging portages of the entire trek. It covered 2 ½ miles of steep ground, although where it levelled off there were two ponds and the plan was to launch the boats on these to reduce the distance that the boats would need to be dragged. Fortunately the water between these two ponds was high enough that the men were able to move the boats along the creek that connected them. This was still hard work, however, because, while it was shallow, it was also choked with reeds necessitating that " ... all men had to get out of the boats into the water and pull the boats through."[47]

The sheer effort required at Height of Land Portage meant that it took some brigades two or three days to get across. To make matters worse, when John Kerr's brigade crossed over on July 25th rain soaked the exhausted men once they had gone to sleep.[48] Nevertheless, the soldiers were beginning to learn the business of portaging and Captain Huyshe was full of praise for the way all ranks, 'officers and men alike', performed.[49] Once across Height of Land, while a great many difficulties lay ahead, the expedition was now traveling with the current rather than against it, and this would remain the case until they entered the Red River itself during the final approach to Fort Garry.

After crossing into the Hudson's Bay watershed, the men found themselves on Lac des Mille Lacs, and the scenery here was, according to Lieutenant Harman of the Ontario battalion, 'very fine'.[50] The lake is about thirty miles long and six to ten across. Unsurprisingly given its name, which means Lake of a Thousand Lakes, it is 'studded with islands'.[51] There were so many in fact that the boat crews frequently found themselves losing their way and it became necessary to steer by compass. "What looks to be one enormous island at a little distance resolves itself on a nearer approach to an infinity of small ones, which, separated only by narrow channels, overlap and fit into one another like the pieces of a Chinese puzzle, so that the traveller may wander on from one little lake to another, for miles."[52] Many accounts speak of the guides losing their way with the loss of valuable time.[53] The canoe carrying the *Globe* reporter was lost for two days and eventually returned to Height of Land Portage to wait for a guide. It was here, as well, that for the first time the expedition encountered the First Nations people of the interior. They approached the force's boats in canoes looking to barter fish for pork and flour, though the supplies of the expedition had been calculated with such knife edge precision, that there was precious little to offer.

The route across Lac des Mille Lacs began in a northerly direction and then turned west to Baril Portage, described by John Kerr in his diary as " ... an awful one, over rocks fifteen and twenty feet high, almost

42 Huyshe, *Red River*, p107.
43 Sissons, *Kerr*, p34.
44 Tennant, *Rough* Times, p37.
45 Huyshe, *Red River*, p108.
46 Huyshe, *Red River*, p108.
47 PPP 568, Correspondence and Journal, Appendix, p82.
48 Sissons, Kerr, p35.
49 Huyshe, *Red* River, p112.
50 PPP 570, Harman, *26 Years*, p21.
51 Huyshe, *Red River*, p118.
52 Huyshe, *Red River*, p118.
53 PPP 589, Riddell, *60th*, p114.

perpendicular. Distance four hundred yards."[54] As well, there was a difficult hill a hundred feet high about half way along. One chronicler noted that it was 'very hard work'.[55] On the other side was Baril Lake, a narrow body of water about 8 ½ miles long.

The men were working hard and eating hard as well, though the monotony of the diet was beginning to tell. Captain Wallace recalled that the inevitable refrain from the men after they had carried their last loads over the final portage of the day was "what have you got for dinner?" The reply was "nice hot boiled pork, beans and tea … ." Wallace sarcastically wrote, "what a delicious change … hot boiled pork instead of cold boiled pork."[56] Captain McCalmont described the daily rations as a mixture of pork and flour known as " … choke dog, … which one would not have found either appetizing or digestible under any other circumstances."[57]

John Kerr's version of the experiences of the men in his boat was different and he does seem to have been a bit of a dab hand with the limited foodstuffs at his disposal:

> But, oh boy! How those boat crews could stow away the grub! Ten or twelve hungry men can clean up a lot of stuff… . Then I had to have enough to serve for dinner and supper, because we stopped only about an hour at noon. So I usually had pork and beans and bannock enough to warm up at noon and night. Sometimes I let the bannock go, and then we had hard-tack, desiccated potatoes, dried apples and little else. The hard-tack I soaked in water for awhile [sic] till it split, and I'd fry it in good pork lard. It made tasty eating, with a little sugar sprinkled on it … .The cubes of desiccated potatoes made a sticky mess when cooked, but, like beans and rice, swelled up a lot.[58]

By the time he neared the end of Baril Lake, Captain Huyshe was clearly tiring of the 'salt diet'. His canoe stopped early for the day and a net was set across a little bay. He and his crew wanted some fresh fish. They were to be sadly disappointed when the following morning the net was found to be empty. Nevertheless, he commented that the men remained very healthy, a case that he firmly believed was due to the absence of 'spirituous liquor', a state of affairs which he hoped would soon be the case throughout the whole army.

Brulé Portage at the end of Baril Lake was five hundred yards long, with a steep hill about two hundred feet high in the middle. It was described as having luxuriant vegetation not dissimilar to an English wood. Forty-seven feet below Baril Lake the troops embarked on a 'winding rushy stream.' This led them into Lake Windegoostigwan, " … which is rather several small lakes connected by creeks."[59] Riddell found the wind blowing strongly against them here, resulting in slow progress for his brigade.[60] Next they came to the French River, " … a strong stream … with numerous rocks and shoals" making navigation dangerous.[61] French Portage was fifty-five feet below Lac des Mille Lacs, " … 2 miles long, very hilly and swampy."[62] About ¾ of a mile along there was a waterfall and a new portage was cut out to avoid " … the long and very bad old one."[63] Huyshe caught up with Colonel Feilden and the three leading brigades on July 25th as they were building the new portage road. He reported that the old one would have taken three to four days to navigate and " … would have been dreadful to contemplate."[64]

Following along three days behind the leading elements, just before reaching French Portage John Kerr recorded that they met Dawson and some of his men. At that time, they were passing through lakes and creeks with nice sandy bottoms, "but we soon entered the rapids and had to wade up to our breasts, holding back the boats for fear of their being dashed to pieces against the rocks. Charlie Bell nearly broke his leg between a large

54 Sissons, *Kerr*, p35.
55 PPP 589, Riddell, 60th, p116.
56 Wallace, *Rebellion*, p14.
57 Callwell, *McCalmont*, p52.
58 Sissons, *Kerr*, pp34/35.
59 PPP 568, Correspondence and Journal, Appendix, p83.
60 PPP 589, Riddell, *60th*, p116.
61 PPP 589, Riddell, *60th*, p116.
62 PPP 568, Correspondence and Journal, Appendix, p83.
63 PPP 568, Correspondence and Journal, Appendix, p83.
64 Huyshe, *Red River*, pp122/123.

The Ontario Battalion at Deux Rivières Portage.(Toronto Public Library, JRR2432. (Artist: William Armstrong)

stone and the boat. But, by this same wading, we saved nearly two miles of portaging ... ."[65] Bell was Charles Napier Bell, future businessman and Manitoba historian. He was just sixteen years old when he left his hometown of Perth, to enlist in the Ontario battalion where his cousin was already serving as an ensign.

> Charlie didn't enlist at Perth. He was only sixteen years old, but he hiked it to Toronto then found that his cousin ... was appointed Ensign to our company. I was setting my kit in order ... , when in walked Charlie! We hunted up Captain Scott and Ensign Bell, and they fixed it up that I was to act as Captain Scott's batman, and Charlie as Ensign Bell's.[66]

On the morning of July 26th, five days after having left McNeill's Bay, Huyshe recorded that he was travelling along a stream which became 'deep and sluggish'. It was too narrow to row and too deep to pole, but luckily the current carried them along to French Lake, " ... a pretty circular basin 1 ½ miles in diameter, surrounded by low hills timbered with an extensive forest of red pine" one hundred fifty feet below Lac des Mille Lacs.[67] He also noted that the temperature was much milder on the western side of the watershed. Pigeons and partridge were in abundance, but they had no shotguns to supplement their cooking pot, possibly an oversight when setting out the equipment for the expeditionary force.

They crossed two smaller lakes and then came to Pickerel Lake " ... a fine sheet of water thirteen miles long by two to four broad ... ."[68] Here Lieutenant Riddell was overtaken by the mail canoe from Fort William to Fort

65 Sissons, *Kerr*, p36.
66 Sissons, *Kerr*, p38.
67 Huyshe, *Red River*, p124.
68 Huyshe, *Red River*, p125

Another view of a portage which looks like it could also be the one at Deux Rivières. (Library and Archives Canada, Acc. No. R9266-3428)

Frances.[69] After crossing Portage des Pins, where the timber was the finest they had seen, a mile long row across Doré Lake brought them to Deux Rivières Portage, 750 yards long and very steep and rocky. Lieutenant Riddell felt that this was one of the most difficult portages so far encountered.[70] Sam Steele was in agreement. There was a large hollow in the centre, which Ignace and his men had bridged with two tall pine trees with skids, made secure with notches, laid across them. In this way the boats could be dragged over. The men referred to it as 'Jacob's Ladder.'[71] Lieutenant Harman went even further and was unequivocal in his view that it was the most difficult of all the portages, though it is possible that his opinion may have been coloured by the "tremendous storm of thunder and lightning, accompanied by heavy rain ... " that greeted him there.[72] The steep grade of the portage made it difficult to lay down the rollers, but the Iroquois boatmen set to work and " ... a capital road was made by 5 o'clock the next evening."[73] This was the afternoon of the July 28th and Colonel Wolseley arrived to join the headquarters camp of the KRRC.

From Deux Rivières Portage, " ... a narrow winding channel, overgrown with rushes and lilies ... " flows into Sturgeon Lake.[74] Huyshe felt this was the most beautiful lake that they had yet traversed, a view with which Harman concurred. "The sudden contraction of the lake into a river breadth for a few yards amongst islands, and

69 PPP 589, Riddell, *60th*, p117.
70 PPP 589, Riddell, *60th*, p117.
71 Steele, *Forty* Years, p24.
72 PPP 570, Harman, *26 Years*, p21.
73 Huyshe, *Red River*, p125.
74 Huyshe, *Red River*, p127

its abrupt opening out into wide expanses of water, with deep and gloomy bays stretching into the dark forests as far as the eye could reach, offered a picture of ever-changing beauty."[75] Lieutenant Riddell described how a First Nation *voyageur* in his boat jumped into the water and returned in triumph with a sturgeon. "He undertook to prepare it for our supper; and the roe artistically cooked by one of the officers, was voted most delicious by all who tasted it."[76] It was here that Weymss Simpson returning from Fort Frances in a canoe manned by Iroquois boatmen met Wolseley. After many weeks negotiating with the First Nations of the interior for the passage of the expeditionary force, he was returning to meet up with Wolseley's men and inform the colonel that there would be no opposition from this quarter.

Sturgeon Lake drains into Lac la Croix through the eighteen mile long Sturgeon River with its various falls and rapids, of which the expedition had received gloomy reports from, " ... those who professed to know them well."[77] There were four rapids in quick succession. The men and supplies were unloaded and the Iroquois ran the boats down, with only one being damaged. Captain Huyshe wrote that "the celebrated guide Ignace and his crew were invaluable at this work, and Colonel Wolseley left them at the rapids to take the boats of the succeeding brigades down too."[78] So much confidence did the colonel have in Ignace's capabilities that he left a notice at the first rapid addressed to the following brigade commanders. It said that, should the Ignace be absent working with another brigade when they arrived, a halt was to be made until he had returned. They were to follow his orders to the letter.[79]

Lieutenant Harman left a highly descriptive account of how these rapids were run and it is worth quoting at length.

> The men were disembarked except for four picked oarsmen and two guides, ... one at the bow, with his pole to direct the course, and the other at the stern, who was to steer by means of one of the sweeps shipped in a rowlock; this you can see gave him great leverage ... . As they near the broken water, the bowman, who has the post of honour, and who has been intently watching the current, hails his chum at the stern. Some words pass between them, at first quietly, and then excitedly: the helmsman takes it up and calls upon the men to pull ... and now they are in it: away they go tearing along, every man pulling for dear life, with his eyes starting out of his head. As they strike the roaring, seething waters the boat makes a bound which fairly lifts them off their seats. Now they are in the middle of it, with the water dashing and foaming around them. Should they touch anything, a rock ahead, or a back eddy, God help them is the thought which flashes through the minds of those on shore, but the guides know their work too well; they are now on the reach below, safely over, and with a shout, which is taken up by those on shore, land below the portage.[80]

Kerr's brigade came through on August 3rd and Ignace and his men ran the boats down without incident. They did not, however, fare so well at a later rapid where there was no experienced guide to assist them. Kerr reported that:

> We ran her against a large rock. The water came pouring in, and we had not time to get her ashore before all the cargo was floating around. I jumped out and swam with the rope a little distance, and gave it to one of the men on the shore; all the crew, save the Captain, jumped in before the boat was twenty yards from the bank, and swam, holding to her side. We got everything we owned wringing wet, and were obliged to throw away seven barrels of hard-tack and two bags of beans. Our rifles, belts and accoutrements were all wet, rusty and blue moulded ... . [81]

75 Huyshe, *Red River*, p127 & PPP 570, Harman, *26 Years*, p22.
76 PPP 589, Riddell, *60th*, p118.
77 PPP 568, Correspondence and Journal, Appendix, p84.
78 Huyshe, *Red River*, p128.
79 PPP 568, Correspondence and Journal, Appendix, p85.
80 PPP 570, Harman, *26 Years*, p22.
81 Sissons, *Kerr*, p39.

The skill of the Iroquois and other First Nations boatmen was repeatedly demonstrated throughout the expedition's trek. (Library and Archives Canada, Acc. No. R9266-3428)

Island Portage. (Library and Archives Canada, Acc. No. R9266-3428)

After crossing Portage de L'Isle, the expedition came to Lac la Croix and here deviated from the old North West Company route, where Donald Smith had recently had great difficulty on the Maligne River. They went instead to the western end of Lac la Croix, turned south onto Loon Lake, and then crossed north-west into Lake Namakan, where they would re-join the traditional Nor'Wester highway. Between Loon Lake and Lake Namakan were a series of short portages.[82] The first of these was 223 yards long, the second stretched a bit longer to 340 yards, and the third, a mile further on, was only 71 yards and very easy. Nevertheless, roads still had to be cut at each, but this was still a much less dangerous alternative to the original route.[83]

After crossing Lake Namakan they arrived at Portage Nu, or Bare Portage, the last before reaching Fort Frances. It was really two portages " ... with a narrow sluggish stream between."[84] It was also swampy and infested with mosquitos, black flies and leeches, the latter meaning that a refreshing swim was out of the question. A new road had just been cut and the rollers laid as Colonel Feilden's detachment arrived.

82 PPP 568, Correspondence and Journal, Appendix, p85.
83 PPP 568, Correspondence and Journal, Appendix, p85.
84 Huyshe, *Red River*, pp132/133.

> It was quite a sight to see the men spring out, unload the boats, and haul them over, the crews vying with each other as to who should get everything over first. No delay or hesitation: as soon as the barrel was landed from the boat, somebody seized it, tied his portage strap around it, and off to the other end of the portage, running back to get another load.[85]

Team work, however, did not always prevail amongst expeditionary force members.

> A London cockney whose name was Smith, and who had served in the Royal Navy, took a fancy to an oar, and got into argument over it with Private Jack Cade, a tall and lanky young fellow from the Canadian backwoods. Both claimed it and struggled for possession. Smith was of short, stout build. They were fairly matched in strength, but the Cockney could easily out-slang Cade. Still the tug-of-war continued, each striving to wrench the oar from the other. Men passing back and forth over the portage would rest a few minutes to look on and encourage the scrappers to 'go to it'. The contestants were in an ugly mood and it looked like a fight to the finish. They slipped, and both fell, but did not let go holds. A bugler named Harry Walker (in later years the popular bandmaster of the Royal Northwest Mounted Police in Regina), was a witness to the latter part of the scrap. He drew close to the winded men struggling on the ground, neither of them quitters, and with no sign of let up. Harry asked to be allowed to settle the matter, and promised to act fair for both. They were about all in and agreed. Walker knew a good thing when he saw it. He told them so and mentioned his great need for a good oar. With a hearty 'Thank you boys for this', he placed the oar over his shoulder, smiled and passed on. The crowd laughed.[86]

From Bare Portage the boats entered Rainy Lake, "an enormous sheet of water, the largest we had yet passed through, being about 50 miles long by 30 to 40 broad."[87] Huyshe's party was greeted by a strong north westerly gale and could make no headway. They took shelter on an island which, they were delighted to discover, was covered in blueberries " ... as large as cherries and delicious as grapes ... .We ate them until we could not stand, and then we lay down and ate them again, and fell asleep to wake up and attack them again."[88]

The shores of the Rainy Lake were noted for being desolate and the timber very poor and bleached. They were now 225 miles west of Prince Arthur's Landing and approximately 420 feet above the height of Lake Superior, meaning they had descended roughly 400 feet from Shebandowan Lake and almost 600 feet from Height of Land Portage. On August 4th, after delays resulting from contrary winds, Colonel Feilden and the leading brigades of the expeditionary force crossed Rainy Lake and entered the Rainy River. After three miles they arrived at Fort Frances.

The HBC post here was " ... composed of two or three wooden houses surrounded by a palisading and situated on a large plateau, amidst gardens and fields overlooking the fine falls which are about 300 yards wide, and which dash over a ledge of rocks about 22 feet in height."[89] The land had the appearance of 'great fertility' " ... and glad indeed were we to see signs of the abode of man after the desolate and inhospitable region we had passed through."[90]

The men had worked tirelessly, being up at 4:30am with limited breaks until late into the evening. They had been at the mercy of the elements and were frequently so tired by the end of the day that they did not pitch their tents if the weather was fine. Of course, it did not always remain fine throughout the night and, between the weather and their exertions on the river, the men were constantly soaked, often for days. They had had little to eat other than salt pork and biscuits and the effect of the constant sliding around on the boat's benches as they rowed had worn out the seats of their trousers. These they had patched using the canvas from empty biscuit bags. And then there were the insects. The mosquito oil had proven to be useless and the nets to protect their heads and faces

85 Huyshe, *Red River*, p133.
86 Tennant, *Rough* Times, pp44/45.
87 Huyshe, *Red* River, p136.
88 Huyshe, *Red* River, p134.
89 HA 170A12W/D/0438, Wallace, *Rebellion*, p17.
90 Huyshe, *Red River*, p136.

impractical. It was seen that the First Nations guides rubbed their hands and faces with pork fat. The soldiers " ... accordingly tried the experiment and were delighted to find it worked like a charm."[91]

The men of the expeditionary force no doubt must have presented a sorry sight even to the residents of such an isolated post as Fort Frances after their twenty days in the wilderness. There was, however, no respite. D and E Brigades arrived at 4:00pm and left again that evening.[92] Any *voyageurs* deemed unfit were discharged here as well to await return to Thunder Bay. Twelve of these men from six of the brigades, one in seven, were left behind. Huyshe commented on this being a high proportion, especially " ... considering they had already been freely weeded before leaving Shebandowan."[93]

Fort Frances was to be established as an advanced base and so Wolseley remained for a few days to ensure that all was properly prepared. A Hospital was established with a thirty-six bed capacity and a field oven and bakery set up. The supply situation was also reviewed. Lindsay and Wolseley intended that the force would have 60 days of supplies accumulated here, in addition to the 30 days of supplies that the troops would carry with them.[94] It had also been decided that John Kerr's company would go no further for the time being. They would form the base garrison until the return of the British regulars.

The expedition was at last making steady progress, but time was still of the essence if the British troops were to reach Fort Garry and execute their return before the winter weather closed in. At this point too, Wolseley received information regarding the state of affairs at the Red River Settlement. After a journey through the United States to Fort Garry, including a meeting with Louis Riel himself, Lieutenant Butler had rendezvoused with the expeditionary force.

---

91 PPP 570, Harman, *26 Years*, p23.
92 PPP 568, Correspondence and Journal, Appendix, p86.
93 Huyshe, *Red* River, p153.
94 PPP 568, Correspondence and Journal, May, 23, 1870, No. 9 Inclosure 3, Lindsay to Governor-General Sir John Young.

17

Butler's Travels

Lieutenant William Francis Butler, the special intelligence officer for the expedition, had had an interesting time since his meeting with Wolseley in Toronto in May. His instructions from Lieutenant-General Lindsay left him with something of an open commission.

> We must leave matters to yourself, I think ... you will be best judge of how to get on when you know and see the ground. I will not ask you to visit Fort Garry, but if you find it feasible, it would be well if you could drop down the Red River and join Wolseley before he gets to the place. You know what I want, but how to do it, I will leave altogether to yourself.[1]

Butler knew that Wolseley was anxious regarding the attitude of the people of Assiniboia, as well as the mood in the American states bordering Canada and the HBC territory. It was also rumoured that the Fenians were amassing weapons, and knowledge of the presence of men like William Bernard O'Donoghue in Riel's immediate circle was a cause of concern.

Lieutenant Butler crossed into the state of Michigan from Toronto on June 10th. In contrast to the experience of the expeditionary force, he traveled by rail in relative comfort. He passed through Chicago, Milwaukee, and St. Paul, ending up in St. Cloud, Minnesota. It was, however, not one continuous journey and he wrote that "business connected with the supply of troops during the coming winter detained me for some weeks in Minnesota ... ."[2] He also visited the shores of Lake Superior to gather intelligence on any planned Fenian opposition to the progress of the expeditionary force.

While in St. Paul he read a newspaper article reporting the difficulties being encountered on the road from Thunder Bay to Shebandowan Lake.

> Of course the American press held high jubilee over this check, which was represented as only the beginning of the end of a series of disasters. The British Expedition was never destined to reach Red River – swamps would entrap it, rapids would engulf it; and if, in spite of these obstacles, some few men did succeed in piercing the rugged wilderness, the trusty rifle of the Metis would soon annihilate the presumptive intruders[3]

Butler's questionings on matters of supply and Fenian activities meant that it was not long before it became common knowledge that he was a British intelligence officer. Consequently, in the first week of July he took the train to St. Cloud on the Mississippi River, seventy miles closer to the border and 400 miles from Fort Garry. The railway went no closer to his destination and Butler next spent three days travelling 180 miles by stagecoach to Fort Abercrombie on the Red River. Constructed in 1858 as the first permanent fort in North Dakota, it was here that Butler heard of a succession of disasters that had either befallen or were about to befall the expedition. "An

1 Butler, *Lone Land*, p30.
2 Butler, *Lone Land*, p61.
3 Butler, *Lone Land*, p77.

A later picture of the expedition's Special Intelligence Officer, William Francis Butler, from 1898. (*Illustrated London News*, ILNO-1898-1119-0007-F)

Indian coming from beyond Fort Francis [sic], somewhere in the wilderness north of Lake Superior, had brought tidings to the Lake of the Woods, that forty Canadian soldiers had already been lost in one of the boiling rapids of the route."[4] Another story involved a large band of Sioux who were ready to move in support of the Métis. The general consensus at Butler's hotel was that the expedition would not get through.

The steamboat *International* was lying at Frog Point, about one hundred miles downriver from Fort Abercrombie. By chance, Butler learned that the riverboat's captain would shortly be arriving from St. Paul by stagecoach and a horse and Red River cart had been organized for him. Butler arranged to travel with the captain and on July 17th, the day after the first brigades of the Red River Expeditionary Force had set out on Shebandowan Lake, the two men set off, together with a dog that had attached itself to the British intelligence officer.

Butler was aghast at the mosquitos they encountered during the journey to the *International.* "I thought my experiences of mosquitos in Indian jungles and Irrawaddy swamps, to say nothing of my recent wanderings by the Mississippi forests, had taught me something about these pests ... ."[5] However, the onset of a prairie thunder and lightning storm brought on clouds of the pestilential insects " ... humming and buzzing along with us as we journeyed on, and covering our faces and heads with their sharp stinging bites."[6] When the rain broke, the two men took shelter under the cart, but as the first streaks of daylight began to show, they set out again. Soaked to the skin, cold and shivering, they knocked on the door of a shanty to ask for shelter and food.

Butler had nothing good to say about the settler he encountered here, a Prussian by the name of Probsfeld, though he was more positively disposed towards his wife and family. Herr Probsfeld was " ... a terribly self-opinionated North German, with all the bumptious proclivities of that thriving nation most fully developed."[7] When writing of the events the following year, Butler realized that, at almost the precise moment he was taking shelter in the Probsfeld cabin, the Franco-Prussian War was getting under way. Setting his prejudices against his host onto the higher plain of international relations, Butler later speculated that:

> ... it is more than probable that had Herr Probsfeld realized the fact, that just at that moment, when the sun was breaking out through the eastern clouds over the distant outline of the Leaf Hills, 700,000 of his countrymen were moving hastily toward the French frontier for the special furtherance of those ideas so dear to his mind – it is most probable, I say, that his self-laudation and cock-like conceit would have been in no ways lessened.[8]

4 Butler, *Lone Land*, p91
5 Butler, *Lone Land*, p97.
6 Butler, *Lone Land*, p98.
7 Butler, *Lone Land*, p99.
8 Butler, *Lone Land*, p100.

Pursued by hordes of mosquitos, Butler and the steamboat captain set out again on their journey, finally arriving at the *International* the following day. They sought shelter by rushing aboard, but to no avail. "They came in after us in millions" and in a short time " ... the interior of the boat became perfectly black with insects. Attempts at eating were to no avail. "They got into the coffee, they stuck fast in the soft, melting butter, until at length, feverish, bitten, bleeding and hungry, I sought refuge beneath the gauze curtains in my cabin, and fell asleep from sheer exhaustion." By morning the boat was underway and "the air was fresh and cool; not a mosquito was visible."[9]

The *International* was a sternwheel paddle boat, 130 feet in length and drawing only two feet of water. Butler described that she had seen better days and "her engines were a perfect marvel of patchwork – pieces of rope seemed twisted around crank and shaft, mud was laid thickly on the boiler and pipes, little jets and spirts of steam had a disagreeable way of coming out from places not supposed to be capable of such outpourings. Her capacity for going on fire seemed very great."[10]

When they crossed the international boundary from the United States, the captain told Butler that he was surprised they had not been boarded and searched as it was suspected there was a British intelligence officer on board. Now on his guard, he made his way to the high roof of the riverboat and noted two horsemen riding speedily in the direction of Fort Garry. Determined to avoid arrest, he decided to somehow disembark before the steamboat's final stop at the settlement. He believed the best course would be to make his way to Lower Fort Garry, located firmly within the settlement's English parishes, where the local population was likely to be more welcoming. Onboard he had met William (Willie) Drever, a resident from a family who had long resided at the Red River Settlement and who was opposed to Riel.[11] Drever informed Butler that the sternwheeler made a sharp turn from the Red onto the Assiniboine River at slow speed just prior to tying up at Fort Garry. At this point, its bow momentarily touched the north bank of the river. In the darkness it would be possible to leap ashore and so avoid any reception committee waiting at the dock. Together with the nameless dog, this is what Butler and Drever did, scrambling up the steep river bank and quickly making their way to Winnipeg village. Butler would later find out that Riel and O'Donoghue, together with 'a strong body of guards', were in fact on the Fort Garry landing stage awaiting his arrival.[12]

Drever said he could provide Butler with a horse to make his way to the lower fort and gave him directions to a bridge where he was to await his return. Butler remained at the meeting place for some time, but there was no sign of Drever. By this stage the dog had wandered off as well, and the British Army lieutenant determined it was time to move on. He later discovered that, after his non-appearance on the Fort Garry dock, the Métis reception party had boarded the *International* and " ... commenced to ransack her from stem to stern."[13] It was discovered that two men had left the boat just prior to its docking. One was quickly identified as Willie Drever and he was found at his home and arrested twenty minutes after the two men had separated. Butler's identity was not immediately clear and it was noted by one Red River resident that "the stranger said to be one Butler or Baker left some luggage on the boat."[14] For his troubles, the *International's* captain also found himself under arrest.

Walking hard through the night, by dawn Butler was only about four miles from the lower fort. He found refuge in the rectory of St. Andrew's Church. While there he met Mary Drever, Willie's sister, who six years later would marry James Macleod, the Brigade Major with the expeditionary force. She agreed to carry a letter back to the *International* so that it could be posted to Ottawa once the boat had returned to United States territory. Hiding it in her blouse, while her buggy was searched by a group of Métis, they did not search her person and the letter got through.[15] What information was contained in this letter, however, is unknown as Butler makes no mention of either the letter or Mary Drever in his account.

9 Butler, *Lone Land*, pp102/103.
10 Butler, *Lone Land*, pp103/104.
11 Maclaren, *Braehead*, p111.
12 Butler, *Lone Land*, p117.
13 Butler, *Lone Land*, p120.
14 Alexander Begg, "Alexander Begg's Red River Journal," Greenwood Press, New York 1969, July 20, 1870, p391.
15 Maclaren, *Braehead*, p112.

With a search for him actively underway, Butler was taken to St. Peter's Indian Settlement near the mouth of the Red River on Lake Winnipeg. In the Intelligence Officer's memoir, *The Great Lone Land*, he speaks at length on the assertions of loyalty made to him by Henry Prince, the First Nations Salteaux chief. The description found in Butler's account is paternalistic and colourfully old fashioned with comments such as them being "faithful children of the Great Mother."[16] Despite the language, which seems so condescending and anachronistic to the modern ear, Butler was certainly safe here and could set off in the direction of Wolseley's approaching force at his convenience. At this point, however, he received an invitation from none other than Louis Riel requesting that he pay him a visit at the upper fort.

Despite the inherent risks, Butler chose to accept the invitation, but under certain conditions. He had heard that Willie Drever had been sentenced to death and so the first condition was that he be released. By this point the *International*, together with her captain, had been freed. In addition, all of Butler's baggage had been left on the riverboat where it had been confiscated and he wanted it returned to him. Finally, he said he would not visit if the Métis flag, "a fleur-de-lis and a shamrock on a white background symbolizing Métis and Fenian unity against a common foe," was flying over the fort.[17] Riel replied that he would order a halt to the work on the road between Fort Garry and Lake of the Woods if Butler did not visit, though such a threat would have likely had no impact on the special intelligence officer's decision making.

As Butler recounts the story, he was on the verge of setting off in the direction of the approaching expeditionary force when word arrived that his first two conditions had been met. He decided to take a chance. He arrived at Upper Fort Garry on July 23rd and found that, while his third condition had not been completely satisfied, a Union Flag, albeit tattered and worn, now flew alongside the one he had taken exception to. This was a compromise he was willing to accept.

The meeting however almost immediately became unstuck. The intelligence man had commenced playing billiards when Riel entered the room. Butler described him as " ... a short stout man with a large head, a sallow, puffy face, a sharp, restless, intelligent eye, a square-cut massive forehead overhung by a mass of long and thickly clustering hair, and marked with well-cut eyebrows – altogether, a remarkable looking face ... . He was dressed in ... a black frock-coat, vest, and trousers, [and] a pair of Indian mocassins [sic]."[18] Butler asked if Riel played billiards and received the terse reply 'never'. Butler's response, referring to it as 'a capital game', caused Riel to leave the room muttering that he could see he was intruding. Persuaded by one of his men to return, he was back shortly afterwards.

When Riel stated his regret that Butler had shown a lack of trust by making his way to Lower Fort Garry, the intelligence officer replied that this resulted from his American sympathizers on the frontier who spoke of the preparations the Métis leader was making to oppose the expeditionary force. Riel said this was not true and that his " ... only wish was to retain power until I can resign it to a proper government. I have done every thing, [sic]" he continued, "for the sake of peace, and to prevent bloodshed amongst the people of this land."[19]

They spoke of the expeditionary force; Riel was interested to know where it was and its size and composition. Butler did not know the answer to the first question, but expressed his view that it was in the area of Lake of the Woods. As for its size, "I told him exactly, setting the limits as low as possible, not to deter him from fighting if such was his intention."[20] This is an interesting response given the British Government's stated position that it was not a punitive expedition, though Butler likely had not received the Standing Orders and so presumably was in the dark as to its professed purpose.

The one subject that was not touched upon was the question of amnesty. As Butler put it, this was a topic of grave concern to a number of the Métis at Red River, and he gave credit to Riel for not broaching the matter. The meeting ended as abruptly as it had begun. Riel reiterated that he had been humiliated by Butler's failure to

16 Butler, *Lone Land*, pp126-128.
17 McCourt, *Butler*, p49.
18 Butler, *Lone Land*, p133.
19 Butler, *Lone Land*, p134.
20 Butler, *Lone Land*, p135.

come and see him and spoke of his 'pacific inclinations'. On that note he left the room, leaving Butler with the impression that he had had enough of the interview.[21]

An hour later Butler had left the upper fort and by dusk was at the lower one. His canoe was ready and, after a 'hasty supper', he was on his way down the Red River. "The crew, with paddles held high for the first dip, gave a parting shout, and like an arrow from its bow we shot out into the current."[22] After spending the night at St. Peter's Settlement, Butler and his party crossed Lake Winnipeg and then began the arduous journey up the multitude of rapids on the Winnipeg River. We will learn more about hazards of these when the expeditionary force navigates the same route in the opposite direction in the next chapter.

Seven days later Butler and his party arrived at Rat Portage, the site of modern day Kenora, Ontario. No one at the HBC post could tell him anything regarding the progress of Wolseley's force. He was warned that strange men had been sited on the islands of Lake of the Woods and it was assumed that these were Riel's men sent to observe the size and progress of the expeditionary force. In fact, there is no evidence that Riel sent Métis scouts out for this purpose and they may in fact have been the forward elements of the expeditionary force itself.

At Rat Portage Butler boarded an HBC York Boat, a larger version of the type being used by Wolseley's men, and set sail across the seventy miles of Lake of the Woods to the mouth of the Rainy River. To Butler's delight, he met a group of indigenous people who confirmed that the expeditionary force was not far distant.

The York Boat moved swiftly up the Rainy River with a 'spanking breeze' driving her forward. Twenty miles from Fort Frances, they found themselves suddenly becalmed. Butler, though, had anticipated just such a situation and had brought a canoe with them. This canoe sprang a leak, but another was obtained and they reached Fort Frances by daybreak. There was no sign of Wolseley, but the news from the HBC factor there was that he was expected before breakfast.

Butler had covered over 400 miles in twelve days across very rough country. He had travelled 200 miles further than he had thought would be necessary to meet Wolseley's men. Despite the imminence of the expeditionary force's arrival, Butler decided he did not wish to supinely wait at the HBC post and set out in the direction of Rainy Lake. He and his men went ashore and climbed a rock where they had a clear view across the lake. It was August 4th and in the early morning light Butler was the first to catch sight of "... the glint of something strange on the lake."[23] It was Wolseley himself in his North Canoe, his eight Iroquois paddlers powering him swiftly towards his destination. Butler and his crew got back into their canoe and the two craft drew together. "Where on earth have you dropped from?" asked the colonel. "Fort Garry, twelve days out, sir," was his reply.[24]

It is not at all clear what intelligence Butler conveyed to Wolseley. No mention is made in the Official Journal of Operations. In the *Narrative of the Red River Expedition*, Colonel Wolseley does not name Butler, but speaks of a 'sharp, intelligent officer' sent to the Northwest via the United States by Lieutenant-General Lindsay. He said that when they met at Fort Frances this officer described the people at Red River as being "... panic-stricken – the English and French populations being mutually afraid of one another, and both being in the direst dread of the Indians."[25] As we will see in the next chapter, however, this is a near verbatim report he would ascribe to '... a loyal and trusty half-breed' who he dispatched to the Red River Settlement to make contact with the Protestant Bishop there when the force was still at Prince Arthur's Landing.[26] This was Joseph Monkman and he also met the colonel at Fort Frances.[27] While *The Great Lone Land* is silent as to the intelligence Butler passed along to

21 Butler, *Lone Land*, p136.
22 Butler, *Lone Land*, p136
23 Butler, *Lone Land*, p167.
24 Butler, *Lone Land*, p168.
25 Wolseley, *Narrative Part 2*, p72.
26 Wolseley, *Soldier's Story*, p203.
27 Mention is made of Monkman's arrival with two guides in PPP 568 Correspondence and Journal, August, 9, 1870, No. 23 Enclosure 1, Wolseley to Military Secretary. The same communication also speaks to the six guides who arrived with Butler and two who were sent by the First Nations chief, Henry Prince.

the colonel, the description in Wolseley's *Narrative* is not really in keeping with the record Butler leaves us of his meeting with Riel. In Butler's account, published in 1872, while he was clearly disdainful of Riel, he also recorded the Métis leader's professed desire for peace and his willingness to turn over the reins of power to a legally constituted government. When he had been on the run, Butler had naturally gravitated to those who opposed Riel and no doubt contact with these elements of the community would have influenced his report to Wolseley. In all likelihood, the expeditionary force commander's comment in his later memoirs that "the important news I received at Fort Francis [sic] from Lieutenant William Butler was that Riel was in a perplexed state of mind ... " was probably closer to the mark.[28] Perhaps Butler's biographer sums matters up best. "What he had done was – as events proved – of no great importance in the sum of things, but he had carried out a difficult assignment with efficiency and dash and with a complete disregard of personal danger. He had every reason to be pleased with himself."[29]

28 Wolseley, *Soldier's Story*, p204.
29 McCourt, *Butler*, p54.

18

Fort Frances to Fort Alexander

The arrival of the advance elements of the expeditionary force at Fort Frances was anything but a rest for the men after their toil from Shebandowan Lake. Three brigades arrived with Colonel Feilden on August 4th and two more arrived the following day. On the 6th and 7th the wind blew so strongly from the west that no boats could reach the fort, but on August 8th four more brigades arrived, including the first of the Ontario volunteers. On the 9th a second Ontario brigade arrived. All moved on the day of their arrival other than the first of the Ontario brigades, I Brigade, with Captain Scott, Lieutenant Macdonald, Ensign Bell, and of course the redoubtable cook, John Kerr, which would remain to form the garrison.[1] With the departing units went the First Nations boatmen who had brought Butler up the Winnipeg River, and would now serve as guides with the expeditionary force.

From Fort Frances the next stage of the journey would take Wolseley's men down the Rainy River and then across Lake of the Woods to Rat Portage. From here they would descend the treacherous Winnipeg River to Fort Alexander. The Rainy River and parts of Lake of the Woods formed the border between Canadian and American territory. Wolseley cautioned Feilden about straying across the border during the next stage of the trek and ordered him to be careful when approaching Rat Portage. Wolseley would have been concerned about Fenian intervention so close to the United States, though it was certainly an isolated spot and the colonel was likely more concerned about creating an incident with the Americans if his men happened to set foot on United States territory. However, he saw Rat Portage as an ideal spot for the Métis to attempt an ambush and wanted his men to be on high alert when they arrived there. To guard against this, Butler had been sent on ahead in a light boat to reconnoitre the approaches prior to the arrival of Feilden and his men.

Wolseley did not continue immediately and paused at Fort Frances for a few days to ensure that all was in order. As mentioned in the previous chapter, here he met with Joseph Monkman who had arrived from Fort Garry carrying letters from Robert Machray, the Anglican Bishop of Rupert's Land, and Henry Prince, the First Nations chief who Butler had taken refuge with before and after his meeting with Riel. Monkman, an English-speaking mixed race resident of Red River, had fled Fort Garry after aiding Schultz in his escape. When he passed through the camp at Prince Arthur's Landing on his way back in June, he agreed to gather information about the state of affairs there and return to meet with Wolseley at some point along the route. Wolseley could never be sure that Butler would get through and, even assuming he did, Monkman would provide a second source of intelligence as to the state of affairs at Fort Garry.

The refrain of the letters from Bishop Machray was that the expeditionary force should come as quickly as possible. Tensions were high in the community and he also spoke of fear of an outbreak of violence amongst the First Nations peoples, though this latter concern was most likely in regard to the several hundred Sioux refugees who were camping in and around the settlement. As regards the troubles at the settlement itself, as we have seen, when Machray realized that the Métis were simply too strong, he worked to restrain the more hot-headed elements of the English-speaking communities.[2] He also acted as a delegate for the English parishes during the

1 PPP 568, Correspondence and Journal, August, 9, 1870, No. 23 Enclosure 1, Wolseley to Military Secretary.

2 For Machray's views of the Canadian takeover and his views on the troubles at Red River, see Chapter 6.

Provisional Government negotiations, while at the same time writing letters to the Canadian Government urging them to take action.[3]

Monkman advised Wolseley of the welcome news that six of the HBC's York Boats " ... well manned by experienced boatmen, to assist the expedition in descending the dangerous rapids ... ," were waiting at Rat Portage.[4] The cost for these had been provided by the loyal inhabitants of the Red River Settlement. Simon Dawson would voice his views on the comparison of the boats he had ordered for the expedition and the York Boats when he wrote his report on the expedition. Perhaps unsurprisingly, he found his boats were "the fastest sailers, the most easily managed in the portages and rapids and in every way the best adapted to the purposes of the Expedition."[5]

The expedition would shortly be passing the Northwest Angle. This was the intended start of the western half of the settler road from Canada to the Red River Settlement. Wolseley had directed that work on it be recommenced and it was this work that Riel had threatened to halt if Butler did not meet with him. From the Northwest Angle to Fort Garry was 90 miles in a straight line, as opposed to 163 miles down the difficult rapids of the Winnipeg River between Rat Portage and Fort Alexander, and there was still the distance from the Northwest Angle across Lake of the Woods to Rat Portage and from Fort Alexander to Fort Garry to be added to the water route as well. This meant that the journey by boat was considerably longer than that by the Northwest Angle road; and then there were the hazards of the Winnipeg River, which will be related shortly.

In his memoirs Wolseley says that it was at Fort Frances that he learned, 'as expected' that it would not be possible for the expeditionary force to use the road.[6] This is not the case and he had known since the outset that the road was not a viable option. Rather contradictorily, Wolseley stated on the preceding page of the same book that he had never intended to use the road, but had 'begged' Mactavish at the Red River Settlement to finish it without delay as a ruse so that Riel would think the force was coming that way.[7] In fact, the road was far from complete. The first thirty-five miles was over boggy ground and, in any case, virtually no work had been undertaken on this section.

In a memorandum from Simon Dawson on April 18th, the Public Works Department man had written of the hard work still to be undertaken to finish the road. The men he said would be " ... terribly harassed with insects, such as mosquitos, black flies etc,. among the marshes." There was also the question of obtaining sufficient land transport to carry the expedition's troops and supplies.[8] After the expedition, when he later viewed the road for himself, he found, "the party sent out with Mr. Snow, in the fall of 1868, had not even penetrated to the Lake of the Woods, with their Exploratory lines, and much of the road they had opened was a mere preliminary track, on which nothing more had been done than cutting down or rolling off the trees."[9]

Dawson had from the beginning urged the use of the Winnipeg River for the penultimate leg of the journey, though he seriously underplayed its challenges. "The Winnipeg River presents no serious difficulties to the largest class of canoes and it has been navigated by the Hudson's Bay Company's Boats. In the navigable sections, the depth of the water is sufficient for large boats and there are but few heavy rapids to be run, and these are short."[10] After the expedition's arrival at Fort Garry he wrote, "upon the whole, the Expedition experienced *no difficulty whatever on the Winnipeg*. [Author's emphasis]'[11] Many of the expedition's men would have begged to differ with

---

3 Hackett, Machray.

4 Huyshe, *Red River*, p155.

5 PPP 559, Dawson, "Report", p30. Simon J. Dawson is an interesting character study. He certainly had much to be annoyed with regarding the criticisms levelled by Wolseley at his workers, the conduct of his department and his superiors in the *Narrative of the Expedition*. He had far too much on his plate and mistakes were bound to occur given how thinly he was stretched. Nevertheless, he challenged every criticism no matter how trivial. Nothing was ever his fault. He comes across as tetchy and overly sensitive. Perhaps his personality was unsuited to be working so intimately with a man like Wolseley, whose ability to unwittingly offend was considerable.

6 Wolseley, *Soldier's Life*, p204.

7 Wolseley, *Soldier's Life*, p203.

8 PPP 559, Dawson, "Report", Memorandum of April 18, 1870.

9 PPP 559, Dawson, "Report", Memorandum of April 18, 1870, p39.

10 PPP 559, Dawson, "Report", Memorandum of April 18, 1870.

11 PPP 559, Dawson, "Report", Memorandum of April 18, 1870, p30.

Dawson's estimation and their memories of the journey were seriously at odds with the Public Works Department man's summing up.[12]

Wolseley too had heard from Butler regarding the Winnipeg's challenges and was receiving other intelligence as well from the guides who were beginning to arrive from the Red River Settlement itself. However, when Mr. Monkman tried to convince him that only a small amount of work was required on the road, the colonel was skeptical. Captain Huyshe neatly summed the matter up when he wrote, "Colonel Wolseley had had too much already of one road to risk the success of the expedition on another which he had not seen himself or through the eyes of a British officer."[13] The expedition would, therefore, make the hazardous trek down the Winnipeg River. While fraught with peril, it was the correct course of action, but there was no epiphany moment. Despite how the story would be be relayed in his memoirs, staying with the boats was Wolseley's intention from the beginning.

It was at Fort Frances, as well, that Wolseley met with the principal Ojibwe First Nations Chief referred to as "Crooked Neck". Maintaining good relations was serious business. Prior to the arrival of the expeditionary force, there had been a meeting of the notables of local Ojibwe people with Weymss Simpson. The substance of the discussion had been whether the Ojibwe should oppose the passage of the expeditionary force. Simpson strenuously argued against it and was successful in dissuading them. Huyshe saw this as an important accomplishment, and while he did not view the Ojibwe as being as warlike as the Sioux, they were still great rivals and " ... have old traditions of enmity against the Iroquois."[14] He added that one hundred men knowing the lie of the land could have done considerable damage to the expedition. The Ojibwe were " ... thoroughly acquainted with the vast network of lakes, [and] they could have fired on the boats as they passed through narrow channels, or blocked up the portages, and done much mischief in a variety of ways, while to have attempted to pursue them through the woods and lakes would have been madness."[15] Luckily for the expedition's progress, this did not come to pass and, as with the journey so far, the only difficulties to be faced came from nature.

Wolseley and his party, which included Captain Huyshe, Lieutenant Denison and Assistant-Controller Irvine, left Fort Frances at daybreak on August 10th. The force commander was anxious to catch up with Colonel Feilden and the leading brigades before they reached Fort Alexander. By this point, all of the British brigades and two of the Ontario battalion's brigades had passed through Fort Frances. As usual the colonel travelled in his North Canoe with his eight Iroquois boatmen. The rest of his group were in the expedition's gig. At Fort Frances a new guide joined Huyshe's boat, an Iroquois by the name of Baptiste. Captain Huyshe was high in his praise for the young man, describing him as " ... always cheery and good-humoured, ready either to take an oar or a paddle and a capital fellow on a portage."[16] The Winnipeg River would soon put his skills to the test.

Descending the Rainy River was a relatively easy part of the journey. The river was between 200 and 400 yards wide and the current ran at about 3 knots.[17] There were only two rapids, the Manitou and the Long Sault, thirty-two and thirty-nine miles from Fort Frances, and these were run with ease. Captain Wallace with G Brigade thought:

> ... the banks in some places resemble an old English park, oak, elm, poplar and ash growing luxuriantly; while the thick brushwood, intertwined with honeysuckle and wild convolvulus, forms an abundant shelter for the numerous insects which abound there, the most troublesome of which are the mosquito, the black fly, the sand fly and the moose fly which literally nips a piece out of you.[18]

12 See Huyshe, *Red River* p172; Steele, *Forty Years*, p25; Tennant, *Rough Times*, p47; PPP 570, Harman, *26 Years*, p26; HA 170A12W/D/0438, Wallace, *Rebellion*, p22 and Callwell, *McCalmont* pp.52/53.

13 Huyshe, *Red River*, p155.

14 Ibid. Huyshe, *Red River*, p142.

15 Ibid. Huyshe, *Red River*, pp143/44.

16 Ibid. Huyshe, *Red River*, p156.

17 See: 170A12W/D/0438Wallace, *Rebellion*, p20 and PPP 570, Harman, *26 Years*, p25.

18 HA 170A12W/D/0438, Wallace, *Rebellion*, p20.

Huyshe was similarly impressed with the river's flora and also described an event on the first night where they were enveloped by a swarm of insects " ... moving up river at a great rate, in a solid column about ten feet high and perhaps fifty feet broad, and at a distance gave the appearance of a thick mist; nearer they looked like a storm of driving snow or sleet."[19] As they engulfed the boats, many landed on the river and "the fish were rising all round, devouring them greedily."[20]

At night a number of the brigades adopted the HBC practice of lashing two boats together and drifting with the current. This allowed most of the men onboard to sleep while the journey continued, and for at least two brigades this was a successful tactic. Lieutenant Harman of the Ontario Rifles described it as 'very satisfactory.'[21] Unfortunately this was not the experience of Wolseley's party. What started out as a beautiful night ended with a storm. Confronted by 'a furious westerly wind' that pelted them with rain and drenched them to the skin, by midnight they gave up and put into the shore where they waited uncomfortably for dawn to break.[22]

At the end of the Rainy River was Lake of the Woods, 377 feet above Lake Superior, 977 feet above sea level, 72 miles long and almost as wide.[23] This 'massive sheet of water' is strewn with islands and with a series of low sandy banks forming a bar where the Rainy River drains into it. The islands would cause the men in more than one boat to lose their way.[24] The most notable feature was the lake's green colour. This was caused by a vegetable growth made up of a " ... minute, tubular, needled shaped organism, about half an inch in length, sometimes detached and sometimes clustered together in star-shaped forms ... ."[25] Though some of the lake's deep water bays were free from the plant growth, the further the boats went from the shore, the thicker it became until its surface gave the impression of " ... a vast expanse of dirty, green mud" that extended for a few miles beyond Rat Portage onto the Winnipeg River itself. [26] Others described it as resembling green pea soup and it was not fit to drink without boiling and straining it.[27] It was here that the mosquito face nets, distributed to the troops at Thunder Bay, came into their own.

Some of the brigades had an easy crossing to Rat Portage. Travelling with Feilden's men in the van of the expedition, Butler wrote, "Never before had these lonely islands witnessed such a sight as they now beheld. Seventeen large boats, close hauled to a splendid breeze swept in a great scattered mass through the high running seas, dashing the foam from their bows as they dipped and rose under their large lug-sails."[28] Rowing became unnecessary and there were no portages to cross, just " ... a grand day's racing over the immense lake."[29] Wallace with G Brigade described the excitement of racing the boats of Captain Northey's F Brigade. They also saw a Union Flag flying on one of the islands and bore over to find two of the York Boats from Fort Garry. Wallace's Brigade arrived at Rat Portage on August 11th, but unfortunately for Wolseley, as with the drift down the Rainy River, the experience of his group was not quite so simple. [30]

Wolseley's party entered Lake of the Woods at about the same time as Captain Macdonald's K Brigade of the 1st Ontario Rifles. Once they passed the shelter of the sandy islands at the mouth of the Rainy River and entered the lake proper, they found themselves facing a gale and began to ship water. In the gig the sail was taken down and shelter was immediately sought at a place they christened 'Detention Island'. The gale continued to blow for the rest of the day and most of the following day. By 8:00 p.m. on the second day the lake had calmed sufficiently for the boats of K Brigade to continue on their way. It remained too rough, however, for Wolseley's canoe. Shortly thereafter a boat did manage to reach them from Thunder Bay carrying the Toronto newspapers up to July 29th

19 Huyshe, *Red River*, pp157/158.
20 Huyshe, *Red River*, p159.
21 HA 170A12W/D/0438, Wallace, *Rebellion*, p20 & PPP 570, Harman, *26 Years*, p25.
22 Huyshe, *Red River*, p159.
23 Huyshe, *Red River*, p162 & PPP 589 Riddell, *60th*, p121.
24 HA 170A12W/D/0438, Wallace, *Rebellion*, p21 & PPP 570, Harman, *26 Years*, p25.
25 Huyshe, *Red River*, p162.
26 PPP 570, Harman, *26 Years*, p25 & Huyshe, *Red River*, p163.
27 Huyshe, *Red River*, p162 & HA 170A12W/D/0438, Wallace, *Rebellion*,p21.
28 Butler, *Lone Land*, pp171/172.
29 Butler, *Lone Land*, p172.
30 HA 170A12W/D/0438, Wallace, *Rebellion*, p20.

and the London papers from July 15th. Wolseley read for the first time of the outbreak of war between France and Prussia of which the officers of the force took great interest.[31] Captain Huyshe pondered the great events that were unfolding in Europe as they were stranded Robinson Crusoe like on Detention Island.[32] The consensus was that France would handily prevail.

Baptiste had also spotted a Union Flag on a nearby island, although when a boat was sent over to investigate, no trace of it was found. Later, however, two of the HBC York Boats arrived with news from Rat Portage that Colonel Feilden had arrived and was on his way down the Winnipeg River. There was also another letter from Bishop Machray urging that two guns and a hundred men be sent to Fort Garry without delay.[33] With this news Wolseley was even more anxious to get moving. His Iroquois guides, however, were adamant that the lake was still too rough. As a result, he took Lieutenant Denison's place in the gig and set out with Captain Huyshe, but without a guide, to cross the lake and navigate through the labyrinth of islands.

They steered by the stars and at 1:00am pulled into an island to spend the night. They were away again at 5:00am and continued until darkness set in and they could go no further. Believing that they must now be close to Rat Portage, they sailed into a bay only to find it was a cul-de-sac. Pushing the bounds of understatement, Huyshe wrote, " ... the uncomfortable feeling began to creep over us that we had lost our way."[34] They came across a First Nation encampment and, after providing the man they found there with tobacco and the women with tea and biscuit, prevailed on the former to lead them to Rat Portage where they arrived at 8:00 p.m. on August 14th.

The alarm bells had begun to ring when the York Boats and Wolseley's canoe, with its Iroquois crew, arrived at Rat Portage with no sign having yet been seen of Wolseley and Huyshe in the gig. Butler set out to light a beacon at a place known as 'Devil's Rock', an island about fourteen miles into the lake from Rat Portage, but on his way there he met the colonel and his party. Though Huyshe would write of Dawson's inaccurate chart, he would also say, no doubt with a tinge of good humour, "The moral of my story is – Do not attempt to cross Lake of the Woods without a guide!"[35] The official journal somewhat laconically states, "To attempt to cross the Lake of the Woods without a guide is a feat which Colonel Wolseley will not attempt a second time."[36]

Butler had arrived at Rat Portage on August 8th. The HBC post consisted of just three log buildings surrounded by a wooden palisade. Here he found the other four York Boats with full crews made up of indigenous and mixed race people from Red River looking to render assistance to the expedition. As the first boats arrived they fired off their guns in welcome leading the men in the following boats to believe that Wolseley's fears were about to be realized and resistance encountered.[37] However, this was quickly sorted without incident and, as each brigade arrived, it immediately began its descent of the Winnipeg River. Butler waited for Wolseley's arrival and, as we have seen, he had to wait for six days.

Despite the optimistic reports from Dawson, Wolseley already had a good understanding of the perils of the Winnipeg River. Mr. McPherson, the HBC's man at Rat Portage, no doubt added to his consternation as he regaled him with tales of the dangers soon to be encountered.[38] Wolseley immediately sent Butler on his way to Fort Alexander to collect more guides for the brigades that would be following. The same evening Lieutenant-Colonel McNeill arrived by canoe. He had made the journey from Shebandowan Lake in just twelve days and was able to report that all was well with the brigades further back down the line of advance.[39]

Looking at a map of the Winnipeg River, one can see what Dawson meant when he described it as " ... a series of lake-like reaches with short intervals of rapid water between them."[40] One member of the force thought " ... it

---

31 Low, *Wolseley*, pp50/51.
32 Huyshe, *Red River*, p165.
33 Low, *Wolseley*, p51.
34 Huyshe, *Red River*, p168.
35 Huyshe, *Red River*, p169.
36 PPP 568, Correspondence and Journal, Appendix, p88.
37 Butler, *Lone Land*, p174.
38 Huyshe, *Red River*, p172.
39 Low, *Wolseley*, p53.
40 PPP 559, Dawson, "Report", p30.

might well be called "the Lakes of the Winnipeg, so numerous are its broad bays and granite islands, ... bounded by precipitous cliffs ... ."[41] The river flows through several gaps along the northern rim of Lake of the Woods forming a number of channels and about fifteen miles below Rat Portage a number of them join together with the main stream. "The windings of this immense river are very abrupt and opposite, suddenly changing from north-west to south-west and from south-west to north-west, for distances exceeding twenty miles. In the course of its 163 miles, it descends, by a succession of magnificent cataracts 349 feet."[42]

During this plunge, the expeditionary force would have to navigate no fewer than twenty-seven portages, as well as a number of rapids. All of those members who left written records speak to the extreme challenges that were faced. Sam Steele called the Winnipeg " ... one of the most difficult in the world," while Bugler Tennant said "the falls and the rapids ... made it a perilous stream, and the most difficult one on the route to navigate."[43] Lieutenant Harman wrote that the rapids and falls, coming so close together, " ... makes it most difficult of navigation and renders the greatest caution necessary."[44] Captain Wallace described his experience as the "seven anxious days" he spent on the Winnipeg.[45] With considerable understatement, Captain McCalmont said that the river was spectacular, but the cataracts " ... imposed heavy labour on the officers and men ... ."[46] He added that " ... it was perhaps fortunate that this, the most difficult part of the journey since embarking at McNeill's Landing, did not come till towards its close and till the boats' crews had become really efficient."[47] All of this was a far cry from Dawson's summation that " ... the Expedition experienced no difficulty whatever on the Winnipeg River."[48]

At Rat Portage the river is roughly three miles across with three potential routes each with its own waterfall.

> The first is not much used. The second, about two hundred yards further to the south, is three hundred yards long and very rough; it is chiefly used for canoes, and therefore Colonel Wolseley passed over it. The third and regular portage, which is three miles from the post to the south, is one hundred and thirty yards long, and as it is generally used for the Company's boats, Colonel Feilden's and the other brigades passed over it.[49]

On the 16th, Wolseley and McNeill set out in their respective canoes with Huyshe and Denison in the gig. It would take them just four and a half days to get to Fort Alexander as they did not have the same weight to transport over the portages. Seven days was more realistic for the brigades.

Wherever feasible, the boats were run down the rapids. If this could be done without unloading them, so much the better. In most cases, though, they had to be unloaded first. In some instances too, the boats had to be taken out and dragged across the portage road, but this was avoided if possible. When running the rapids Sam Steele wrote:

> ... the bowman always stands up in his place and steers, long paddle in hand, braced against the stem, his keen and practiced eye on the rushing water. The voyageur in the stern, who has shipped a long oar in the stern-rowlock, a ring securely fashioned so that it cannot jump out, keeps the boat from swinging in the current. Down the torrent the craft rushes, propelled by the desperate efforts of the six oarsmen. They row as for their lives so that there may be steerage way for the bowman, who by skilful use of his paddle, brings the vessel safely through the rocks and whirlpools of the passage.[50]

---

41 HA 170A12W/D/0438, Wallace, *Rebellion*, p21.
42 PPP 589, Riddell, *60th*, p121 (Quoting Hind).
Dawson says it was 149 miles from Rat Portage to Fort Alexander. This would make it approximately 151 to Lake Winnipeg.
43 Steele, *Forty Years* p25 & Tennant, *Rough Times*, p47.
44 PPP 570 Harman, *26 Years*,. p26.
45 HA 170A12W/D/0438, Wallace, *Rebellion*, p22.
46 Callwell, *McCalmont*, p53.
47 Callwell, *McCalmont*, p52
48 PPP 559, Dawson, "Report", p30.
49 Low, *Wolseley*, pp52/53.
50 Steele, *Forty* Years, p25.

One of the Voyageurs carries a 528 pound pack at one of the portages on the Winnipeg River. (Courtesy of Bruce Peel Special Collections, University of Alberta (2008.1.1.1.3.18.1)

Steele also recorded perhaps the heaviest weight that any expedition member carried across a portage when a recent arrival demonstrated what he could do:

> One of the Company's guides, a tall, dark, and powerful-looking voyageur, with a full black beard and moustache, hearing of the exploits of the Iroquois and others in our brigades, was anxious to show what he could do, so he carried two barrels of pork and 1000 rounds of ammunition across. The load had to be carefully secured and placed so that he could stand well under it. The weight was 528 lbs., but the burden was an awkward one and nothing to be gained by it except to show the man's great strength, which was patent to everyone as he moved quickly under the load without any apparent distress.[51]

One KRRC officer was also noted as having a considerable carrying capability. Ensign Algernon St. Maur, later the Duke of Somerset, " ... a tall, handsome young man ... frequently packed two barrels of pork on his back, 400 lbs ... ."[52] Ensign St. Maur had been educated at Britannia Royal Naval College, but chose to join the 60th Rifles. His wife would later write that, given his boating experience, " ... he steered many of the boats down the most dangerous part of the rapids."[53] Whether or not he played the prominent role his proud wife ascribed to him is not known. However, given his strength and his boating skill, he would certainly have been a reliable man to have along on the expedition. Twenty years later he made the journey once again, this time with his wife and by rail. They covered the same distance in forty-five hours.[54]

From Rat Portage it is nine miles to Les Dalles Rapids, 440 yards long with a drop of three feet. Twenty-one miles further along was La Grande Décharge with a fall of six feet.[55] This must have been a challenging obstacle as two force members describe near disasters here. Captain Huyshe was there on August 17th. The unloaded boats were to be run down the rapids with two guides, one in the front and one in the stern, and four men rowing. Captain Huyshe described what followed:

51 Steele, *Forty* Years, pp25/26.
52 Steele, *Forty* Years, p26.
53 Mrs. Algernon St. Maur, *Impressions of a Tender Foot During a Journey in Search of Sport in the Far West*, (London: John Murray, 1890), p28.
54 St. Maur, *Impressions*, p28. Mrs. St. Maur also says that at 'Savenne,' presumably Savanne on Lac de Mille Lacs, they saw two of the boats from the expedition, pp27/28.
55 PPP 589, Riddell, *60th*, p123.

> Whilst at Rat Portage Baptiste had cut and fashioned a fine broad paddle … and took his place in the bow … .We went over at a tremendous pace, so close to the cliff at one side (in order to avoid a half sunken rock) that the starboard oars had to be unshipped and run to avoid the cliff. Scarcely realizing the speed at which we were going, I was late in running in my oar, and consequently lost a rowlock by it, besides nearly breaking the oar and upsetting the boat. Of course when the oar touched the cliff it partially turned the boat's head, and Baptiste had to give a superhuman heave with his paddle to clear the sunken rock. In doing this his paddle broke in two like a stick of sealing-wax, and had he not, quick as lightning, seized a scull, which was fortunately at hand, and forced the boat's head round with it, we should have been on the rock and upset in the twinkling of an eye. It was a close shave … . [56]

Sam Steele recounted how, as they approached the crest of the same rapid with Captain Daniel Hunter McMillan aboard, the stern oar:

> … snapped like a pipe stem and the boat swung into the tremendous waves on our right, rolling and pitching over them, and hurling several of the crew from their oars into the bottom of the boat … we were quite helpless and, death stared us in the face as we surged past the rocks and whirlpools at a great speed, while Big Mike, [their 'powerful and skilful Iroquois' boatman] stood towering in the bow wielding a heavy oar as if it were a light paddle … .and he handled his oar with such effect that the boat came safely through … .[57]

It is interesting to see how often disaster was averted by the skill of the Iroquois boatmen and not surprising that Wolseley, along with the other chroniclers, spoke so highly of them. Captain Huyshe felt that the expedition's Ojibwe guides also did good work, but that they would avoid the rapids if they could. The Iroquois on the other hand, he believed actually preferred the rapids to smooth water.[58] In spite of the dangers, there was no difficulty in getting volunteers from among the expedition's soldiers to man the boats during the running of the rapids and some men had " … the thrilling experience of taking every boat in their brigade over a dangerous chute."[59]

The Yellow Mud Falls and Pine Portage, " … with the dangerous Cave Rapids, which have often proved so destructive to the bateaux of the Company … ," followed.[60] Next came Portage de l'Isle, the second portage to be so named during the trek to Fort Garry, and Huyshe believed the rapids here were the worst of them all.

> Imagine an enormous volume of water hurled headlong down a steep incline of smooth, slippery rock against a cluster of massive boulders, over which it dashed madly with a roar like thunder, foaming along until it reached the level below, where its exhausted fury subsided into circling eddies, and deep treacherous whirlpools. Into this fearful abyss of waters we dashed, old Michel [Baptiste's uncle] boldly steering straight down the centre of it; and as we tore down the incline at railroad speed with the green white-tipped waves curling their monstrous heads high over the gunwale of the boat, we held our very breath for awe, and for a second or two forgot to row, till the sharp admonition from Michel roused us from our stupor.[61]

Here the gig was practically the only boat to run the river, the rest being taken across the portage road.

Next came the Chûte-à-Jacquot where the river falls thirteen feet, then Point des Bois Rapids where it drops thirty seven feet. This was followed by Slave Falls, where legend had it that the Ojibwe had sent two Sioux slaves over the falls tied together in a canoe.[62] Huyshe felt that Slave Falls was one of the two most beautiful on the river, but thought the canoe portage was " … very dangerous to approach, except for a skilled boatman well acquainted

56 Huyshe, *Red River*, p175.
57 Steele, *Forty Years*, pp26/27
58 Huyshe, *Red River*, p176.
59 Tennant, *Rough Times*, p47.
60 PPP 589, Riddell, *60th*, p123.
61 Huyshe, *Red River*, pp179/180.
62 PPP 589, Riddell, *60th*, p123.

with the place."[63] It was here that Colonel Wolseley passed Lieutenant Harman's brigade as he drove forward to catch up with the leading elements of the expedition.[64]

Barrière and Otter Falls were the next two obstacles. Butler had an uncomfortable time here. Travelling in a canoe with three First Nations men, a father and his two sons, it was the weather rather than the challenges of the river that caused his discomfiture. "A wild storm burst upon us … , and our bivouac was a damp and dreary one." His oil cloth was not sufficiently large to cover him completely and, as two bags of letters and papers had been entrusted to his care, presumably to be sent via the United States postal service, he had a great deal of trouble trying to keep them dry. By the break of daylight it was still raining. "How bleak and wretched it all was!" he wrote. The following night, August 17th, they had reached Otter Falls. "It came a night of ceaseless rain, and again the mail bags underwent a drenching. The old Indian cleared a space in the dripping vegetation, and made me a rude shelter with branches woven together, but the rain beat through, and drenched body, bag and baggage." The following day Lieutenant Butler felt he had to stop and examine his bags of papers. He found their consistency was now that of a 'pulpy mass.' Realizing that he needed to dry them, he made a large fire and, " … placing cross sticks above proceeded to toast and grill the dripping papers."[65]

Seven miles from Otter Falls were the dreaded seven portages. "These are about three miles long, and are simply an unbroken series of rapids, falls, whirlpools, and eddies, necessitating seven distinct portages, some of the approaches to and departures from which are very dangerous."[66] While suffering no losses in his brigade, Riddell reported seeing the wrecks of boats hauled up on the shore here.[67] At one of the last rapids that Huyshe's boat ran, they again came close to disaster when the gig grazed a rock.

> Instantly she heeled over on to her side, my oar was whipped out of my hand, and I myself thrown violently on my back, and for a moment I thought it was all up with us, but she had only grazed, and the rush of water carried her past; and as she righted Michel picked up my oar and handed it to me, and we went on as if nothing had happened.[68]

At Silver Falls, in fact two waterfalls, a vast torrent descends a slope about 200 yards long. This was the second of the two waterfalls that Captain Huyshe felt were the most beautiful on the river. The drop in the river was sixteen feet, " … in the form of five or six giant swells."[69] After Silver Falls there was just one more rapid to overcome, Pine Portage, the second on the river to be so named. "Only those who have been through this trip can properly appreciate the feeling of relief that came over us as we stood safe and sound on the west of Pine Portage."[70]

When they grounded their boats at Fort Alexander, they were tired, wet, cold and hungry, but they knew there were no more portages, they were as good as there and the " … hateful portage-strap would cease to gall our foreheads for some time to come … ."[71] A couple of miles further along was the mouth of the river and Lake Winnipeg. As Butler put it, after many "close shaves, … from the 600 miles of wilderness there emerged 400 soldiers [the Canadian troops had not yet arrived] whose muscles and sinews, taxed and tested by continuous toil, had been developed to a pitch of excellence … ."[72] Butler added that not a man had been lost and this was certainly his belief and has become the accepted truth of the expedition. It may not, however, be accurate.

While it had been a significant accomplishment that the expedition had travelled so far, under such difficult conditions and without any major disaster, it seems likely there had been one fatal casualty. On Saturday August 20th, the day that Wolseley arrived at Fort Alexander, Captain Daniel Hunter McMillan, in command of No. 4

---

63 Huyshe, *Red River*, p181.
64 PPP 570, Harman, *26 Years*, p26.
65 Butler, *Lone Land*, pp180-182.
66 Huyshe, *Red River*, p183.
67 PPP 589, Riddell, *60th*, p123.
68 Huyshe *Red River*, p183.
69 PPP 589, Riddell, *60th*, p124 (Quoting Hind).
70 PPP 570, Harman, *26 Years*, p26.
71 Huyshe, *Red River*, p185.
72 Butler, *Lone Land*, p186.

Company in the 1st Ontario Rifles, reported in his diary the details of an accident. In the course of unloading Ensign Mulvey's boat at one of the portages, Private Butcher had tossed his bag containing a loaded colt revolver, to Captain McMillan. The bag slipped from the captain's grasp and struck a rock causing the pistol to discharge. Butcher was hit. "I saw him in the boat holding his side with his hand and the blood spurting from the wound." The injured man was removed from the boat and was found to have been shot through the right side of the chest, with the ball lodged under his shoulder blade. There was little that could be done for him. Two men were left with him and he was made as comfortable as possible. "He cried when we parted and mentioned what would become of his wife and child … . We left him and moved off at 5 o'clock. I hope we will see him again, but I am afraid it will prove fatal."[73] The following day McMillan's diary mentions that he has had no further word on 'poor Butcher' and that is the last we hear of the man. It is more than likely that he succumbed to a wound of such magnitude, isolated as they were in the wilderness, and seems to have gone unrecorded in the official records of the expeditionary force.

Feilden and the regular troops arrived at Fort Alexander on August 18th and Wolseley two days later. Donald Smith was waiting for him and gave some of his staff supper. "Seldom have I enjoyed anything more thoroughly than the fresh bread and butter which he set before us … ."[74] Sam Steele arrived with Macleod's brigade on the 25th, but Wolseley and the regulars were not there. On the 21st they had set out in fifty boats on the last leg of the journey.

73 Sir Samuel Steele Collection (2008/1/1/3/1/1), Diary of Captain Daniel Hunter McMillan No. 4 Company 1st Ontario Rifles.

74 Huyshe, *Red River*, p185.

19

Fort Alexander to Fort Garry

Fort Alexander is situated on the left bank of the Winnipeg River about two miles from Lake Winnipeg.[1] Lieutenant Harman described it as 'very prettily situated' perched on a high bank. "It is larger and more important than Fort Francis [sic] and is far more imposing in importance."[2] This is true, though his view may have been coloured by the fact that here he and his men ate their first fresh meat since embarking on Shebandowan Lake.

As Wolseley prepared to set out on the final leg of the journey, the question first and foremost on the minds of the men of the expedition pertained to whether or not there was going to be a fight when they reached Fort Garry. W.L. Morton, in his classic book *A History of the Canadian West*, wrote that "Riel does not seem to have made the slightest attempt to oppose Colonel Wolseley."[3] Back in June while still at Prince Arthur's Landing, the expeditionary force commander had sent a proclamation to 'The Loyal Inhabitants of Manitoba.' Delivered by Donald Smith, it spoke of the mission being one of peace with 'the sole object' being " ... to secure her Majesty's sovereign authority." It talked of courts of law for all, promised strict order and discipline, and guaranteed protection of private property.[4] Riel had personally supervised the printing of the proclamation for the people of Red River on July 23rd.[5] This is hardly the action of someone bent on militarily opposing the expedition. If the matter of amnesty had been dealt with, Riel would likely have gone out to welcome Wolseley.[6] As we have seen, however, the response in Ontario to the killing of Scott had made the granting an amnesty a very thorny issue for Macdonald and the British were unwilling to become involved, viewing the matter as a Canadian concern. Riel had made a cardinal blunder when he sanctioned Scott's execution.

One can only imagine Wolseley's response had the Métis leader come out to greet him upon his arrival. Despite the conditions placed on the use of Imperial troops by the British Government, and the orders for the expeditionary force stating categorically that it was in no way a punitive expedition, Wolseley had without doubt fallen in with the views of his friend George Denison of the Canada First movement. On August 21st the colonel wrote to his wife:

> I hope Riel will have bolted, for though I should like to hang him to the highest tree in the place, I have such a horror of rebels and vermin of his kind, my treatment of him might not receive from the civil powers that be that amount of approval which in these puling times of weaknesses and timid policy, is only accorded to the mildest policy.[7]

1 The banks of the river are described as left or right based on the assumption that one is facing down river. This will become important when the story of the expedition's trip up the Red River is described later in this chapter. Here they are travelling up river and so when describing the left bank, it is actually on their right, and vice versa.

2 PPP 570, Harman, *26 Years*, p26.

3 Morton, *Canadian West*, p918.

4 See Appendix 3 for the full text of the proclamation.

5 Begg, *Journal*, p392.

6 Morton, *Canadian West*, p918.

7 Hove Public Library, WP.1/1, Letter from Garnet Wolseley to Lucy Wolseley, August 21, 1870.

In his memoirs, written over thirty years later, he said "Personally I was glad that Riel did not come out and surrender, as he at one time said he would, for I could not then have hanged him as I might have done had I taken him prisoner when in arms against his sovereign."[8] In Hove Public Library there is copy of *A Soldier's Life* annotated in Wolseley's own hand detailing how he would like the book amended should it be re-printed. He did not change one word in this passage, other than to capitalize Arms and Sovereign.[9]

It is doubtful Riel ever seriously toyed with the idea of resistance. Indeed, during their meeting he had told Butler that he was only holding power so that could turn it over to a 'proper government.' He had taken no steps to impede the expedition's progress while it was at its most vulnerable, strung out across the lakes and rivers of the interior. In fact, he did not even know where it was because he had not sent out scouts to track its progress. There is also no evidence he did anything to stir the First Nations people to resistance. By the time the expeditionary force arrived at Fort Alexander it also seems that many of the Métis military arm were away from the settlement " ... on the plains and rivers to the north."[10]

Nevertheless, when Donald Smith arrived at Fort Alexander on August 10th, he reported that:

> ... he heard rumours that Riel had called a meeting of about 600 Métis 'the purpose being to oppose the entrance of the troops until an amnesty should be granted covering the shooting of Scott and all other acts done by the insurgents. It appears that the meeting pronounced against resistance' ... 'and were not sparing in their abuse of 'President' Riel and the other members of the 'Provisional Government ... .'[11]

Wolseley also said that he had received intelligence of the Métis leader calling a 'secret conclave,' and while it was not known what had transpired at this, an order had followed that the HBC was forbidden to sell gunpowder or bullets. According to the colonel, the informant said that this had been done " ... to prevent the supply of ammunition running short should they require it."[12] This he took as evidence of Riel intending to make a stand.

Wolseley spins a good yarn in his various writings dealing with the Red River Expedition. The settlement with its loyal population being held in check against its will. The relief force, having hacked its way through the wilderness, is almost there. Time is of the essence and the vanguard must press on with all speed. The truth is somewhat more prosaic. This is not to downplay that there was a significant section of the Red River population which had been cowed into silence and submission by the actions of Riel and the military arm of the Métis since the outbreak of the troubles. Riel's motivations may have been justifiable when confronted by the high-handed actions of the Canadian surveyors and road builders, not to mention the haughty and derisory attitude of the Canadian Party, but there was no escaping the fact that there were a great many people within the community whose views did not align with his and towards these he had used the threat of force, and on occasion force itself, to keep them in check.

Nevertheless, in spite of the letters he was receiving from loyalist elements at Fort Garry to move quickly, the preponderance of intelligence indicated that an outburst of violence at the settlement was decidedly unlikely, as was any serious opposition to the entry of the expeditionary force. Yet in his memoirs Wolseley concluded that "on the whole, the general tenor of the news indicated that Riel would fight." This was his justification for pressing on without waiting for the arrival of the Ontario battalion, even though its two forward boat brigades were known to be close by, Wolseley and his party having passed them on the Winnipeg River.[13]

The rumoured meeting where the Métis had refused their support in opposing the expeditionary force would, of course, not have precluded Riel and a few of his close supporters from making a last stand. With the gift of hindsight it is easy to see that this was unlikely, though it was still incumbent on Wolseley to take all necessary precautions to ensure he was not caught off guard as he embarked on the final leg of his journey to Fort Garry. To

8 Wolseley, *Soldier's Life*, p220.
9 Hove Public Library, Wolseley, *Soldier's Life*, Annotated Version, p220.
10 Stanley, *Riel*, p153.
11 McDonald, *Strathcona*, p169.
12 Wolseley, *Narrative Part 3*, p172.
13 Wolseley, *Soldier's Life*, p214.

have done otherwise would have been foolish and Wolseley was no fool. However, if he truly believed that his force of roughly 350 men was about to be confronted by an army of six hundred Métis warriors, or even Riel and a few of his adherents, it seems logical that he would have waited for the two additional nearby boat brigades of Ontario volunteers. Wolseley may have simply been exhibiting the common view of the time that a small band of British troops was more than a match for a larger force of indigenous levies; nevertheless, one could also take the view that not waiting for the Ontario men, who he knew were close by, was a strong indication that he expected the opposition to be at worst limited.

In all likelihood Wolseley's reasoning in deciding to move on from Fort Alexander as quickly as he did had little to do with a fear of serious Métis resistance and the evidence for this comes from two members of the expeditionary force's staff. Huyshe was clear that Riel's adherents had no intention of putting up a fight and, " ... in view of the certainty of being warmly welcomed by the loyal section of the inhabitants, Colonel Wolseley resolved not to wait for the Militia, but to push on at once with the Regulars."[14] In a similar vein, McCalmont believed that there was no reason to wait for the militia " ... in view of the intelligence to hand as to Riel's adherents deserting him."[15]

There were also practical considerations behind Wolseley's decision to move when he did. From Fort Alexander the force would proceed down the last two miles of the Winnipeg River to Lake Winnipeg, swing west round Elk Island and then turn south towards the mouth of the Red River. Wolseley knew that the wind could change quickly when the weather was foul, making it difficult to navigate around Elk Island. He had already been caught by an adverse wind once on Lake of the Woods and would take all necessary steps to ensure this did not happen again. The fair wind on August 21st could not be counted upon to last and, for this reason alone, Wolseley was right to go when he did. Time was still of the essence to ensure the British troops returned to Canada before the winter weather set in and, as we shall see, the weather was about to become very nasty. This would delay the forward brigades of the Ontario volunteer battalion when they set out to cross the lake just a few days later. Had Wolseley waited for them, he would have been delayed as well.

So what do we make of Wolseley's assertions in his subsequent writings regarding his expectation of a fight at Fort Garry? He certainly received letters from the settlement urging that he press on with haste, though the preponderance of the evidence available indicated opposition was unlikely. Nevertheless, the colonel clearly had to make preparation for all eventualities during the final stages of his advance. Wolseley's achievement in getting the expeditionary force to Fort Garry was significant. However, his later pronouncements of an impending battle smacks of exaggeration, perhaps in an attempt to emphasize the drama of the moment rather than providing an accurate representation of actual events. It could be argued with some justification that he was writing for posterity.

At 3:00pm on August 21st the bugles sounded advance and fifty boats containing the 60th Rifles, together with the artillery and engineer components of the expeditionary force, set off down the Winnipeg River to Lake Winnipeg. Huyshe likened it to a Viking flotilla making a descent on an enemy coast. Wolseley attested that the fleet made 'a pretty sight', worthy of the attentions of an artist.

In warm and sunny weather with a light breeze blowing from the southwest, the flotilla made good time. Wolseley accompanied Donald Smith in one of the larger HBC boats. Its square sail " ... towered over the little lugs of the smaller boats, and led the way steering well 'out to sea' to make a good offing. The fleet followed as fast as oars and sails would take them ... ."[16]

They spent the night " ... in a broad, curving, sandy bay ... " on Elk Island eighteen miles north of Fort Alexander.[17] "The boats drew up in a long line, side by side, with their bows on the beach. Fires were soon lighted,

14 Huyshe, *Red River*, p186.
15 Callwell, *McCalmont*, p53.
16 Huyshe, *Red River*, p187.
17 Butler, *Lone Land*, p186.

and a few tents pitched here and there … . One looked down from the high bank upon the busy scene below, where all was cheerful bustle, the hum of voices, the noise of axes chopping wood … ."[18] The men were soon " … bent over the frying-pans or peering into the kettles with anxious interest … ."[19]

The expedition was sheltered from the wind as their bay faced north and the wind was blowing from the southwest. The lack of a breeze, however, would temper this picture of bucolic paradise as it gave free rein for the insect life of the island to descend on the troops in full force. " … Not even the veils, or smoky fires called 'smudges' lighted in the tents could keep off the insects; the mosquitos and sand flies on that desert island have never tasted human blood before; not one of them can say so now."[20] Huyshe speculated on whether their picturesque bay might one day become " … a favourite summer resort of the wealthy inhabitants of the Red River … . When emigration shall have covered the fertile prairies … with a teeming population, and towns and cities have sprung up over the length and breadth of the land … ."[21] Today it is one of Manitoba's provincial parks.

The following morning, the wind, while not as good as the day before, was still favourable. They set off across the lake in the direction of the Red River, sailing in " … a wide scattered mass … ."[22] With intended understatement, Huyshe described Lake Winnipeg as "not a bad sized pond!"[23] It is in fact 264 miles long, with an average width of thirty-five miles and a maximum width of sixty miles. It covers an area of around 9000 square miles with a drainage basin of 400,000 square miles.[24] At its southern end it was found to be very shallow with the result that even a little wind could raise a heavy swell. The mouth of the Red River was reached in the early afternoon and a number of boats grounded due to the shallowness. The land was marshy and abounded with wild-duck and geese. They had travelled six or seven miles upstream before the ground became solid.

The progress was slower now. The wind was blowing against them and for the first time since the Height of Land Portage they were pulling against the current. Butler and Irvine were sent in Wolseley's canoe to scout ahead and the boats of the expedition advanced with Wolseley in the lead followed by Feilden and then the rest of the force in two lines.[25]

Wolseley had hoped to reach the Stone Fort at Lower Fort Garry by nightfall. When they halted, they had travelled fourteen miles upriver from Lake Winnipeg but were still twelve miles short of their goal. They camped on the left bank near the First Nations settlement where Butler had received refuge during his stay at Red River. Chief Henry Prince " … with a number of his warriors came across the river to pay a visit to the commander-in-chief."[26] There was virtually no information as to what was going on in the settlement and, rather surprisingly, Prince did not know of the approach of the expeditionary force either. The last he had heard was that it was in the vicinity of Lake of the Woods. A messenger was sent up river to the Stone Fort and returned with Mr. Flett, the HBC's man there. He confirmed that that there was no knowledge in the community that the troops were as close as they were; his understanding had also been that they were still in the Lake of the Woods area.[27] This ignorance by the local population as to the force's whereabouts was a state of affairs that Wolseley was determined to maintain. When asked if Riel would fight, Flett said that opinions differed in the community, but it was thought that, if he could get some of his supporters to stand with him, he would.[28] Given the comments already made regarding Riel's intention to resist the expedition, the author's view that the evidence is solidly against this can only be reiterated.

It had rained thirteen days in August up until the 20th and on the evening of the 22nd the mild weather of the past two days again gave way to precipitation. By 3:30 a.m. it had slowed to a drizzle, but this was only a foretaste

18 Wolseley, *Narrative Part 3*, p173.
19 Huyshe, *Red River*, p188.
20 HA 170A12W/D/0438, Wallace, *Rebellion*, pp23/24.
21 Huyshe, *Red River*, p188.
22 Butler, *Lone Land*, p186.
23 Huyshe, *Red River*, p189.
24 Wolseley, *Narrative Part 3*, p173 & PPP 589 Riddell, *60th*, p126.
25 Wolseley says three in his *Narrative*, but all other accounts at this point say two.
26 PPP 589, Riddell, *60th*, p126.
27 Wolseley, *Narrative Part 3*, p174.
28 Huyshe, *Red River*, p191.

Lower Fort Garry, also known as The Stone Fort. (*Illustrated London News.* ILNO-1870-0212-0013-F)

of what was to come. After an early start, by 8:00 a.m. on August 23rd they had arrived at the Stone Fort where breakfast awaited the officers.

> The officials had prepared for us officers what really seemed to be a most sumptuous breakfast, and I look back upon that repast as quite the most satisfactory meal that I have partaken of anywhere. For although the fare was simple enough in itself, there was fresh meat, and there was butter, and there was properly baked bread. Those were articles of diet that to us pilgrims seemed to be extraordinary luxuries after more than a month of 'choke dog' or worse.[29]

There is no mention of what the men ate. As they are not mentioned, presumably it was their regular rations. This reversion to a more traditional relationship between the officers and men flies in the face of Wolseley's thinking as outlined in his *Soldier's Pocketbook*, not to mention the more egalitarian approach that had been adopted towards the heavy work and risks of the expedition thus far.

Upper Fort Garry was 21½ miles by road from the Stone Fort. Before setting out, Wolseley ordered that the boats be lightened and only four days of provisions taken. The colonel's goal was to reach the upper fort by nightfall. Captain Wallace's company was detached to act as an advance guard and flanking party. They would move up the more settled left bank of the river, keeping the bulk of the company on the road about a quarter mile ahead of the boats, with a line of men back to the river and an advanced section about five hundred yards ahead. Signal flags were provided to both the advanced section and the main body of the company to ensure communication was maintained with the main force on the river.

A motley group of horses, ponies and mules was accumulated so that Wallace's company would have a mounted component. Carts were also organized for the rest. There was a fair degree of amusement as men who had never ridden before found themselves having to come to grips with their new equine companions. As a cavalry officer, Captain McCalmont was placed in command of this section. "Some of my troopers could ride and others said they could ride, while one of them who declared that he did not know whether he could ride or not until he tried,

29 Callwell, *McCalmont*, p54.

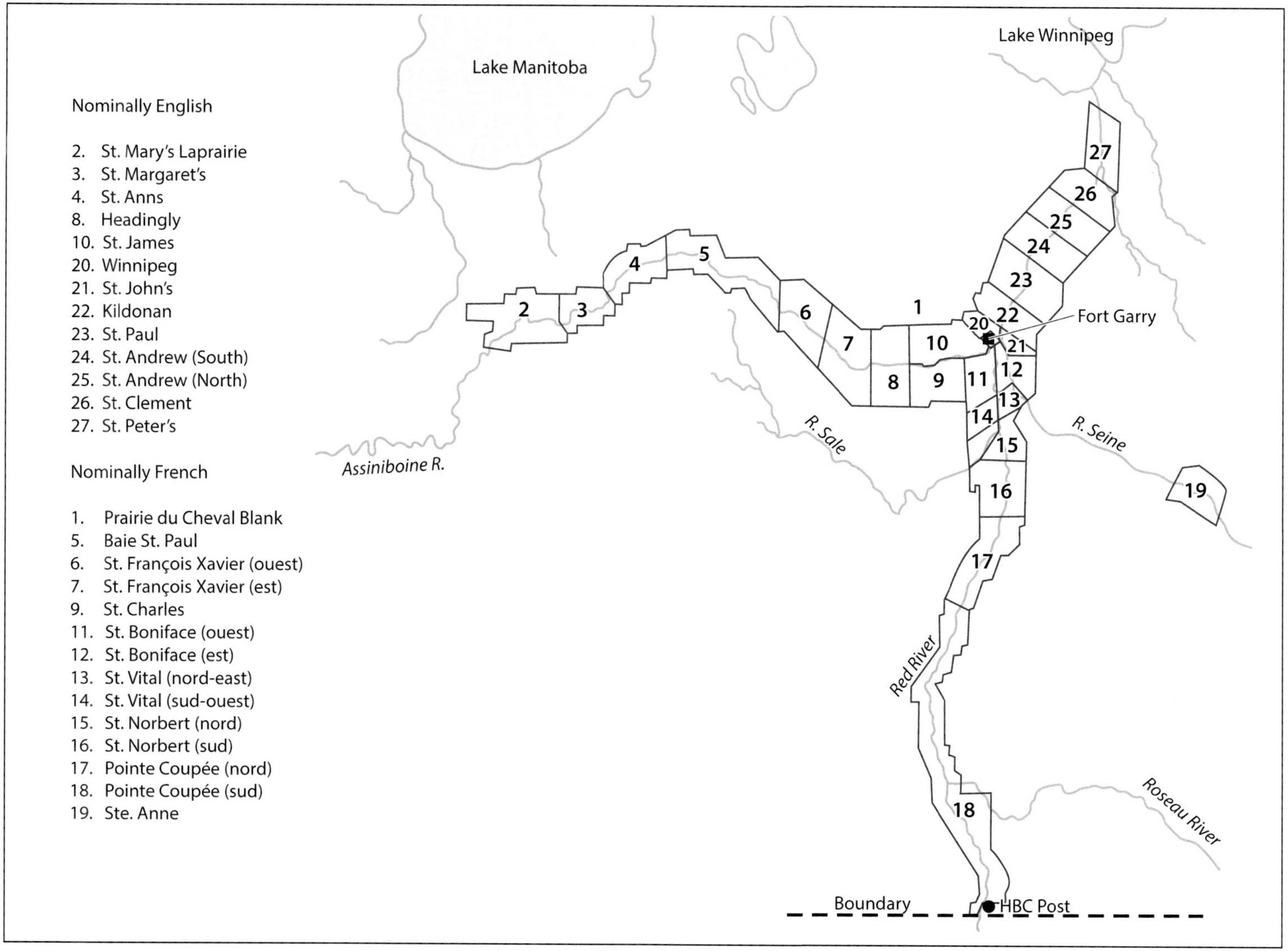

The parishes of the Red River Settlement.

proceeded to clamber up his pony on the wrong side.[30] Wallace described an incident where, owing to the unit having advanced too far ahead of the boats:

> I said to my bugler, 'Sound the halt.' He was mounted on a mare, whose foal was at her heels – a common sight in the Northwest; a considerable time elapsed while he tried to fasten himself securely by the mane, and by dint of coaxing, ... persuade his animal to stand. At last he gave the call; just as the last note rang out, the foal took advantage of the halt to partake of some refreshment. The effect was instantaneous. This liberty combined with the noise of the bugle was too much for the maternal nerves, and the bugler and his bugle were sent flying to the ground.[31]

Huyshe noted that the left bank was fairly well settled with " ... clean white houses and neat farms abutting on the river."[32] The right bank was much less so and Butler rode through the woods here to ensure there were no surprises hidden in the trees, emerging periodically to report on his progress. The rest of the expedition moved up the river by boat with the 7 pounders mounted in the bows of the two boats manned by the Royal Artillerymen.

The advance was something of a triumphal procession. The parishes through which they were passing were English-speaking; 'English and Scotch' according to Butler, and the troops were viewed as liberators. "As we advanced ... , people turned out from every house ... , the men cheered, the women waved handkerchiefs, and the bells of the churches, which are all Protestant below Fort Garry, were rung to manifest the universal joy felt at seeing us. At some places numbers of Indians were encamped, who welcomed us by the discharge of firearms."[33] All who left a record of the day tell of similar scenes of jubilation as the force passed by.[34]

There were some rapids a few miles above the Stone Fort, but these were passed easily by poling and tracking. As their journey continued the banks became steeper and it was clear to see that the surface was made up of alluvial clay. "When wet, the mud formed from these substances is of such a soapy and sticky nature that it is almost impossible to walk over it without losing your shoes."[35] This would soon become readily apparent to the men of the force.

Wolseley gave orders to the flanking party that all who attempted to move in the direction of the upper fort were to be detained with the result that the parishes they passed through became cut off from Upper Fort Garry. The colonel was determined to ensure that " ... the actual appearance of the boats was the first intimation the people had of the arrival of the Expedition ... ."[36] It was later discovered that vague rumours of the expedition being on the river had in fact reached Fort Garry, but that Riel discounted them. Contradictorily, there is also some evidence that during the night he and O'Donoghue rode out in their direction to ascertain for themselves, but due to the heavy rain that was by then falling, and fearful of capture if the troops were indeed there, they turned back.

By nightfall on the 23rd the expeditionary force was still six miles short of the upper fort and orders were given to halt for the night. They made camp on the left bank with advanced pickets spread out on both sides of the river. Wallace's company continued in this role on the left bank. "Everyone who came within the line of sentries was detained, and several of Riel's counsellors were made prisoners."[37]

About 10:00 p.m. a violent storm blew in from the northwest and it continued relentlessly all through the night. Huyshe says that the left bank party were about 600 yards off in a farmhouse, but Wallace makes no mention of being under cover. "It blew a gale and the rain fell in sheets, and as we stood by the fire, knee-deep in mud, with no great coats or tents, it was as much as we could do to keep ourselves alive, by burning the neighbouring

30 Callwell, *McCalmont*, p54.
31 HA 170A12W/D/0438, Wallace, *Rebellion*, p27.
32 Huyshe, *Red* River, p192.
33 Wolseley, *Narrative Part 3*, p174.
34 PPP 589, Riddell, *60th*, p127, HA 170A12W/D/0438, Wallace, *Rebellion*, p26 & Bulter, *Lone Land*, p187.
35 Wolseley, *Narrative Part 3*, pp174/175.
36 Low, *Wolseley*, p64.
37 PP 589, Riddell, *60th*, p129.

farmers' fences."[38] Given the conditions, he also pondered what might have happened if they were faced with a more determined opponent. "The night was black and wind so strong, that although sentries were posted round the camp, I am confident had Riel had the pluck, he might easily have surprised us."[39] Wallace refers to those that were caught in the net as 'spies,' though whether or not they were is debateable. Most were likely settlers who went to see the camp; "but once they got within the picket lines they stayed there, to their surprise, all night."[40] 'One or two' were overhead plotting their escape, but when told they would be fired on if any attempt was made, they quieted down. The force had its own 'spies' as well, and local loyalists were dispatched to Winnipeg village and the upper fort to try and determine if anything was afoot there.

As the night bore on, the wind howled and the rain fell in torrents, " ... till the tents flapped and fell and drenched soldiers shivered shelterless, waiting for the dawn. The occupants of tents which stood the pelting of the pitiless storm were no better off than those outside; the surface of the ground became ankle-deep in mud and water, and the men lay in pools during the last hours of the night."[41]

The onset of daylight saw no break in the relentless downpour. "As we bent over our fires ... trying to get some warmth for our bodies, and sufficient heat to boil the kettles, a more miserable-looking lot of objects it would be impossible to imagine. Every one [sic] was wet through; we were cold and hungry; our very enemies would have pitied our plight."[42] Breakfast, such as it was, put a bit of life back into the men, but "the unfortunate picquets and sentries looked more liked drowned rats than human beings, and the men were so done up with cold and wet ... ."[43] The one positive that could be said for the horrible weather of the night was that it had also kept the majority of the inhabitants of the settlement indoors. The secret of the force's presence was largely intact.

With daylight, Wolseley surveyed an unpleasant scene before him. The surrounding countryside was flooded and the roads, mere tracks at the best of times, were ankle deep in 'black gluey mud.'[44] The intention had been to march the last six miles to Fort Garry, but given the conditions, Wolseley knew he had to amend his plan. By 6:00 a.m. the men, wet through and cold, were back at their oars " ... rowing up the river in three columns, and the advanced guard resuming its skirmishing."[45] In places the flank company had to wade across the flooded landscape; however, they were still in the English-speaking part of the settlement and, as they passed the Protestant cathedral, the Union Flag was run up and the tintinnabulation of the bells was heard by all.

Two miles by road below Fort Garry the Red River makes a sharp bend to the east before turning equally sharply westward once again. Known as Point Douglas, the left bank is not so steep here and this is where at 8:00 a.m. the boats turned into the shore and the troops disembarked. The force was quickly formed up with the boats left in the charge of the *voyageurs*. Captain Wallace's skirmishers remained out front. The rest of the companies of the 60th were formed up in open column. Wallace and his men had secured some waggons to carry the ammunition, engineer's equipment and the hospital, as well as some 'wretched ponies' for Wolseley and his staff to ride. They set off, " ... ankle deep in a thick black mud, and the rain still pouring in torrents," behind the skirmishers with all but one of the remaining companies at the front, followed by the waggons with the two 7-pounder cannons limbered up trundling along behind, and then the final company acting as a rearguard.[46] It was heavy going over the waterlogged and muddy ground with the rain in their faces and the visibility reduced to no more than a few hundred yards.

Rumours as to whether Riel would fight had abounded throughout the night and this continued into the morning. While Wolseley must have known there was little chance of serious opposition, there would still have

38 HA 170A12W/D/0438, Wallace, *Rebellion*, p28.
39 HA 170A12W/D/0438, Wallace, *Rebellion*, p28.
40 R.G. Macbeth, *The Romance of the Canadian West*, (Toronto: Ryerson, 1920), p161.
41 Butler, *Lone Land*, p188.
42 Wolseley, *Narrative Part 3*, p176.
43 Huyshe, *Red* River, p194.
44 PPP 568, Correspondence and Journal, Appendix, p92.
45 PPP 589, Riddell, *60th*, p130. There is a sketch of the positions of the boats on the river in Wallace's Journal held at the Hampshire Archives.
46 Huyshe, *Red* River, pp194/195 & Low, *Wolseley*, p66.

been a question in his mind as to whether Riel and his immediate followers intended to make a stand. This was certainly his hope, and if we believe the accounts left to us by those in the force, it was the hope of the men as well.[47] One said it was understood that Riel had fifty men with him, while another wrote the belief was two hundred.[48] Those locals sent out the night before to attempt to ascertain what was going on in Winnipeg and at the fort now returned and reported that the 'rebel' flag was still flying and Riel was still in residence.

Most accounts state that, as the force proceeded on its final march to Fort Garry, the local intelligence was that those inside intended to fight. "It certainly looked as if our labours were not to be altogether in vain," wrote Huyshe and the pace quickened as word spread among the ranks that a battle was in the offing.[49] Interestingly, there is one dissenting voice among the British as the climax of the expedition was reached. Captain McCalmont, the young cavalry officer, wrote that "from the information that had been extracted out of the settlers, it seemed more than doubtful whether Riel meant to offer resistance."[50]

Winnipeg village was about 800 yards north of Fort Garry connected to it by a straight road. The fort itself, located at the confluence of the Red and Assiniboine Rivers, was described as " ... a collection Hudson's Bay Company's buildings, surrounded by a stone wall on three sides, and by a wooden palisading on the fourth, with circular towers at each corner, the whole loopholed for guns and musketry. It is about 100 yards long by 85 yards wide; in the centre is Government House."[51] At the southern gate on the Assiniboine River was a boat bridge.[52] As the expeditionary force neared Winnipeg village, it wheeled slightly to bypass the buildings and made its final approach towards the northern gate (actually facing northwest) with Winnipeg on its left flank and the Assiniboine River on its right.[53] The gate was closed, but there was no flag flying and no signs of life to indicate that the fort was occupied. Gun muzzles could be seen in the bastion and at one or two embrasures, " ... but no sign of defence or resistance was visible throughout the place."[54] They continued across the open plain, affording no cover, between the village and the fort wondering if they would soon see puffs of smoke reporting from the guns. Riddell noted that at their approach, " ... several persons were observed hurrying off across the prairie, in buggies and on horseback ... ."[55] Some of these, said to be Riel's counsellors, were taken into custody, but Wolseley was unable to ascertain from them if the Métis leader was actually in the fort.

The force commander needed to know what was going on around the other side of Fort Garry; the side facing the Assiniboine River. What is clear is that one or more of his staff officers went to find out. What is not clear is which of the staff officers it actually was. Most frequently it is mentioned as McNeill and Denison.[56] George Denison would later write:

> When approaching Fort Garry Colonel Wolseley sent my brother on to reconnoitre. He rode on to the fort, and around it to the rear gate, out of which Riel's followers were running. He rode into the gate, glanced hurriedly around and rode out and back to carry the information there would be no resistance. As he was the first man in Fort Garry, Colonel Wolseley ordered him with Sir John McNeil [sic] to raise once more the Union Jack to the top of the flagpole ... .[57]

47 See Butler, *Buller* p25 and HA 170A12W/D/0438, Wallace, *Rebellion*, p28. Buller said " ... he was disgusted to have come so far to hear the band play 'God Save the Queen.'" Wallace said " ... we had been told the night before that Riel meant fighting with his 200 men ... this report was now confirmed by several idlers to our great joy."

48 PPP 589, Riddell, *60th*, p130 & HA 170A12W/D/0438, Wallace, *Rebellion*, p28.

49 Huyshe, *Red River*, p195.

50 Callwell, *McCalmont*, p55.

51 HA 170A12W/D/0438, Wallace, *Rebellion*, p29.

52 Alexander Begg described this as a boat ferry with a hawser connecting it to each bank. See: Alexander Begg, *Creation of Manitoba; A History of the Red River Troubles*, (Toronto: Hunter, Rose & Co., 1871), p390.

53 PPP 568, Correspondence and Journal, Appendix, p92.

54 Butler, *Lone Land*, pp189/90.

55 PPP 589, Riddell, *60th*, p130

56 Low, *Wolseley*, p68.

57 Denison, *Soldiering*, p179.

Upper Fort Garry at the confluence of the Red and Assiniboine Rivers. The seat of power for Louis Riel during the troubles at the settlement and the objective of the Red River Expeditionary Force. (*Illustrated London News*. ILNO-1870-0212-0013-F)

Hugh McCalmont, however, had a different tale to tell, claiming the honour of being first into the fort for himself. He wrote that, as Wolseley gazed at the closed northern gate, the colonel said, "Will somebody go and see what's the other side?" and so he galloped off to reconnoitre the situation by himself. Finding the southern gate was open, he rode into the fort and was confronted by a man standing by the flagstaff, from which the flag of the provisional government still flew.

> So I rode up to the sportsman with my revolver out and ordered him to haul it down – which he did. I thereupon extracted a Union Jack from under my saddle, where I had been carrying it, bent it on to the halyard, and ran our own colours up to the peak. In the meantime the force was moving round the fort, and it now marched into the enclosure through the southern gate.[58]

McCalmont's version loses some credibility in that it is at odds with all other accounts which state that no flag was flying as the expeditionary force approached the fort. It will have to suffice to say that one or more of staff officers entered the fort, determined that it was unoccupied, following which Wolseley and the rest of the force marched in. Loaded weaponry was found throughout and this was said to be evidence of Riel's intent to resist. It had been a volatile few months at the Red River Settlement and a few loaded weapons was hardly overwhelming evidence when weighed against all the indicators on the other side of the question as to Riel's intent to fight.

It was something of an anti-climactic end and perhaps Wallace summed it up best when he wrote, "Then wet, weary, and disappointed, on the 24th August, 1870, thirty six days out from Shebandowan, with band playing, we marched, if not indeed under heavy fire at least under heavy rain, into Fort Garry."[59] It was somehow fitting that the vanguard of the expedition arrived in the rain. Of the 94 days since they had first landed at Thunder Bay, it had rained on 45 of them. Regardless, the expeditionary force had accomplished its mission. Fort Garry had been retaken, the Union Flag was again flying and in celebration a twenty-one gun salute was fired off. There was also no question of the haste of Riel's exit. Captain Wallace said that he and O'Donoghue were seen 'skedadaddling'

58 Callwell, *McCalmont*, pp55/56.
59 HA 170A12W/D/0438, Wallace, *Rebellion*, p29.

across the Assiniboine River. His uneaten breakfast was found as well, " ... beefsteaks smoking on the table, and the tea hot in the pot ... ."[60]

The rain was still pelting down, and given the state of the weather, it made no sense to establish camp on the waterlogged ground. The troops were, therefore, housed for the time being within the walls of Fort Garry. After their weeks in the wilderness the men promptly got down to foraging, and " ... boxes, cupboards, drawers, were turned inside out, and the contents overhauled; everything of use was appropriated, under clothing [sic] being in most request, the hard works of the past months having left its mark on every one [sic]."[61] Documents of political significance were sent to Wolseley, and "A further search revealed the welcome secrets of the larder and cellar."[62] Captain Wallace took for himself a number of items, including a carbine which he said had belonged to Riel.

Donald Smith of the HBC complained that the troops had pillaged Company stores, although the fort was in a shambles when the troops arrived and it is hard to believe that the stores had not already been well gone over by Riel's men during the course of the winter. The activities of the troops were brought to a halt only when informed that the fort's contents were private property.[63] According to Smith's biographer, sorting out compensation on behalf of the HBC would take up a considerable amount of his time in the coming months. However, in the immediate aftermath of the occupation, the soldiers had only done what soldiers usually do when new digs are occupied; they made themselves comfortable and went in search of food and souvenirs. The men of the expeditionary force were tired and hungry and their clothes were falling to pieces. Sometimes there is a fine line between foraging and looting, and after their travails in the wilderness, it is unlikely that Wolseley's men gave much consideration to the distinction.

Butler described Winnipeg as "The most miserable-looking village" and said it " ... produced, as if by magic, more saloons than any city of twice its size in the States could boast of."[64] On the first night of the force's arrival there were scenes of public drunkenness and brawling in the village's muddy streets. The unrest was ascribed largely to "Voyageurs, Indians and half-breeds," though there is an admission of some troops being involved as well, although not to any great extent after the first night.[65] The Reverend George Young, a Red River resident and supporter of Schultz, who had pleaded with Riel for Scott's life and been present at his execution, wrote of the scenes he personally witnessed on that first night.[66]

> It was most distressing for me to see, on that first night especially, so many of these men – soldiers, voyageurs and Indians – who had abstained from all intoxicants so advantageously to themselves and the entire force, now so crazed with the vile stuff they were buying at very high rates from these abominable rum shops, as to be actually rolling and fighting in the miry mud holes of Winnipeg.[67]

The rank and file of the British Army during this era were hardly the cream of society, and after going without their daily ration of spirits for the past several weeks, it is hardly surprising that some men got out of hand on their first night, but it was far from a case of the discipline of the British regulars breaking down. In fact, Alexander Begg, an English-speaking resident who had not been ill-disposed towards Riel wrote:

60 HA 170A12W/D/0438, Wallace, *Rebellion*, p30.
61 HA 170A12W/D/0438, Wallace, *Rebellion*, p30.
62 HA 170A12W/D/0438, Wallace, *Rebellion*, p32.
63 McDonald, *Strathcona*, p170.
64 Butler, *Lone Land*, p192.
65 PPP 568 Correspondence and Journal, Appendix, p93.
66 Angel, Michael R., "YOUNG, GEORGE," in Dictionary of Canadian Biography, vol. 13, University of Toronto/Université Laval, 2003–, accessed September 21, 2016.
67 The Reverend George D.D. Young, *Manitoba Memories, Leaves From My Life in the Prairie Province, 1868-1884*, (Toronto: William Briggs, 1897), pp189/190.

> Too much praise cannot be accorded to the 60th, for their honorable and just behaviour on their arrival at Fort Garry. Their conduct at that time is a page in the history of their regiment, which they may be proud of; and the people of Red River will never forget their short stay amongst them. No one was insulted; no one was interfered with; no one was harmed; everything went on pleasantly. Coming off a trip such as the men had gone through, it is not to be wondered at if they indulged rather freely in liquor , – what body of men would not do so. There were several fights in consequence; but, invariably it was a fair and square stand-up battle, – and in every case between two men belonging to the same regiment. No citizen was molested at any time."[68]

Nevertheless, determined to maintain discipline, "Colonel Wolseley ordered a strong picquet to patrol the village every night till everything was quiet."[69] Shortly thereafter Donald Smith hired special constables and banned the serving of alcohol between the hours of 7:00 p.m. and 6:00 a.m.

While it had been hoped that Lieutenant-Governor Adams Archibald would arrive at Fort Garry before Wolseley, this had not happened. Bishop Taché had certainly argued that this should happen, and it is interesting to ponder whether Riel would have chosen to bolt had this taken place. Archibald's absence did leave a gap, however, in that there was no civil authority at the settlement and Wolseley, although he had coveted it before the expedition set out, was not willing to take it on at this point. He wanted to keep the army out of civil affairs and strongly believed that until Archibald arrived, *de jure* power remained vested with the HBC. Donald Smith was prevailed upon to assume this role and he did so, albeit reluctantly.

A lack of civil authority was a considerable oversight on the part of the Canadian Government with public drunkenness far from the most serious cause of unrest in the community. With the power of the Métis in check, there was no shortage of loyalist residents who were more than willing to track Riel down and bring him back dead or alive. Immediately after the arrival of the force such individuals were petitioning Wolseley to issue them with a warrant; a step the colonel steadfastly refused to take. Archibald finally arrived on September 2nd and was sworn in a few days later.

The boat brigades of the 1st Ontario Rifles were now beginning to arrive. The storm that had greeted Wolseley and the vanguard of the expeditionary force on the Red River had also caught the first of the Ontario boat brigades out on Lake Winnipeg. Captain Cook's force had not experienced the favourable wind that Wolseley had on August 21st and 22nd.

> After leaving the river there was little progress against the headwind, and a landing had to be made at Elk Island ... .It blew from the northwest and rose to the violence of a hurricane. Three times during the night the boats had to be dragged further up the beach to save them from the pounding waves and the rush of the invading waters. The wind drove the water up as if it were a rising tide. At break of day the boats were actually on the timber line. Towards noon it began to go down.[70]

As the storm abated somewhat the following brigade under Captain Smith was seen approaching from the mouth of the Winnipeg River and Cook did not relish the prospect of being overtaken. "The wind had fallen but the waves were high and great difficulty was found in getting the boats out of the surf. By this time the rear brigade was almost abreast, out on the lake. It would be a great feather in their cap if they passed. Captain Cook would not stand for that."[71] It was a close race, but Cook just about prevailed and both brigades entered the river before dark, making a triumphal procession similar to that experienced by the 60th Rifles. They arrived at Upper Fort Garry on August 27th.

The rest of the Canadian brigades continued to trickle in for some time to come. James Macleod and Sam Steele reached Fort Alexander on the evening of the 25th, leaving early on August 27th. They too received a hero's

68 Begg, *Creation*, p391.
69 PPP 568, Correspondence and Journal, Appendix, p93.
70 Tennant, *Rough* Times, p48.
71 Tennant, *Rough* Times, p49.

welcome and reached the Forks on the 29th, thirty-eight days after embarking on Shebandowan Lake. By August 31st Lieutenant-Colonel Jarvis and the rest of the Ontario battalion were at the upper fort. S, T, V, and X brigades of the 2nd Quebec Rifles passed Fort Frances between August 17th and 19th.[72] The Ontario battalion would spend the winter at Upper Fort Garry, other than I Company which would be based at Pembina. The Quebec battalion was quartered at the Stone Fort.

The British troops embarked on their return journey almost immediately. The first men left on August 29th and they were all on the way by September 3rd. Virtually all went by way of the Winnipeg River, though Captain Buller's company went overland along the incomplete road to the Northwest Angle. After an attempt by Lieutenant-Colonel Bolton to find the route had been unsuccessful, Lieutenant Denison and Joseph Monkman were dispatched, the latter knowing the way. The two men caught up with Buller and a rendezvous was affected with Captain Scott's brigade of the Ontario Rifles which was known to be passing through Lake of the Woods on or about September 3rd/4th. Buller's men took Scott's boats and Monkman and Denison led the Ontario men to the Red River Settlement by way of the road.[73]

Wallace's company left by boat at 3:00am on August 29th. The journey back, other than the Red River itself, was all against the current until they reached Height of Land Portage. There were great difficulties on the Winnipeg River and they had problems finding guides willing to haul the expedition's boats up the perilous rapids. They crossed over to the Great Lakes watershed on September 23rd and the following day landed at McNeill's Bay. Two days later they marched into Prince Arthur's Landing. By early October all of the British troops were in barracks in Quebec in preparation for their departure from Canada.

Lieutenant-Colonel McNeill returned through the United States, as would Captain McCalmont. In the latter's case he had departed almost immediately, sent by Wolseley with a guide who would accompany him as far as the American border. He was to carry the force's despatches, a signal honour for one so young. Unfortunately McCalmont did not fully appreciate the importance of his undertaking, although to be fair, he had found a copy of the *Times* at Fort Garry with an announcement in the *Gazette* stating that he was being transferred from the 9th Lancers to the 7th Hussars. He was not certain that he favoured this course and this might partially explain his distraction when it came to the despatches.

According to McCalmont's telling of the tale, Colonel Wolseley told him to make his way to St. Paul, the nearest city of consequence south of the international boundary. At dawn, while the rest of the expeditionary force was resting peacefully, he set off on horseback with this guide. "When we had covered a few miles we came upon a party of three mounted and armed scallywags, one of whom, a man of about my own age, the half-breed [McCalmont's guide] indicated to me as being Louis Riel. We passed quite close to them, but they gave no indication of wishing to interfere with us."[74]

After a few days more they came upon another fellow, who said he was the correspondent of the *New York Daily Herald*. "He tacked himself on to us and, as he had a revolver which he was fond of loosing off rather recklessly, he was not in all respects the ideal travelling companion."[75] Later, while McCalmont was bringing his kettle to the boil to make tea, he and the correspondent got into a heated debate about the merits of their respective countries and his companion quickly became a 'typical Yankee.' He said that if anyone said anything against the United States he would plug them just like he would plug the kettle, at which point he put a round from his revolver through the vessel, just as it had finally come to the boil. That was the end of the tea, lamented the cavalry officer, who with intended sarcasm, noted that his companion was "Just the helpful, accommodating, meet-you-half-way sort of comrade one likes to have to hob-nob with in the wilds."[76] From Pembina he travelled by stage coach to St. Paul, which he described as a civilized town with a post office.

---

72 PPP 568, Correspondence and Journal, Appendix, p94.
73 PPP 568, Correspondence and Journal, Appendix, p95.
74 Callwell, *McCalmont*, p58.
75 Callwell, *McCalmont*, p58.
76 Callwell, *McCalmont*, p59.

It was at St. Paul that he committed his cardinal sin, which he put down to his own inexperience. He sent the expedition's despatches to the British Army's military headquarters in Montreal by way of the United States Post Office, though at least he did send them by registered mail.

> It was a bad blunder. To be entrusted with despatches by the commander of an army in the field at the end of his operations, had always been regarded as something of an honour in the Service. In the old days, an officer who under such circumstances brought the despatches home was wont to be awarded recognition. This particular case was, no doubt, somewhat different, still, I ought as a matter of course to have pushed on with my packet, to have travelled through the United States till I could find a railway connection to take me to Montreal, and to have handed over the papers that I had been entrusted with to the general-officer commanding in Canada [Lindsay] in person.[77]

He learned later that Lindsay and his staff 'had been somewhat scandalized' and he speculated that Wolseley no doubt was not pleased. "But in the meantime, unaware of the impropriety of which I had been guilty, I journeyed to New York and took ship for the United Kingdom."[78] His *faux pas* does not appear to have hurt his career prospects unduly, however, as he would be employed by Wolseley again and retired a major-general.

In fact several other officers from the expedition would serve with Wolseley on subsequent operations. The expeditionary force commander became known for repeatedly calling on the same officers as his star continued to rise and the operations he conducted increased in number. These officers became known as the Wolseley Ring, sometimes the African or Ashanti Ring. It was a state of affairs that was not much liked throughout the army as a whole as it limited opportunities for others to make names for themselves on active service.[79] While the start of the ring is normally associated with Wolseley's next command, the Ashanti Expedition of 1873-1874, its beginnings can be clearly seen on the Red River Expedition and Buller, Butler, McNeill, as well as the errant McCalmont, would all become members.

Wolseley was also flowing in praise for his men both in the expedition's immediate aftermath and many years later when he came to write his memoirs. At the time he thanked the regulars for so successfully carrying out Lieutenant-General Lindsay's orders. He also spoke of the hard physical labour they had endured without complaint in the face of " ... inclement weather, excessive fatigue and the annoyance by flies."[80] He told the Canadians that he had " ... never been associated with a better set of men ... ."[81]

The troops had indeed performed splendidly in the face of considerable adversity and he had every right to be proud of what they had accomplished. He would write, "I can draw no distinction between the relative merits of military value of the regular soldier and the Canadian militia man who went with me to Red River; each had arrived at Prince Arthur's Landing with special attributes peculiarly their own, but by the time Fort Garry had been occupied each had acquired the military virtues of the other."[82] In 1899 the Canadian Government issued a general service medal for British and Canadian forces who had served in Canada on active service between 1866 and 1871. Three clasps were available. These were the Fenian Raids of 1866, the Fenian Raids of 1870 and the Red River Expedition.[83] As such, the Red River Expedition is the only campaign medal ever made available to a British soldier for service in a campaign where there were no casualties.[84]

---

77 Callwell, *McCalmont*, pp59/60.
78 Callwell, *McCalmont*, p60.
79 Leigh Maxwell, *The Ashanti Ring; Sir Garnet Wolseley's Campaigns, 1870-1882*, (London: Leo Cooper in Association with Secker and Warburg, 1985), p2.
80 Low, *Wolseley*, p74.
81 Steele, *Forty Years*, p33.
82 Wolseley, *Soldier's Life*, p224. In his memoirs he would refer to the militiamen as being " ... in some respects ... better than our Regulars, for owing to the colonial bringing-up, they have more initiative, and are more self-reliant." Wolseley, *Soldier's Story*, p211.
83 Government of Canada Website, Veterans Affairs, Medals.
84 Byron Farwell, *Mr. Kipling's army; All the Queen's Men*, (New York: Norton & Company, 1981), p168.
As we have seen, however, there was in fact likely one fatal casualty.

The pressure he found himself under to get the expeditionary force moving, combined with his burning ambition to do well, caused Wolseley to make certain claims and accusations, some of which stand up to scrutiny, while others do not. Nevertheless, his accomplishment in getting his force through the wilderness without a major mishap was something of a masterstroke; a model of planning and organization in fact, and all accomplished at a tiny cost to the British taxpayer.[85] Adams Archibald, the new lieutenant-governor, referred to it as a 'magnificent success.'[86] Lieutenant-General Lindsay wrote that the plan had been 'perfectly carried out' and that it was hardly possible 'to overrate the advantage' to the British and Canadian Governments " ... derived from the employment upon this delicate as well as arduous service of an officer of Colonel Wolseley's attainments, character, and discretion." Lindsay added that he felt himself " ... very fortunate in having such an instrument in my hands to carry out your orders with respect to the Red River Expedition."[87]

Wolseley may have already been something of a rising star before setting out on his trek to Fort Garry; his success made him the man of the moment. He left the Red River Settlement on September 10th. A message from Lindsay reached him while he was at the Northwest Angle suggesting that they travel back to England on the same ship. Wolseley, therefore, made haste and did not stop in Toronto on his way through.[88] He was gone from Canada by the beginning of October.

85 Huyshe says the cost was £400,000 of the British paid 25%. Huyshe, *Red River*, p237. Low says this was inflated and that Huyshe was in error. The actual cost was just £80,000 for which the British taxpayer was liable for just £20,000. Low, *Wolseley*, p78.

86 Huyshe, *Red River*, p235.

87 PPP 568, Correspondence and Journal, October 11, 1870, No. 26, Lindsay to Secretary of State for War.

88 "Colonel Wolseley went through Toronto without stopping on his way home to England from Fort Garry. He telegraphed to me to meet him at the station, but the telegram was not delivered in time for me to see him. He wrote to me from the steamer off Father Point as he was leaving Canada, and I was much pleased with the way in which he spoke of my brother Fred. "A better or nicer fellow in every respect I never knew. He was the best aide-de-camps, and a most zealous hard-working soldier." Denison, *Soldiering*, p180.

20

The Aftermath

The achievement of the Red River Expeditionary Force in establishing a forward base on Thunder Bay, and then making its way through the wilderness from there to Fort Garry, was just one example of the type of operation that the British Army regularly demonstrated an ability to undertake throughout the empire during the Victorian period. It was, nonetheless, a minor masterpiece of logistics and sheer physical effort given the array of problems and challenges encountered along the way, not forgetting the tight timeframes imposed by the politicians in London. The men of the expedition were fully deserving of the praise showered upon them by their commander and Wolseley certainly merited the accolades he received from his superiors. It is, therefore, something of a mystery to the writer that it has received such scant study, particularly in light of its leader rising to such lofty heights in the profession of arms. Perhaps this was because there was no fighting and the British component of the force disappeared from the scene so quickly. Whatever the reason, it remains a remarkable achievement.

From a political perspective, the Canadian takeover of the Hudson's Bay Company lands was finally complete. In 1871 British Columbia entered Confederation and Macdonald's dream of a Canada stretching from the Atlantic to Pacific Oceans was a reality. A trans-continental railway was completed, with Donald Smith driving the last symbolic spike at Craigellachie, British Columbia on November 7, 1885. Prince Edward Island joined the Dominion in 1873, though Newfoundland and Labrador would not do so until 1949.

The acquisition by Canada of Rupert's Land and the North-Western Territory, combined with the creation of the new province of Manitoba, meant that big changes were in store for the inhabitants of what was now the Canadian West. First and foremost was the immigration of ethnic European settlers, although there would be others as well. By 1901 the population of the west stood at 400,000 and would rise to 2.4 million by 1931.[1] When considering that the population at Red River Settlement in 1870 was 12,000, even though this number did not take into account the First Nations people residing throughout the rest of the former HBC lands, the increase still represents a staggering change.

After their terms of enlistment ended, while some of the Canadian militiamen returned to the east, many remained in Manitoba or migrated further west. They " ... found various occupations: Steamboating, rafting and logging on the rivers; and on land building roads, working at trades and farming."[2] Several joined the NWMP and a number rose to prominence in politics and business in Manitoba, as well as other parts of the Canadian West.[3]

Staff Officer Fred Denison remained for a year as aide-de-camp to the lieutenant-governor and then returned to Ontario. He would serve again with Wolseley during the Gordon Relief Expedition in the Sudan in 1884/1885[4] when an attempt was made to effect the rescue of General Charles George Gordon at Khartoum by moving

1 Friesen, *Canadian Prairies,* p242.

2 Tennant, *Rough Times*, p91.

3 See Memorable Manitobans website for many biographies of expeditionary force members: http://www.mhs.mb.ca/docs/people/index_a.shtml

4 Gagan, *Denison Family*, p33.

a relief column up the Nile River. Wolseley remembered the skill of at least some of his Red River Expedition boatmen and recruited almost 400 Canadian *voyageurs*.[5] Denison would go as their commanding officer.

Brigade Major James Macleod would rise to become Commissioner of the NWMP in July 1876 and had to contend with the Sioux leader Sitting Bull leading his followers into Canadian territory after their defeat of George Armstrong Custer's force at the Little Big Horn. Macleod resigned in 1880 to concentrate on his career as a jurist and was appointed to the first Supreme Court of the North West Territories in 1887. He died in 1894.

Sam Steele also joined the NWMP, though only after initially returning to Ontario. He was involved in the negotiations between Sitting Bull and the American military authorities in the aftermath of Custer's defeat and later served with distinction in the suppression of the North-West Rebellion in 1885. After commanding the NWMP in the Yukon during the gold rush, he led Strathcona's Horse during the Second Boer War in South Africa.[6] This was followed by service with the South African Constabulary. He applied for active service during the First World War and, while he commanded the Canadian 2nd Division for a short period, he was clearly too old for such a role and was relieved before the formation went to France. He was knighted in 1918 and died aged 70 in January 1919 during the influenza pandemic. He was buried in Winnipeg.

Hugh Macdonald, the prime minister's son, would also see service during the North-West Rebellion, having moved to Winnipeg in 1882. He became an MP for the city and for a short time was a cabinet minister in the federal government. He would later, also for a short time, become premier of the province of Manitoba. He retired from politics to focus on his law practice. He lived on until March 1929.

John Kerr, the man whose cooking skills enabled him to avoid the rigours of portaging, stayed on in the west. He became a policeman, hunter, trader and interpreter for the government in its dealings with the First Nations. He became well acquainted with many of the personalities of the Canadian West including prominent First Nations chiefs, Métis notables and Canadian political leaders. After a long life, he died in February 1940.

In the immediate aftermath of the arrival of the Canadian component of the expeditionary Force and its establishment in the Red River Valley, the Canadian Government took the view that order had been restored at the settlement. As to whether the residents took the same view is a divisive issue. By and large it would be safe to say that the English-speaking community for the most part took the position that it was. The Métis viewed matters differently and there are documented cases of abuses that occurred after the departure of the British contingent of the force.[7] While it certainly would not be accurate to characterize these as being part of systematic program on the part of the men of the Canadian battalions of the Red River Expeditionary Force, there is little doubt that some of its members were involved.

The first incident was the death of Elzéar Goulet just three days after Wolseley left Fort Garry. Goulet had been a high ranking member of the Métis military hierarchy. He had also been present at the Scott trial, and according to Sam Steele was alleged to have commanded the firing squad.[8] On September 13th he was recognized in Winnipeg village by a member of the Canadian Party and pursued by the Canadian man and two Canadian volunteers. In attempting to escape, Goulet tried to swim the Red River. Rocks were thrown at him as he struggled in the water, one of which struck his head and he drowned.[9] There were other incidents too that resulted in

5 Adrian Preston, "Wolseley, The Khartoum Relief Expedition and the Defence of India, 1885-1900", in Preston, Adrian and Dennis, Peter (Editors) *Swords and Covenants*, (London: Croom Helm Ltd, 1976), p91 & Roy MacLaren, *Canadians on the Nile by Canadians on the Nile, 1882-1898: Being the Adventures of the Voyageurs on the Khartoum Relief Expedition and Other Exploits*, (University of British Columbia Press, 1978).

6 Donald Smith had become Lord Strathcona in 1897. He had paid for the raising and equipping of the regiment. See: https://military.wikia.org/wiki/Lord_Strathcona%27s_Horse_(Royal_Canadians)

7 See for example Lawrence Barkwell, "The Reign of Terror Against the Metis of Red River" https://www.academia.edu/35190134/THE_REIGN_OF_TERROR_AGAINST_THE_METIS_OF_RED_RIVER

8 Steele, *Forty Years*, p34.

9 Jackson, J. A., "GOULET, ELZÉAR," in Dictionary of Canadian Biography, vol. 9, University of Toronto/Université Laval, 2003–, accessed November 28, 2016,

beatings and further deaths. An inquest was held into the Goulet incident, but no charges were brought, nor were they brought in any of the other cases.'

Violent acts such as these, together with English-speaking settlers taking over much of the land that had been set aside for the Métis in the Manitoba Act, caused many Métis to leave the Red River Settlement and move west into what would later become the provinces of Saskatchewan and Alberta.[10]

Riel was on the run for a period of time after the arrival of the expeditionary force. In September of 1870 he split with O'Donoghue. The Irishman had petitioned President Grant for American intervention in the Northwest and looked to Riel to provide Métis support. When he realized that Riel was opposed to the United States taking over, he turned to the Fenians. The result was yet another raid this time in the Pembina region in October 1871. It was an even bigger farce than the original raid at Campobello in 1866. While most of the Irishmen thought they had crossed the border into Canada, most had in fact not and they were taken prisoner by American forces. O'Donoghue did manage to make his way north of the international boundary and was captured by a party of Métis. Riel himself had responded to a call from Adams Archibald to counter the Fenian threat and was in command of a company of Métis irregulars at the time. In the aftermath, Adams Archibald was prevailed upon to review the Métis troops and shook hands with their leaders, including Louis Riel. This was seen in positive terms in Manitoba but in a less favourable light in Ottawa, where it led to a resurgence in Ontario of the powerful and emotional feelings of 1870. The premier of Ontario went so far as to put a price on Riel's head. Ever the deal maker, Macdonald arranged for a payment of $1000 to be made to 'induce' Riel " ... to remain outside Canadian jurisdiction until the political storm had blown over."[11]

Despite his grave error in the killing of Scott, it is not overly difficult to find sympathy for Riel. As we have seen, there is very little evidence that he ever contemplated opposing the expeditionary force and he had demonstrated his loyalty to Canada during the resurgence of the Fenian troubles. He stood aside when nominated to stand for a Manitoba seat in the federal parliament so that Cartier could run, after Macdonald's staunch ally had been defeated in Quebec. When Cartier died in 1873, Riel was again nominated. He was victorious in the by-election, as well as the general election that followed. Given the strength of feeling against him in English Canada, he was never able to take his seat, although he did go to Ottawa and sign the members' registry after his second electoral victory.

Finally, in 1875 amnesty came, conditional on him leaving the country for a period of five years. About this time, however, he suffered a mental breakdown and was for a period of time institutionalized. He eventually moved to the United States, married, became involved in politics in Montana and in 1883 became an American citizen. By 1884 he was teaching school in Missouri.

He was drawn back to Canada and became involved in the events of the North-West Rebellion of 1885. This was a much larger affair than the troubles at Red River in 1869 and 1870, involving many of the aboriginal peoples of the plains as well as the Métis. Ultimately the uprising was put down by the NWMP and Canadian troops. This time Riel chose surrender rather than flight and was put on trial. There was ample evidence of mental instability, but he was found guilty and hanged at Regina on November 16th, 1885. It was a miscarriage of justice and a grave political mistake on Macdonald's part. The fissures already present between English and French Canada became a chasm and the Canadian Government's relations with the Métis, as well as other indigenous peoples, were seriously damaged. If Riel's sanctioning of the killing of Scott had been a major political error, the execution of Riel was an even bigger blunder on the part of the Canadian Government and the ramifications are arguably still being felt up until the present day.[12]

---

10 See footnote dealing with the Manitoba Act in Chapter 6.

11 Stanley, *Canadian West*, p168.
The Fenian threat led to the rush of a second Red River Expeditionary Force from Canada. See, Justus A. Griffin, *An Account of the Second Expedition to Red River, Diary of a Private Soldier*, (Hamilton: 1893). British troops were not involved on this occasion.

12 Thomas, Riel.

Appendix I

The Composition of the Red River Expeditionary Force

Colonel	Garnet Wolseley, Expeditionary Force Commander

Expeditionary Force Staff

Lieutenant-Colonel	W.F. Bolton, Royal Artillery, Deputy Assistant-Adjutant-General
Assistant-Controller	Matthew Bell Irvine, Chief Control Officer
Lieutenant	William Francis Butler, Special Intelligence Officer
Captain	George L. Huyshe, Rifle Brigade, Staff Officer
Lieutenant	F.C. Denison, Staff Officer
Lieutenant-Colonel	John Carstairs McNeill
Major	James Macleod, Brigade Major
Surgeon-Major	Young, M.D., Principal Medical Officer
Assistant Surgeon-Major	Robertson

1st Battalion King's Royal Rifle Corps (60th Rifles)

Colonel	R.J. Feilden
Lieutenant	H.S. Marsham (Adjutant)
Quartermaster	John Toole

A Company

Captain	J.D. Dundas
Lieutenant	D. Bingham
Lieutenant	The Hon. Keith Turnour

B Company

Captain	N.W. Wallace
Lieutenant	R.C. Robinson
Ensign	F.M. Ward

C Company

Captain	Redvers Buller

D Company

Captain	F.V. Northey
Ensign	F.W. Archer

F Company

Captain	J.O. Young
Lieutenant	E.L. Fraser
Lieutenant	R.C. Davies

G Company

Captain	E.H. Ward
Lieutenant	F.J.A. Wood
Ensign	A. St. Maur

H Company

Captain	C.M. Calderon
Lieutenant	F.C. Coulson
Lieutenant	A.F. Mitchell-Innes
Ensign	W.H. Holbech

Royal Artillery

Lieutenant	Alleyne

Royal Engineers

Lieutenant	Heneage

1st Ontario Rifles

Lieutenant-Colonel	Samuel Peters Jarvis
Major	Griffith Wainwright
Paymaster	I. F. B. Morrice
Adjutant	William J. B. Parsons
Quartermaster	Edward Armstrong
Surgeon	Alfred Codd M.D.
Chaplain	Stewart Patterson

No. 1 Company

Captain	Henry Cooke
Lieutenant	James Benson
Ensign	William Hill Nash

No. 2 Company

Captain	William Smith
Lieutenant	Andrew McBride
Ensign	John Biggar

No. 3 Company

Captain	Thomas Macklem
Lieutenant	David Marr Walker
Ensign	Adam John Lang Peebles

No. 4 Company

Captain	Daniel Hunter McMillan
Lieutenant	William Nassau Kennedy
Ensign	Stewart Mulvey

No. 5 Company

Captain	William Macauley Herchmer
Lieutenant	Samuel Bruce Harman
Ensign	Stewart Hamilton

No. 6 Company

Captain	Alexander R. Macdonald
Lieutenant	William T. McMurty
Ensign	Hugh John Macdonald

No. 7 Company

Captain	Thomas Scott
Lieutenant	Donald A. Macdonald
Ensign	Josiah Jones Bell

2nd Quebec Rifles

Lieutenant-Colonel	Louis Adolphe Casault
Major	Acheson Gosford Irvine
Paymaster	C. Auguste La Rue
Captain and Adjutant	F.D. Gagnier
Quartermaster	Frank Villiers
Surgeon	F.L.A. Neilson
Chaplain	Marie Joseph Royer

No. 1 Company (Did not reach Fort Garry)

Captain	L.C.A.L. de Bellefeuills
Lieutenant	Edward T.H.F. Patterson
Ensign	William Wilmount Ross

No. 2 Company

Captain	William John Barrett
Lieutenant	John Price Fletcher
Ensign	Alphonse Tetu

No. 3 Company

Captain	Allan Macdonald
Lieutenant	Leonides de Salaberry
Ensign	John Beresford Allan

No. 4 Company

Captain	John Fraser
Lieutenant	Maurice C.B. Duchesney
Ensign	Alphonse de Montenach Henri D'Eschambault

No. 5 Company

Captain	Jacques Labranche
Lieutenant	Oscar Prevost
Ensign	Gabriel Louis Des George

No. 6 Company

Captain	Samuel Macdonald
Lieutenant	Josephus Wyatt Vaughan
Ensign	George Simard

No. 7 Company

Captain	Jean-Baptiste Amyot
Lieutenant	Henri Bouthillies
Ensign	Edward S. Bernard

This list has been compiled from the following sources:

Butler, Lieutenant-Colonel Lewis, "The Annals of the King's Royal Rifle Corps, Volume 3, The 60th: the K.R.R.C.," John Murray, London, 1926 pp264/65

Peel's Prairie Provinces 568, "Correspondence Relative to the Recent Expedition to the Red River Settlement with Journal of Operations," Harrison and Sons, London, 1871, No. 8 Inclosure 8.

Manitoba Historical Society, http://www.mhs.mb.ca/docs/people/wolseleyexpedition.shtml

Appendix II

The Composition of the Boat Brigades

Departure Date	Brigade Designation	Number of Boats	Commander	Regiment	Numbers embarked				
					Officers	Men	Voyageurs	Guides	Total
July 16th	A	6	Captain Young	1st bn 60th Rifles	5	50	12	1	68
July 16th	B	6	Captain Ward	1st bn 60th Rifles	4	50	12	0	66
July 16th	C	5	Lieutenant Alleyne RA	RA and RE	2	38	10	0	50
July 17th	D	7	Captain Dundas	1st bn 60th Rifles	4	50	14	1	69
July 17th	E	6	Captain Buller	1st bn 60th Rifles	3	50	12	0	65
July 18th	F	6	Captain Northey	1st bn 60th Rifles	3	49	12	1	65
				A.S.C & A.H.C.					
July 19th	G	7	Captain Wallace	1st bn 60th Rifles	5	58	14	1	78
July 21st	H	6	Captain Calderon	Ontario Rifles	4	49	12	1	66
July 21st	I	6	Captain Scott	HQ Staff	6	48	12	1	67
July 21st	Gig	1	Captain Huyshe		2	4	0	2	8
July 22nd	K	6	Captain McDonald	Ontario Rifles	4	49	12	0	65
July 22nd	L	6		Ontario Rifles	3	48	12	1	64
Total		68			45	543	136	7	731
July 23rd	North Canoe	1	Colonel Wolseley						
July 23rd	M&N			Ontario Rifles					
July 26th	O&P			Ontario Rifles					
August 1st	Last Brigade		Lt-Colonel Casault	Quebec Rifles					
Total					42	505	120	8	675
					87	1048	256	15	1406

Note: The numbers are precise until shortly after Wolseley's departure. Lieutenant-Colonel McNeill's records afterwards are much more general in nature. It should also be noted that there is almost no material available regarding the journey of the Quebec Rifles.

Compiled from Peel's Prairie Provinces 568 "Correspondence Relative to the Recent Expedition to the Red River Settlement with Journal of Operations," Harrison and Sons, London, 1871, No. 21 Enclosure 1.

Appendix III

Proclamation to the People of Red River from Colonel Wolseley, June 30, 1870. Delivered to the Red River Settlement by Donald Smith

Her Majesty's Government having determined upon stationing some troops amongst you, I have been entrusted by the Lieutenant-General commanding in British North America to proceed to Fort Garry with the troops under my command. Our mission is one of peace, and the sole object of the Expedition is to secure Her Majesty's Sovereign authority.

The force which I have the honour of commanding will enter your province, representing no party, either in religion or politics, and will afford equal protection to the lives and property of all races and all creeds. The strictest order and discipline will be maintained and private property will be carefully protected. All supplies furnished by the inhabitants to the troops will be duly paid for. Should anyone consider himself injured by any individual attached to the Fore, his grievance shall be promptly inquired into.

All loyal people are earnestly invited to aid me in carrying out the above-mentioned objects.

Bibliography

Ahrens, Merv, 'The First NWMP Trek: From Ottawa to the Stone Fort, 1873', *The Beaver, Canada's National History Society*, Winnipeg June/July 1998.

Angel, Michael R., "YOUNG, GEORGE," in Dictionary of Canadian Biography, vol. 13, University of Toronto/ Université Laval, 2003–, accessed September 21, 2016, http://www.biographi.ca/en/bio/young_george_13E.html.

Arthur, Elizabeth (Editor), *Thunder Bay District 1821-1892*, (Toronto: Champlain Society, 1973).

Arthur, Elizabeth, *Simon J. Dawson, C.E.*, (Thunder Bay Historical Museum Society, 1987).

Arthur, Elizabeth, "Dawson, Simon James," in Dictionary of Canadian Biography, vol. 13, University of Toronto/Université Laval, 2003–, accessed April 4, 2018, http://www.biographi.ca/en/bio/dawson_simon_james_13E.html.

Barkwell, Lawrence, 'The Reign of Terror Against the Metis of Red River', https://www.academia.edu/35190134/THE_REIGN_OF_TERROR_AGAINST_THE_METIS_OF_RED_RIVER.

Barnard E.D. C.D, Lieutenant Colonel W. T., *The Queen's Own Rifles of Canada 1860-1960; One Hundred Years of Canada*, (Don Mills: Ontario Publishing Company, 1960). Edited excerpts found at: https://qormuseum.org/history/timeline-1856-1899/red-river-rebellion-1870/.

Barnes, Major R.M., *A History of the Regiments & Uniforms of the British Army, 5th Edition*, (Seeley Service & Co. Limited, 1962).

Beal, Bob & Macleod, Rod, *Prairie Fire; The 1885 North-West Rebellion*, (Edmonton: Hurtig Publishers, 1984).

Beckett, Ian F. W., "Wolseley, Garnet Joseph, first Viscount Wolseley (1833–1913)", Oxford Dictionary of National Biography, Oxford University Press, 2004; online edn, Jan 2008 http://www.oxforddnb.com/view/article/36995, accessed 25 Nov 2016.

Beckett, Ian F. W., "Buller, Sir Redvers Henry (1839-1908)", *Oxford Dictionary of National Biography*, Oxford University Press, 2004; online edn, Jan 2008, http://oxforddnb.com/view/article/32165, accessed 25 Nov 2016.

Beckett, Ian F. W., "Butler, Sir William Francis (1838-1910)", *Oxford Dictionary of National Biography*, Oxford University Press, 2004; online edn, Jan 2008, http://www.oxforddnb.com/view/article/32219, accessed 25 Nov 2016.

Beckett, Ian F. W., "McNeill, Sir John Carstairs (1831–1904)", *Oxford Dictionary of National Biography*, Oxford University Press, 2004; online edn, Jan 2008 http://www.oxforddnb.com/view/article/34814, accessed 25 Nov 2016.

Begg, Alexander, *Creation of Manitoba; A History of the Red River Troubles*, (Toronto: Hunter, Rose & Co., 1871), https://archive.org/stream/bub_gb_ejceAAAAMAAJ#page/n5/mode/2up.

Begg, Alexander, *Alexander Begg's Red River Journal*, (New York: Greenwood Press, 1969).

Bell, Charles N., *The Selkirk Settlement and the Settlers: A Concise History of the Red River Country*, (Winnipeg: Printed at the Office of "The Commercial", 1887). https://archive.org/details/selkirksettlemen00belluoft.

Bell, Charles N., 'Old Forts of Winnipeg', *Manitoba Historical Society*, MHS Transactions Series 2, No. 3. Read 1927. http://www.mhs.mb.ca/docs/transactions/2/oldfortsofwinnipeg.shtml.

Berger, Carl, *The Sense of Power; Studies in the Ideas of Canadian Imperialism, 1867-1914*, (Toronto: University of Toronto Press, 1970).

Binnema, Theodore, Ens, Gerhard J., & Macleod, *From Rupert's Land to Canada*, (Edmonton: University of Alberta Press, 2001).

Bonenfant, J.-C., "Cartier, Sir George-Étienne," in Dictionary of Canadian Biography, vol. 10, University of Toronto/Université Laval, 2003–, accessed May 3, 2016, http://www.biographi.ca/en/bio/cartier_george_etienne_10E.html.

Bourne, Kenneth, *Britain and the Balance of Power in North American, 1815-1908*, (Longmans, Green and Co. Ltd, 1967).

Bowsfield, Hartwell, "Semple, Robert," in Dictionary of Canadian Biography, vol. 5, University of Toronto/Université Laval, 2003–, accessed March 13, 2018, http://www.biographi.ca/en/bio/semple_robert_5E.html.

Bowsfield, Hartwell, "Snow, John Allan," in Dictionary of Canadian Biography, vol. 11, University of Toronto/Université Laval, 2003–, accessed July 23, 2018, http://www.biographi.ca/en/bio/snow_john_allan_11E.html.

Bowsfield, Hartwell, "Stutsman, Enos," in Dictionary of Canadian Biography, vol. 10, University of Toronto/Université Laval, 2003–, accessed November 28, 2016, http://www.biographi.ca/en/bio/stutsman_enos_10E.html.

Bowsfield, Hartwell, "Taylor, James Wickes," in Dictionary of Canadian Biography, vol. 12, University of Toronto/Université Laval, 2003–, accessed December 14, 2016, http://www.biographi.ca/en/bio/taylor_james_wickes_12E.html.

Bowsfield, Hartwell, 'The United States and the Red River Settlement,' *Manitoba Historical Society Transactions*, Series 3, Number 23 1966-67 Season. http://www.mhs.mb.ca/docs/transactions/3/unitedstatesredriver.shtml.

Boyce, Gerald E, *Canadian Interest in the Northwest, 1856-1860*, Unpublished Thesis mspace.lib.umanitoba.ca 1960.

Brown, Jennifer S. H.: 'The Métis: Genesis & Rebirth', in Francis, R. Douglas and Palmer, Howard (Editors), *The Prairie West, Historical Readings (2nd Edition)*, (Pica Pica Press, Text Book Division of the University of Alberta Press, 1992).

Buck, Ruth M., 'Keeping Touch; Pioneer Mail Services Ended, The North-West's Long Isolation', *The Beaver*, October-November, 1986. https://canadashistory.partica.online/canadas-history/the-beaver-oct-nov-1986/flipbook/4/.

Buckner, Philip, "Macdonald, Sir John Alexander (1815-1891)", *Oxford Dictionary of National Biography*, Oxford University Press, 2004-16, online edn, http://www.oxforddnb.com/view/printable/17444, accessed 28 Nov 2016.

Buckner, Philip A. (Revised by Foot, Richard), 'The Quebec Conference,' *Historica Canada*, 2006, https://www.thecanadianencyclopedia.ca/en/article/quebec-conference/

Bumstead, J.M., *Trials and Tribulations; The Red River Settlement and the Emergence of Manitoba, 1811-1870*, (Winnipeg: Great Plains Publications, 2003).

Butler, Lewis William George, *Sir Redvers Buller*, (Dehli: Facsimile Publisher Delhi, 2013, First published 1909).

Butler, Lieutenant-Colonel Lewis, *The Annals of the King's Royal Rifle Corps, Volume 3, The 60th: the K.R.R.C.*, (London: John Murray, 1926).

Butler, William Francis, *The Great Lone Land; A Narrative of Travel and Adventure in the North-West of America*, (Edmonton: M.G. Hurtig Ltd., 1968, First Published 1872).

Buzzell, Nora (compiler), *The Register of the Victoria Cross*, (Cheltenham: This England, 1988).

Callwell, Major-General Sir C.E. K.C.B. (Editor), *The Memoirs of Major-General Sir Hugh McCalmont K.C.B., C.V.O.*, (London: Hutchinson & Co., 1924).

Campbell, Marjorie Wilkins, *The North West Company*, (Toronto: The Macmillan Company of Canada Limited, 1957).

Cameron, Scott L., *The Frances Smith; Palace Steamer of the Upper Great Lakes, 1867-96*, (Toronto: Natural Heritage Books, 2005).

Careless, J.M.S., *Canada; A Celebration of Our Heritage*, (Mississaauga: Heritage Publishing House, 1997).

Carter, Sarah A., "Macdonald, Allan," in Dictionary of Canadian Biography, vol. 13, University of Toronto/Université Laval, 2003–, accessed November 24, 2016, http://www.biographi.ca/en/bio/macdonald_allan_13E.html.

Chambers, Captain, Ernest J., *The 90th Regiment; A Regimental History of the 90th Regiment Winnipeg Rifles*, 1906, http://peel.library.ualberta.ca/bibliography/2935/5.html.

Clark, Lovell, "Schultz, Sir John Christian," in Dictionary of Canadian Biography, vol. 12, University of Toronto/Université Laval, 2003–, accessed September 21, 2016, http://www.biographi.ca/en/bio/schultz_john_christian_12E.html.

Coates, Kenneth Stephen and Swan, Ruth, "Boulton, Charles Arkoll," in Dictionary of Canadian Biography, vol. 12, University of Toronto/Université Laval, 2003–, accessed September 21, 2016, http://www.biographi.ca/en/bio/boulton_charles_arkoll_12E.html.

Coleman, E.C., *The Pig War; The Most Perfect War in History*, (Stroud: The History Press, 2009).

Cooke, O. A. and Hillmer, Norman, "Cathcart, Charles Murray, 2nd Earl Cathcart," in Dictionary of Canadian Biography, vol. 8, University of Toronto/Université Laval, 2003–, accessed March 26, 2018, http://www.biographi.ca/en/bio/cathcart_charles_murray_8E.html.

Cooke, O. A., "Denison, Frederick Charles," in Dictionary of Canadian Biography, vol. 12, University of Toronto/Université Laval, 2003–, accessed November 2, 2016, http://www.biographi.ca/en/bio/denison_frederick_charles_12E.html.

Cooper, Leonard, *Radical Jack; The Life of the first Earl of Durham*, (London: The Cresset Press, 1959).

Corvi, Steven J., 'Garnet Wolseley', in Corvi, Steven J. & Beckett, Ian F.W. (Editors), *Victoria's Generals*, (Barnsley: Pen and Sword Military, 2009).

Creighton, Donald, *John A. Macdonald; The Young Politician*, (Toronto: The Macmillan Company of Canada, 1952).

Creighton, Donald, *John A. Macdonald; The Old Chieftain*, (Toronto: The Macmillan Company of Canada, 1955).

Creighton, Donald, *The Road to Confederation; The Emergence of Canada, 1863-1867*, (Toronto: Macmillan of Canada, 1964.

Creighton, Donald: John A. Macdonald, 'Confederation, and the Canadian West', *MHS Transactions*, Series 3, Number 23, 1966-67 Season, http://www.mhs.mb.ca/docs/transactions/3/macdonald_ja.shtml

Creighton, Donald, *Canada's First Century, 1867-1967*, (Toronto: Macmillan of Canada, 1970).

Darwin, John, *The Empire Project; The Rise and Fall of the British World-System 1830-1970*, (Cambridge: Cambridge University Press, 2009).

Darwin, John, *Unfinished Empire; The Global Expansion of Britain*, (London: Allen Lane, 2012).

Den Otter, A. A., "Smith, Donald Alexander, first Baron Strathcona and Mount Royal (1820-1914)', Oxford Dictionary of National Biography, Oxford University Press, 2004; online edn, Jan 2011 http://www.oxforddnb.com/view/article/36132, accessed 28 Nov 2016.

Denison, Lt.-Col. George T., *Soldiering in Canada; Recollections and Experiences*, (Toronto: George N. Morang and Co., 1900). https://archive.org/stream/fesoldieringinca00deni#page/n7/mode/2up/search/soldiering+in+canada

Dimbleby, David & Reynolds, David, *An Ocean Apart*, (London: BBC Books Hodder and Stoughton, 1988).

Dorge, Lionel, "Black, John (1817-79)," in Dictionary of Canadian Biography, vol. 10, University of Toronto/Université Laval, 2003–, accessed December 10, 2016, http://www.biographi.ca/en/bio/black_john_1817_79_10E.html.

Ens, Gerhard J., "Lépine, Ambroise-Dydime," in Dictionary of Canadian Biography, vol. 15, University of Toronto/Université Laval, 2003–, accessed November 28, 2016, http://www.biographi.ca/en/bio/lepine_ambroise_dydime_15E.html.

Farwell, Byron, *Mr. Kipling's army; All the Queen's Men*, (New York: Norton & Company, 1981).

Fitzmaurice, Lord Edmond, *The Life of Granville George Leveson Gower, Second Earl Granville K.G., 1815-1891, Volume 2*, (London: Longmans, Green and Co., 1905). https://archive.org/stream/lifegranvillege00unkngoog#page/n12

Friesen, Gerald, *The Canadian Prairies: A History*, (Toronto: University of Toronto Press, 1984).

Gagan, David, *The Denison Family of Toronto 1792-1925*, (Toronto: University of Toronto Press, 1973).

Galbraith, John S., *The Hudson's Bay Company as an Imperial Factor, 1821-1869*, (Berkeley: University of California Press, 1957)

Galbraith, John S., *The Little Emperor; Governor Simpson of the Hudson's Bay Company*, (Toronto: Macmillan of Canada, 1976).

Gentilcore, R. Louis (Editor), *Historical Atlas of Canada; Volume 2 The Land Transformed 1800-1891*, (Toronto: University of Toronto Press, 1993).

Gluek Jr., Alvin C., *Minnesota and the Manifest Destiny of the Canadian Northwest; A Study in Canadian-American Relations*, (Toronto: University of Toronto Press, 1965).

Goldsborough, Gordon, 'Charles Napier Bell (1854-1936)', *Memorable Manitobans*, http://www.mhs.mb.ca/docs/people/bell_cn.shtml.

Goldsborough, Gordon 'McMillan, Daniel Hunter McMillan (1846-1933)', *Memorable Manitobans*, http://www.mhs.mb.ca/docs/people/mcmillan_dh.shtml.

Goldsborough, Gordon, 'O'Donnell, John Harrison (1838-1912)' *Memorable Manitobans*, http://www.mhs.mb.ca/docs/people/odonnell_jh.shtml.

Goossen, N. Jaye, "Mactavish, William," in Dictionary of Canadian Biography, vol. 9, University of Toronto/Université Laval, 2003–, accessed November 28, 2016, http://www.biographi.ca/en/bio/mactavish_william_9E.html.

Gough, Barry, *Britannia's Navy; On the West Coast of North America 1812-1914*, (Heritage House Publishing Company Ltd, 2016).

Government of Canada Website, Veterans Affairs, Medals. http://www.veterans.gc.ca/eng/remembrance/medals-decorations/details/1

Granatstein, J.L., *Canada's Army; Waging War and Keeping Peace*, (Toronto: University of Toronto Press, 2002).

Gray, John Morgan, *Lord Selkirk of Red River*, (Toronto: The Macmillan Company of Canada, 1964).

Gray, John Morgan, "Douglas, Thomas, Baron Daer and Shortcleuch, 5th Earl of Selkirk," in Dictionary of Canadian Biography, vol. 5, University of Toronto/Université Laval, 2003–accessed May 29, 2017 http://www.biographi.ca/en/bio/douglas_thomas_5E.html.

Griffin, Justus A., *An Account of the Second Expedition to Red River, Diary of a Private Soldier*, (Hamilton: 1893). https://archive.org/stream/cihm_28974#page/n9/mode/2up.

Guest, Hal J., "MacDonald, Sir Hugh John," in Dictionary of Canadian Biography, vol. 15, University of Toronto/Université Laval, 2003–, accessed November 24, 2016 http://www.biographi.ca/en/bio/macdonald_hugh_john_15E.html.

Gwyn, Richard, *John A., The Man Who Made Us: The Life and Times of John A. Macdonald Volume One 1815-1867*, (Vintage Canada, 2008).

Gwyn, Richard, *Nation Maker; Sir John A. Macdonald: His Life, Our times, Volume Two: 1867-1891*, (Vintage Canada, 2012).

Hackett, Christopher, "Machray, Robert," in Dictionary of Canadian Biography, vol. 13, University of Toronto/Université Laval, 2003–, accessed May 24, 2018, http://www.biographi.ca/en/bio/machray_robert_13E.html.

Hamelin, Jean, "TACHÉ, ALEXANDRE-ANTONIN," in Dictionary of Canadian Biography, vol. 12, University of Toronto/Université Laval, 2003–, accessed May 3, 2016, http://www.biographi.ca/en/bio/tache_alexandre_antonin_12E.html.

Hamilton, C. F., 'Defence 1812-1912', in Short, Adam and Doughty, Arthur editors, *Canada and Its Provinces, A History of the Canadian People and Their Institutions*, (T. & A. Constable at the Edinburgh University Press for the Publishers Association of Canada, Toronto, 1914).

Harris, Stephen J., *Canadian Brass; The Making of a Professional Army, 1860-1939*, (Toronto: University of Toronto Press, 1988).

Headrick, Daniel R., *The Tools of Empire; Technology and European Imperialism in the Nineteenth Century*, (New York: Oxford University Press, 1981).

Hitsman, J. Mackay, *Safeguarding Canada, 1763-1871*, (Toronto: University of Toronto Press, 1968).

Howard, Joseph Kinsey, *Strange Empire; A Narrative of the Northwest*, (St. Paul: Minnesota Historical Society Press, 1994, First published 1952).

Hutchison, Bruce, *Mr. Prime Minister, 1867-1964*, (Don Mills: Longmans Canada Ltd., 1964).

Hutton K.C.B., K.C.M.G., p.s.c., Lieutenant-General Sir Edward, *A Brief History of the King's Royal Rifle Corps, 1755-1915, (Second Edition)*, (Winchester: Warren and Son Ltd, 1917).

Huyshe, Captain G.L., *The Red River Expedition*, (The Naval & Military Press Ltd, in association with Firepower, The Royal Artillery Museum, Woolwich, first published by Macmillan and Co., London, 1871).

Hyam, Ronald, *Britain's Imperial Century, 1815-1914; A Study of Empire and Expansion (Third Edition)*, (Basingstoke: Palgrave Macmillan, 2002).

Jackson, J. A., "GOULET, ELZÉAR," in Dictionary of Canadian Biography, vol. 9, University of Toronto/Université Laval, 2003–, accessed November 28, 2016, http://www.biographi.ca/en/bio/goulet_elzear_9E.html.

James, Lawrence, *The Rise and Fall of the British Empire*, (London: Little, Brown and Company, 1994).

Jarrell, Richard A., "HIND, HENRY YOULE," in Dictionary of Canadian Biography, vol. 13, University of Toronto/Université Laval, 2003–, accessed December 1, 2016, http://www.biographi.ca/en/bio/hind_henry_youle_13E.html.

Johnson, J. K. and Waite, P. B., "MACDONALD, Sir JOHN ALEXANDER," in Dictionary of Canadian Biography, vol. 12, University of Toronto/Université Laval, 2003-, accessed June 19, 2017 http://www.biographi.ca/en/bio/macdonald_john_alexander_12E.html.

Jones, Howard, *To the Webster-Ashburton Treaty; A Study in Anglo-American Relations, 1783-1843*, Chapel Hill: University of North Carolina Press, 1977).

Judd, Denis, *Empire; The British Imperial Experience from 1765 to the Present*, (London: Harper Collins Publishers, 1996).

Kendle, John E., "MULVEY, STEWART," in Dictionary of Canadian Biography, vol. 13, University of Toronto/Université Laval, 2003–, accessed November 24, 2016 http://www.biographi.ca/en/bio/mulvey_stewart_13E.html.

Kerr, D.G.G., *Historical Atlas of Canada, Third Revised Edition*, (Don Mills: Thomas Nelson & Sons (Canada) Limited, 1975).

Kinross, John S., "Jervois, Sir William Francis Drummond (1821-1897)", *Oxford Dictionary of National Biography*, Oxford University Press, 2004; online edn, May 2009, http://www.oxforddnb.com/view/article/14800, accessed 28 Nov 2016.

Kirk, Sylvia, 'Women in Between: Indian Women in Fur Trade Society in Western Canada'. *Historical Papers/Communications historiques*. 12 (1), 1977.

Knowles, Norman, "DENISON, GEORGE TAYLOR (1839-1925)," in Dictionary of Canadian Biography, vol. 15, University of Toronto/Université Laval, 2003–, accessed November 23, 2016, http://www.biographi.ca/en/bio/denison_george_taylor_1839_1925_15E.html.

Kochanski, Halik, *Sir Garnet Wolseley; Victorian Hero*, (London: The Hambledon Press, 1999).

Lamb, R.E., *Thunder in the North; Conflict Over The Riel Risings*, (New York: Pageant Press Inc., 1957).

Latham, David, "MAIR, CHARLES," in Dictionary of Canadian Biography, vol. 15, University of Toronto/ Université Laval, 2003–, accessed November 23, 2016, http://www.biographi.ca/en/bio/mair_charles_15E.html.

Lehmann, Joseph, *All Sir Garnet; A Life of Field-Marshal Lord Wolseley, 1833-1913*, (London: Jonathan Cape, 1964).

Low, Charles Rathbone, *A Memoir of Lieutenant-General Sir Garnet J. Wolseley In Two Volumes, Volume 2,"* (London: Richard Bentley & Son, 1878).

MacArthur, Peter, 'The Red River Rebellion', in *Manitoba Pageant*, Spring 1973, Volume 18, Number 3, http://www.mhs.mb.ca/docs/pageant/18/redriverrebellion.shtml.

Macbeth, R. G., *The Romance of the Canadian West*, (Toronto: Ryerson, 1920).

MacKay, Douglas, *The Honourable Company; A History of the Hudson's Bay Company*, (Toronto: McClelland and Stewart, 1949).

MacLaren, Sherrill, *Braehead; Three Founding Families of Nineteenth Century Canada*, (Toronto: McClelland and Stewart, 1986).

Roy MacLaren, *Canadians on the Nile by Canadians on the Nile, 1882-1898: Being the Adventures of the Voyageurs on the Khartoum Relief Expedition and Other Exploits*, (University of British Columbia Press, 1978).

Macleod, R. C., "Macleod, James Farquharson," in Dictionary of Canadian Biography, vol. 12, University of Toronto/Université Laval, 2003–, accessed May 10, 2016, http://www.biographi.ca/en/bio/macleod_james_farquharson_12E.html.

Macleod, Roderick C. "Butler, Sir William Francis," in Dictionary of Canadian Biography, vol. 13, University of Toronto/Université Laval, 2003–, accessed April 29, 2016, http://www.biographi.ca/en/bio/butler_william_francis_13E.html.

Macleod, Roderick Charles, "Steele, Sir Samuel Benfield," in Dictionary of Canadian Biography, vol. 14, University of Toronto/Université Laval, 2003–, accessed May 10, 2016, http://www.biographi.ca/en/bio/steele_samuel_benfield_14E.html.

Mailhot, Philippe R., "Ritchot, Noël-Joseph," in Dictionary of Canadian Biography, vol. 13, University of Toronto/Université Laval, 2003–, accessed November 28, 2016, http://www.biographi.ca/en/bio/ritchot_noel_joseph_13E.html.

Manore, J.I., 'William Francis Butler and the Great Lone Land', *The Beaver*, October-November, 1986, https://canadashistory.partica.online/canadas-history/the-beaver-oct-nov-1986/flipbook/42/.

Manore, Jack, 'Mr. Dawson's Road', *The Beaver*, January-February, 1991, https://canadashistory.partica.online/canadas-history/the-beaver-feb-mar-1991/flipbook/6/.

"Maritime History of the Great Lakes," http://images.maritimehistoryofthegreatlakes.ca/6873/data?n=44

Martin, Ged, 'Sir John A. Macdonald and the Bottle', *Journal of Canadian Studies/Revue d'études Canadiennes*, Volume 40, Number 3, Fall 2006.

Martin, Ged, *Britain and Origins of Canadian Confederation, 1837-67*, (London: Macmillan Press Ltd, 1975).

Maurice, Major-General Sir F. and Arthur, Sir George, *The Life of Lord Wolseley*, London: William Heinemann Ltd., 1924).

Maxwell, Leigh, *The Ashanti Ring; Sir Garnet Wolseley's Campaigns, 1870-1882*, (London: Leo Cooper in Association with Secker and Warburg, 1985).

Mays, Herbert J., "MacDonell, Miles," in Dictionary of Canadian Biography, Vol 6, University of Toronto/ Université Laval, 2003-accessed June 9, 2017 http://www.biographi.ca/en/bio/macdonell_miles_6E.html.

McArthur, Alex: 'The Causes of the Rising in the Red River Settlement 1869-70', *Manitoba Historical and Scientific Society*, Publication No. 1, Winnipeg, October 10th, 1882 http://peel.library.ualberta.ca/bibliography/580.html.

McCourt, Edward, *Remember Butler; The Story of Sir William Butler*, (London: Routledge & Kegan Paul, 1967).

McDonald, Donna, *Lord Strathcona; A Biography of Donald Alexander Smith*, (Toronto: Dundurn Press, 1996).

McElwee, William, *The Art of War, Waterloo to Mons*, (Bloomington: Indiana University Press, 1974).

McPherson, James M., *The Battle Cry of Freedom; The Civil War Era*, (New York: Oxford University Press, 1988).

Melville, Colonel C.H. C.M.G., *Life of the Right Hon. Sir Redvers Buller, V.C., G.C.B., G.C.M.G.*, (London: Edward Arnold and Company, 1923).

Merk, Frederick, *The Oregon Question; Essays in Anglo-American Diplomacy*, (Cambridge, Massachusetts, The Belknap Press of Harvard University Press, 1967).

Miller, J.R., Riel, 'Louis David (1844-1885)', *Oxford Dictionary of National Biography*, Oxford University Press, 2004; online edn, May 2008, http://www.oxforddnb.com/view/article/23638, accessed 28 Nov 2016.

Miller, Stephen M., 'Redvers Buller', in Corvi, Steven J. & Beckett, Ian F.W. (Editors), *Victoria's Generals*, (Barnsley: Pen and Sword Military, 2009).

Mitchell, Dr. Ross, 'Wolseley's Intelligence Officer: William Francis Butler (1838-1910)', *Manitoba Pageant*, April 1959, Volume 4, Number 3. http://www.mhs.mb.ca/docs/pageant/04/wolseleyintelligence.shtml

Morris, David A., *The Canadian Militia From 1855 – An Historical Summary*, Erin: The Boston Mills Press, 1983).

Morris, James, *Heaven's Command; An Imperial Progress*, (London: The Folio Society, 1992).

Morrison, William R., 'The Second Battalion, Quebec Rifles at Lower Fort Garry', in *Canadian Historic Sites: Occasional Papers in Archaeology and History – No. 4,* (Ottawa, 1970).

Morrison, William R., 'The Sixth Regiment of Foot at Lower Fort Garry', in *Canadian Historic Sites: Occasional Papers in Archaeology and History – No. 4*, (Ottawa, 1970).

Morton, Arthur S., *A History of the Canadian West to 1870-71*, (London: Thomas Nelsons & Sons Ltd).

Morton, Desmond, *Ministers and Generals; Politics and the Canadian Militia 1868-1904*, (Toronto: University of Toronto Press, 1970).

Morton, Desmond, *The Canadian General, Sir William Otter*, (Toronto: Hakkert, 1974).

Morton, Desmond, *A Military History of Canada*,(Edmonton: Hurtig Publishers, 1985).

Morton, Desmond, *A Short History of Canada (Fifth Edition)*, (Toronto: McClelland & Stewart, 2001).

Morton, Desmond, "Lindsay, Sir James Alexander," in Dictionary of Canadian Biography, vol. 10, University of Toronto/Université Laval, 2003–, accessed April 29, 2016, http://www.biographi.ca/en/bio/lindsay_james_alexander_10E.html.

Morton, Desmond: 'The Militia Lobby in Parliament: The Military Politicians and the Canadian Militia, 1868-1897', in Preston, Adrian and Dennis, Peter (Editors) *Swords and Covenants*, (London: Croom Helm Ltd, 1976).

Morton, Desmond: 'Yes, think of Nov. 11 – but 1871, not 1918', *The Globe and Mail*, published Nov. 11, 2008.

Morton, W.L., *Manitoba: A History*, (Toronto: University of Toronto Press, 1957).

Morton, W.L., *The Critical Years; The Union of British North America 1857-1873*, (Toronto: McClelland and Stewart, 1964).

Morton, W.L., *The Kingdom of Canada; A General History from Earliest Times (Second Edition)*, (Toronto: McClelland Stewart, 1969).

Morton, W. L., "Scott, Alfred Henry," in Dictionary of Canadian Biography, vol. 10, University of Toronto/Université Laval, 2003–, accessed November 28, 2016, http://www.biographi.ca/en/bio/scott_alfred_henry_10E.html.

Nelles, H.V., *A Little History of Canada, Third Edition*, (Don Mills: Oxford University Press, 2017).

Northcote, Sir Stafford Henry, *Diaries of the First Earl of Iddesleigh*," (Printed for private circulation 1907, Accessed at the British Library).

O'Donnell, John H., *Manitoba As I saw It, From 1869 to Date; With Flash-Lights on the First Riel Rebellion*, (Clark Bros. & Co. Limited, 1909). http://peel.library.ualberta.ca/bibliography/3323.html.

Ordnance Survey History, https://www.ordnancesurvey.co.uk/about/overview/history.html.

Owram, Doug, *Promise of Eden; The Canadian Expansionist Movement and the Idea of the West 1856-1900*, (Toronto: University of Toronto Press, 1992).

Payment, Diane P., "Nolin, Charles," in Dictionary of Canadian Biography, vol. 13, University of Toronto/Université Laval, 2003–, accessed November 28, 2016, http://www.biographi.ca/en/bio/nolin_charles_13E.html.

Pope, Sir Joseph, *Correspondence of Sir John Macdonald; Selections from the Correspondence of the Right Honourable Sir John Alexander Macdonald, G.C.B.,"* (New York and Toronto: Doubleday, Page and Company, 1921).

Porter, A.N. (Editor), *Atlas of British Overseas Expansion*, (New York: Simon and Schuster, 1991).

Porter, Bernard, *The Lion's Share; A Short History of British Imperialism 1850-1970*, (London: Longman Group Limited, 1975).

Geoffrey Powell, *Buller: A Scapegoat? A Life of General Sir Redvers Buller, 1839-1908*, (Pen and Sword Books, 2005).

Preston, Adrian: Wolseley, 'The Khartoum Relief Expedition and the Defence of India, 1885-1900', in Preston, Adrian and Dennis, Peter (Editors) *Swords and Covenants*, Croom Helm Ltd, London, 1976.

Preston, Richard A., "Robertson-Ross, Patrick," in Dictionary of Canadian Biography, vol. 11, University of Toronto/Université Laval, 2003–, accessed April 29, 2016, http://www.biographi.ca/en/bio/robertson_ross_patrick_11E.html.

Pryke, K. G., "Archibald, Sir Adams George," in Dictionary of Canadian Biography, vol. 12, University of Toronto/Université Laval, 2003–, accessed November 28, 2016, http://www.biographi.ca/en/bio/archibald_adams_george_12E.html.

Ramm, Agatha, *The Political Correspondence of Mr. Gladstone and Lord Granville, 1868-1876, Volume 1, 1868-71*, (London: Offices of the Royal Historical Society, 1952).

Rea, J. E., "Bannatyne, Andrew Graham Ballenden," in Dictionary of Canadian Biography, vol. 11, University of Toronto/Université Laval, 2003–, accessed November 28, 2016, http://www.biographi.ca/en/bio/bannatyne_andrew_graham_ballenden_11E.html.

Rea, J. E., "Scott, Thomas (d. 1870)," in Dictionary of Canadian Biography, vol. 9, University of Toronto/Université Laval, 2003–, accessed November 28, 2016, http://www.biographi.ca/en/bio/scott_thomas_1870_9E.html.

Rea, J.E. 'Red River Stand-off', *Horizon Canada*, Centre for the Study of Teaching Canada Inc., April 1986

Read, Colin Frederick, "Dennis, John Stoughton," in Dictionary of Canadian Biography, vol. 11, University of Toronto/Université Laval, 2003–, accessed July 23, 2018, http://www.biographi.ca/en/bio/dennis_john_stoughton_1820_85_11E.html.

Reford, Alexander, "Smith, Donald Alexander, 1st Baron Strathcona and Mount Royal," in Dictionary of Canadian Biography, vol. 14, University of Toronto/Université Laval, 2003–, accessed November 28, 2016, http://www.biographi.ca/en/bio/smith_donald_alexander_14E.html.

Rich, E.E., *The Hudson's Bay Company, Volume 3 1821-1870*, (Toronto: McClelland and Stewart, 1960).

Rich, E.E., *The Fur Trade and the Northwest to 1857*, (Toronto: McClelland and Steward Limited, 1967).

Richards, Denis and Hunt, J.W., *An Illustrated History of Modern Britain 1783-1964*, (London: Longman Group Limited, 1973).

Roberts, Rick, 'Records of the Royal Canadian Rifles', Global Genealogy & History Store, http://globalgenealogy.com/globalgazette/canada-military/british-in-cda/roal-cdn-rifles-1840.htm

Ross, Alexander Ross, *The Red River Settlement; It's Rise, Progress, and Present State*, (London: Smith, Elder and Co., 1856). https://archive.org/stream/redriversettlem00rossgoog#page/n0.

Ross, David & Tyler Grant, "Canadian Campaigns 1860-70," Osprey Publishing Inc., Oxford, 1992.

Senior, Elinor Kyte, *The Roots of the Canadian Army: Montreal District 1846-1870*, (Montreal: Historical Publications; The Society of the Montreal Military & Maritime Museum, 1981).

Senior, Hereward, *The Last Invasion of Canada; The Fenian Raids of 1866-1870*, (Toronto: Dundurn Press, 1991).

Silver, A.I., "Cartier, "Sir George- Étienne, baronet (1814-1873)", *Oxford Dictionary of National Biography*, Oxford University Press, 2004 http://oxforddnb.com/view/article/4811, accessed 28 Nov 2016.

Sissons, Constance Kerr, *John Kerr*, (Toronto: Oxford University Press, 1946).

Smith, W. D., "Ross, James (1835-71)," in Dictionary of Canadian Biography, vol. 10, University of Toronto/Université Laval, 2003–, accessed November 28, 2016, http://www.biographi.ca/en/bio/ross_james_1835_71_10E.html.

Spiers, Edward, *The Late Victorian Army, 1868-1902*, (Manchester: Manchester University Press, 1992).

Spiers, Edward: 'The Late Victorian Army, 1868-1914', in Chandler, David (General Editor) and Beckett, Ian (Associate Editor) *The Oxford Illustrated History of the British Army*, (Oxford: Oxford University Press, 1994).

Spry, Irene M., "Palliser, John," in Dictionary of Canadian Biography, vol. 11, University of Toronto/Université Laval, 2003–, accessed Decembrr 1, 2016, http://www.biographi.ca/en/bio/palliser_john_11E.html.

Stacey, C.P., *Canada and the British Army 1846-1871 (Revised Edition)*, (Toronto: University of Toronto Press, 1963).

Stacey, C.P., *Canada and the Age of Conflict; Volume 1: 1867-1921*, (Toronto: University of Toronto Press, 1984).

Stacey, Colonel C.P. (Editor), 'Introduction to the Study of Military History for Canadian Students (Sixth Edition)', (Ottawa: Directorate of Training Canadian Forces Headquarters). http://www.cmp-cpm.forces.gc.ca/dhh-dhp/his/docs/Intro_MilHist_e.pdf.

Stacey, C.P., "Michel, Sir John," in Dictionary of Canadian Biography, vol. 11, University of Toronto/Université Laval, 2003–, accessed April 19, 2018, http://www.biographi.ca/en/bio/michel_john_11E.html.

Stanley, George F.G., *The Birth of Western Canada; A History of the Riel Rebellions*, (Toronto: University of Toronto Press, 1960, First Published 1936).

Stanley, George F.G., *Canada's Soldiers, 1604-1954; The Military History of an Unmilitary People*, (Toronto: The Macmillan Company of Canada, 1954).

Stanley, George F.G., *Louis Riel*, (Toronto: The Ryerson Press, 1963).

Stanley, George F.G., *Toil and Trouble; Military Expeditions to Red River*, (Toronto & Oxford: Dundurn Press, 1989).

Stanley, George F.G., 'A Soldier at Fort Garry', *The Beaver*, Governor and Company of Adventurers trading into Hudson's Bay, Winnipeg, Autumn 1957.

Stanley, George F. G., "Casault, Louis-Adolphe," in Dictionary of Canadian Biography, vol. 10, University of Toronto/Université Laval, 2003–, accessed November 24, 2016, http://www.biographi.ca/en/bio/casault_louis_adolphe_10E.html.

Stanley, George F. G., "O'Donoghue, William Bernard," in Dictionary of Canadian Biography, vol. 10, University of Toronto/Université Laval, 2003–, accessed November 28, 2016, http://www.biographi.ca/en/bio/o_donoghue_william_bernard_10E.html.

St. Aubyn, Giles, *The Royal George; The Life of H.R.H. Prince George Duke of Cambridge, 1819-1904*, (London: Constable, 1963).

Steele, Sam, *Forty Years in Canada; Reminiscences of the Great North-West with Some Account of His Service in South Africa*, (Toronto: Prospero Books, 2000, originally published 1915).

St. Maur, Mrs Algernon, *Impressions of a Tender Foot During a Journey in Search of Sport in the Far West*, (London: John Murray, 1890).

Sutherland, Alex H., *The Selkirk Settlement on the Red River*, (Victoria, British Columbia).

Swan, Ruth and Reynolds, Janelle, "Nault, André," in Dictionary of Canadian Biography, vol. 15, University of Toronto/Université Laval, 2003–, accessed November 28, 2016, http://www.biographi.ca/en/bio/nault_andre_15E.html.

Sweeny, Alastair, *George-Etienne Cartier*, (Toronto: McClelland and Stewart Limited, 1976).

Tennant, Bugler Joseph F., *Rough Times 1870-1920; A Souvenir of the 50th Anniversary of the Red River Expedition and the Formation of Manitoba*, (Winnipeg: Facsimile Publication, Originally self-published, 1920).

Thomas, Lewis H., "Riel, Louis (1844-85)," in Dictionary of Canadian Biography, vol. 11, University of Toronto/Université Laval, 2003–, accessed April 9, 2018, http://www.biographi.ca/en/bio/riel_louis_1844_85_11E.html.

Thomas, Lewis H., 'The Hind and Dawson Expeditions 1857-58', *The Beaver*, Winter 1958, https://canadashistory.partica.online/canadas-history/the-beaver-winter-1958/flipbook/38/.

Thompson, Charles A., "Young, Sir John, Baron Lisgar," in Dictionary of Canadian Biography, vol. 10, University of Toronto/Université Laval, 2003–, accessed November 28, 2016, http://www.biographi.ca/en/bio/young_john_1807_76_10E.html.

Turner, Allan R.: 'Palliser of the Triangle', in *The Beaver*, Governor and Company of Adventurers trading into Hudson's Bay, Winnipeg, Autumn 1957.

Van Kirk, S. (1977). 'Women in Between: Indian Women in Fur Trade Society in Western Canada.' *Historical Papers*, 12(1), 30–46. doi:10.7202/030819ar.

Vetch, R. H., "Williams, Sir William Fenwick, baronet (1800-1883)", rev. H. C. G. Matthew, Oxford Dictionary of National Biography, Oxford University Press, 2002, online edn, Jan 2008, http://www.oxforddnb.com/view/article/29561, accessed 28 Nov 2016.

Waite, Peter: 'Between Three Oceans: Challenges of a Continental Destiny (1840-1900)', in Brown, Craig (Editor), *The Illustrated History of Canada*, (Toronto: Lester & Orpen Dennys, 1987).

Waite, P.B., "Williams, Sir William Fenwick," in Dictionary of Canadian Biography, vol. 11, University of Toronto/Université Laval, 2003–, accessed November 22, 2016, http://www.biographi.ca/en/bio/williams_william_fenwick_11E.html.

Wallace, Captain Nesbit Willoughby, *A Regimental Chronicle and List of Officers of the 60th or the Royal American Regiment of Foot*, (London: Harrison and Sons, 1879). https://archive.org/details/aregimentalchro00wallgoog.

Webb, R.K., *Modern England (Second Edition)*, (Harper & Row, Publishers Inc., 1980).

Wilson, Keith, 'Fur Wars', *Horizon Canada*, Centre for the Study of Teaching Canada Inc., August 1985.

Wilson, Keith, 'Settlement at the Forks', *Horizon Canada*, Centre for the Study of Teaching Canada Inc., October 1985.

Wilson, Keith, 'Napoleon of the West', *Horizon Canada*, Centre for the Study of Teaching Canada Inc., January 1986.

Wilson, Keith, "Crofton, John Ffolliott," in Dictionary of Canadian Biography, vol. 11, University of Toronto/Université Laval, 2003–, accessed January 8, 2017, http://www.biographi.ca/en/bio/crofton_john_ffolliott_11E.html.

Winks, Robin W. Winks, "Jervois, Sir William Francis Drummond," in Dictionary of Canadian Biography, vol. 12, University of Toronto/Université Laval, 2003–accessed May 13, 2016. http://globalgenealogy.com/globalgazette/canada-military/british-in-cda/roal-cdn-rifles-1840.htm.

Wolseley, Field-Marshal Viscount, *The Story of a Soldier's Life Volume 2*, (New York: Charles Scribner's Sons, 1904). https://archive.org/stream/storyasoldiersl04wolsgoog#page/n10/mode/2up.

Wolseley, Colonel Sir Garnet J., *The Soldier's Pocket-Book for field service*, (London: Macmillan and Co., 1871). https://archive.org/details/soldierspocketb00wolsgoog.

Wolseley, Garnet (An English Officer), 'A Month's Visit to the Confederate Headquarters', in *Blackwood's Edinburgh Magazine,* Volume 93 No. DLXVII January 1863, https://babel.hathitrust.org/cgi/pt?id=uc1.b5227817;view=1up;seq=9.

Wolseley, Garnet (An Officer of the Expeditionary Force), 'Narrative of the Red River Expedition', in *Blackwood's Edinburgh Magazine*, Vol. CVIII July – Dec 1870 and Vol CIX Jan – Jun 1871, London 1870 and 1871 (Published in 3 parts Dec, 1870 and Jan. and Feb. 1871. https://babel.hathitrust.org/cgi/pt?id=uc1.b5227832;view=1up;seq=7 https://babel.hathitrust.org/cgi/pt?id=uc1.b5227833;view=1up;seq=54.

Wood, Herbert Fairlie, *The King's Royal Rifle Corps (The 60th Regiment of Foot)*, (London: Hamish Hamilton, 1967).

Woodcock, George, "Robertson, Colin," in Dictionary of Canadian Biography, vol. 7, University of Toronto/Université Laval, 2003–, accessed March 13, 2018, http://www.biographi.ca/en/bio/robertson_colin_7E.html.

Young, The Reverend George D.D., *Manitoba Memories, Leaves From My Life in the Prairie Province, 1868-1884*, (Toronto: William Briggs, 1897). https://archive.org/stream/manitobamemories00youn#page/n5/mode/2up.

Zeller, Suzanne, "Mcdougall, William," in Dictionary of Canadian Biography, vol. 13, University of Toronto/Université Laval, 2003–, accessed December 1, 2016, http://www.biographi.ca/en/bio/mcdougall_william_13E.html.

Archives and Documents

Early Canadiana Online, http://eco.canadiana.ca/

Canadian Sessional Papers, "Correspondence and Papers Connected Recent Occurrences in the North-West Territories," Printed by Order of Parliament, I.B. Taylor, Printer, Ottawa, 1871

Canadian Sessional Papers No12, 1870, communications 6031, 6032, 6033, 7513, 9193, 9194, 6121, January 1870

"Correspondence and Papers Connected with the Recent Occurrences in the North-West Territories," I. B Taylor Ottawa 1870, http://eco.canadiana.ca/

Glenbow

Dundas, Captain James Durham Dundas, "The Letters and Journal of James Durham Dundas, 60th Rifles, written during The Red River Expedition," James D. Dundas Fonds, M-9560-1, M-9560-2, M-9560-3, Glenbow Archives http://www.glenbow.org/collections/search/findingAids/archhtm/dundas.cfm

Hampshire Archives

70A12W/D/0406, Anonymous, "Some Recollections of the Return Journey of C Company from the Red River Expedition"

170A12W/D/0438, Wallace, Captain N. Willoughby: "The Rebellion in the Red River Settlement; Its causes and suppression, A Lecture." Delivered at Clifton October 25th, 1871, Henry T. Cook, Barnstaple, 1872. Also found at: https://archive.org/details/cihm_30529

170A12W/D/1049/1-2, Wallace, Captain N.W., "Field Diary"

Hove Public Library

SS2/11, Rough notes pertaining to the Red River Expedition, written shortly after the event.

W/P.1/1-21, Personal correspondence from Wolseley to his wife written in Canada in 1870.

W/W.2, Rough Draft of Red River Report.

Wolseley, Field-Marshal Viscount, "The Story of a Soldier's Life Volume 2," Archibald Constable & Co., 1903, Annotated Version.

Peel's Prairie Provinces, University of Alberta

"Correspondence Relative to the Recent Expedition to the Red River Settlement with Journal of Operations," Harrison and Sons, London, 1871, http://peel.library.ualberta.ca/bibliography/568.html

Dawson, C.E., Simon J., "Report, the Line of Route Between Lake Superior and the Red River Settlement Printed by Order of the House of Commons, Ottawa, 1869 http://peel.library.ualberta.ca/bibliography/481.html

Dawson, C.E., Simon J., "Report of the Red River Expedition of 1870, and Addenda" Times Printing and Publishing, Ottawa, 1871, http://peel.library.ualberta.ca/bibliography/559.html

Harman, Captain S. Bruce, "T'Was 26 Years Ago; Narrative of the Red River Expedition 1870," Toronto, 1896, http://peel.library.ualberta.ca/bibliography/570/4.html

Hind, Henry Youle, Gladman, George, Dawson, Simon James, Napier, W. E., "Report on the Exploration of the Country between Lake Superior and the Red River Settlement," John Lovell, Printer, Toronto, 1858, http://peel.library.ualberta.ca/bibliography/350/2.html

Irvine, C.M.G., Assistant Controller M. Bell, "Report on the Red River Expedition of 1870," Harrison and Sons, London, 1871, http://peel.library.ualberta.ca/bibliography/576.html

James R.E., F.R.S., Colonel Sir Henry: "Notes on the Routes from Lake Superior to the Red River and On The Settlement Itself; Compiled from Reports by Captain Palliser, Professor Hind, and Messrs. Dawson and Napier with Notes Relating to the Transport of Troops &c., by Colonel Crofton and Captain, (Now General) Lefroy, R.A.," Compiled in the Topographical Department of the War Office, March 31st, 1870, http://peel.library.ualberta.ca/bibliography/558/2.html

Riddell, Lieutenant H.S.H., 60th Rifles, The Red River Expedition of 1870,: Transactions of the Literary and Historical Society of Quebec, Session of 1870-71, Printed by Middleton & Dawson, at the "Gazette," http://peel.library.ualberta.ca/bibliography/589.html

Wainwright, Major Griffiths 1st Ontario Rifles, "Field Diary," University of Alberta, Sam Steele Collection, https://steele.library.ualberta.ca/units/2008/1/1/3/1/2

The National Archives

CO 42/684, Committee of Canadian Privy Council, dealing with the sending of an expeditionary force.

CO 42/686, Report of Jas. J. Hill.

CO 42/695, Correspondence from Macdonald to Granville.

CO 43/157, Correspondence pertaining to use of British Troops.

CO 880/4/26, Correspondence relative to recent disturbances at Red River.

WO 32/7583, "Correspondence Relative to the Recent Expedition to the Red River Settlement with Journal of Operations," Harrison and Sons, London, 1871

WO 32/7584, Red River Reports and Dispatches.

WO 32/7585, Lindsay to Secretary of State for War, reports.

WO 32/7586, Irvine, C.M.G., Assistant Controller M. Bell, "Report on the Red River Expedition of 1870," Harrison and Sons, London, 1871

WO 33/21A, James R.E., F.R.S., Colonel Sir Henry: "Notes on the Routes from Lake Superior to the Red River and On The Settlement Itself; Compiled from Reports by Captain Palliser, Professor Hind, and Messrs. Dawson and Napier with Notes Relating to the Transport of Troops &c., by Colonel Crofton and Captain, (Now General) Lefroy, R.A.," Compiled in the Topographical Department of the War Office, March 31st, 1870.

WO 33/22, Report of the Control Department on Red River Expedition.

WO 107/9, Wolseley, Colonel Garnet, "Memorandum Regarding the Despatch of an Armed Force to the Red River Territory."

FO 925/1849, Sketch of road from Prince Arthur's Landing, Thunder Bay, Lake Superior to Lake Shebandowan

Sir Samuel Steele Collection, University of Alberta

Hubbard, William: "The Red River Expedition; Recollections by William Hubbard, of Toronto, one of the Force, written during the Winter of A.D. 1914," University of Alberta, Sam Steele Collection, https://steele.library.ualberta.ca/units/2008/1/3/1/3

McMillan, Captain Daniel Hunter and Mulvey, Ensign Stewart of No 4 Company 1st Ontario Rifles: "Field Diaries," University of Alberta, Sam Steele Collection, https://steele.library.ualberta.ca/units/2008/1/1/3/1/1

Index